CLAMP in Context

ALSO BY DANI CAVALLARO AND FROM MCFARLAND

Art in Anime (2012)

The Fairy Tale and Anime: Traditional Themes, Images and Symbols at Play on Screen (2011)

The World of Angela Carter: A Critical Investigation (2011)

Anime and the Art of Adaptation: Eight Famous Works from Page to Screen (2010)

Anime and the Visual Novel: Narrative Structure, Design and Play at the Crossroads of Animation and Computer Games (2010)

Magic as Metaphor in Anime: A Critical Study (2010)

The Mind of Italo Calvino: A Critical Exploration of His Thought and Writings (2010)

Anime and Memory: Aesthetic, Cultural and Thematic Perspectives (2009)

The Art of Studio Gainax: Experimentation, Style and Innovation at the Leading Edge of Anime (2009)

Anime Intersections: Tradition and Innovation in Theme and Technique (2007)

The Animé Art of Hayao Miyazaki (2006)

The Cinema of Mamoru Oshii: Fantasy, Technology and Politics (2006)

CLAMP IN CONTEXT

A Critical Study of the Manga and Anime

Dani Cavallaro

McFarland & Company, Inc., Publishers
Jefferson, North Carolina, and London

LIBRARY OF CONGRESS CATALOGUING-IN-PUBLICATION DATA

Cavallaro, Dani.
    CLAMP in context : a critical study of the manga and anime / Dani Cavallaro.
        p.   cm.
    Includes bibliographical references and index.

    ISBN 978-0-7864-6954-3
    softcover : acid free paper ∞

    1. CLAMP (Mangaka group)   2. Comic books, strips, etc.— Japan — History and criticism.   3. CLAMP (Mangaka group)— Influence. I. Title.
    NC1764.5.J3C5632   2012
    741.5'952 — dc23   2011052668

BRITISH LIBRARY CATALOGUING DATA ARE AVAILABLE

© 2012 Dani Cavallaro. All rights reserved

No part of this book may be reproduced or transmitted in any form or by any means, electronic or mechanical, including photocopying or recording, or by any information storage and retrieval system, without permission in writing from the publisher.

Front cover: Illustration from the 1989 manga *RG Veda* (CLAMP)

Manufactured in the United States of America

McFarland & Company, Inc., Publishers
   Box 611, Jefferson, North Carolina 28640
     www.mcfarlandpub.com

To Paddy, with all my love

Contents

Preface 1

1 — CLAMP's Philosophy 3
2 — Epic Reinventions 43
3 — Transworld Migrations 82
4 — Technologies of Subjectivity 136

Filmography 179
Appendix: Selected Manga 188
Bibliography 189
Index 195

A line is a dot that went for a walk. — Paul Klee

Preface

Film will only become an art when its materials are as inexpensive as pencil and paper. — Jean Cocteau

Since the serialization in *Wings* magazine of its debut manga *RG Veda*, CLAMP has steadily asserted itself as one of the most widely renowned teams of manga artists, leaving a durable imprint in every established genre while also devising some novel formulae along the way. Taking a selection of CLAMP manga and anime inspired by those manga as its object of study, this book seeks to document the team's incremental creation of a graphic constellation of unparalleled appeal. Endowed not solely with stylistic distinctiveness but also the caliber of a comprehensive cultural structure, CLAMP's output ultimately stands out as a veritable multiverse — or ensemble of multiple hypothetical universes — abetted by both worldbuilding flair and visual vitality.

The book comprises four chapters. Chapter 1, "CLAMP's Philosophy," examines a salient range of aesthetic perspectives and artistic experiments which can help us appreciate the broader philosophical underpinnings — and attendant conceptual import — of the works under scrutiny in the chapters to follow. In Chapter 2, "Epic Reinventions," the analysis focuses on CLAMP's dedication to the invention of elaborate narrative constructs which appear to replicate the classic epic modality in their complexity and breadth, yet challenge many of its fundamental objectives and mores in a courageous pursuit of alternative world pictures. *RG Veda*, *Tokyo Babylon*, *Magic Knight Rayearth* and *X* are of special relevance to this segment of the discussion. *X — X2 Double X* and *X: An Omen* are also briefly examined. Chapter 3, "Transworld Migrations," engages with CLAMP's legendary passion for multilayered universes affording virtually infinite opportunities for cultural, historical and stylistic leaps of often vertiginous intensity across time and space. *Cardcaptor Sakura, Tsubasa: RESERVoir CHRoNiCLE, xxxHOLiC* and *Kobato* constitute this chapter's pivotal titles. Additional productions deserving rapid inspection in this context are the two *CLAMP in Wonderland* videos, *Miyuki-chan in Wonderland, Sweet Valerian* and the *Wish* special. The manga *Legend of Chun Hyang, Shirahime-Syo: Snow Goddess Tales, Legal Drug* and *Gate 7* are also referred to in the course of the discussion. In this chapter, the discussion devotes special attention to one of CLAMP's most prominent and most cherished achievements of recent years, *Tsubasa: RESERVoir CHRoNiCLE*. In so doing, it comments on the relationship between the original drawn version of the saga and its anime adaptation across two TV series, two OVAs and a movie, while also engaging with portions of the parent manga which have not been translated into moving images. Insofar as the analysis of *Tsubasa: RESERVoir CHRoNiCLE* is situated approximately halfway through the book, this title's central significance to both CLAMP's own corpus and this particular study is here highlighted in structural, as well as conceptual, terms. With Chapter 4, "Technologies of Subjectivity," the discussion concentrates on CLAMP's symbolic interpretation of human identity as an unstable outcome of the intersection of science, fantasy and politics: a process to which humor and pathos contribute in equal measures. *Angelic Layer, CLAMP School Detectives, Chobits, Mouryou no Hako* and *Code Geass* are the key works examined in this chapter. Reference is also made, where relevant, to the *Chibits* and the *Clover* specials, and to the manga *Duklyon: Clamp School Defenders, Man of Many Faces, Suki,* and *The One I Love*.

The book's primary texts comprise a selection of manga issuing from the CLAMP team's prolific imagination alongside their anime adaptations. In addition, they include two anime series, *Mouryou no Hako* and *Code Geass*, to which the CLAMP artists have contributed in the capacity of character designers. Comprehensive information regarding the production details of the anime explored is provided in the filmography. A further category of materials on which this study assiduously relies includes the twelve-volume series *CLAMP no Kiseki*: a set of books released in 2004 to celebrate CLAMP's fifteenth anniversary, each of which features articles, interviews, original art, original short manga and chess pieces portraying *chibi* versions of characters from various CLAMP manga.

Chapter 1

CLAMP's Philosophy

Good design begins with honesty, asks tough questions, comes from collaboration and from trusting your intuition. — Freeman Thomas

From its modest beginnings in the mid–1980s as a group of *doujinshi* artists, CLAMP has risen to the status of an internationally acclaimed presence in the interdependent areas of manga and anime, while the dozen members of the original circle have shrunk to just four artists: Ageha Ohkawa, Tsubaki Nekoi, Satsuki Igarashi and Mokona. As Leslie Smith has observed, "since *RG Veda*, CLAMP has released one big hit after another, transcending countries, languages and cultures. Their appeal continues to grow, with the majority of their manga now available to English-speaking readers" (Smith, p. 31). There is no doubt that CLAMP has made a crucial contribution to the sensational success of manga in the United States, impacting not only on the creations of several American manga authors but also on the evolution of the distribution and marketing initiatives undertaken by major American publishers such as Tokyopop, Viz, Del Rey Manga and Dark Horse. Notably, the launch of the Del Rey Manga imprint in 2004 incorporated two eminent CLAMP titles, *Tsubasa: RESERVoir CHRoNiCLE* and *xxxHOLiC*, both of which remain to this day among Del Rey Manga's main bestselling series. The CLAMP artists themselves have never exhibited any complacency or smugness in the face of their overseas success. If anything, wonder or even a sense of defamiliarization have tended to be their most likely responses to that phenomenon. "It's very strange to think of our work being translated into all these other languages and read by people all over the world," Ohkawa has maintained. "When I was in America ... I saw a bunch of our titles lined up in a bookstore, and it felt like meeting an old friend who kept trying to talk to me in a foreign language for some reason. It was very strange. Seeing our speech bubbles filled with non–Japanese lettering is just weird" (cited in Smith, p. 28).

This book's chief objective is to offer an original contribution to the ongoing growth of manga and anime scholarship with a focus on CLAMP as one of the most esteemed collectives of manga artists all over the world: a creative team who has not merely made a durable contribution to those art forms as a first-class entertainer but actually redefined the boundaries of genres as diverse as fantasy and horror, comedy and psychodrama, romance and action adventure, the magical girl and the bildungsroman, the historical saga and the apocalyptic epic. It might come as a surprise, given CLAMP's current stature, to discover that the group actually came into being in an utterly informal, indeed almost accidental, fashion. As Ohkawa amusingly explains, "Satsuki Igarashi, Tsubaki Nekoi and Mokona were all in the same grade at the same school, so they knew each other from the beginning. I was introduced to them by a mutual friend. That's how we met. We were originally just a group of friends who got together to have fun ... we haven't lost that high school/college enthusiasm. As for the actual work ... we've gotten faster. Just a little, though" (cited in Smith, p. 28).

In focusing both on CLAMP's manga and on anime they have inspired, this book posits as its implied protagonists the moving images born from those manga's latently animate lines. This could indeed be regarded as the crux of the analysis here provided. As the relationship between the two forms manifests itself in an intriguing variety of guises, one realizes that from a conceptual point of view, there is far less of a gap between the manga created by CLAMP and the anime based upon them than one might at first suspect. This is not to claim that in the process of translation of one art form into another, the original text remains unchanged. Not only would such a contention be absurd, especially when media as substantially different as those deployed in manga and anime production are at stake: it would also crudely disregard the energizing beauty of the aesthetic, technical and conceptual journeys occurring across the two forms. As argued in *Anime and the Art of Adaptation*, moreover, a "text can be transposed to a different form without altering substantially, acquiring fresh meanings and inaugurating novel perspectives. This is because the divergence of the expressive vehicle used by the adaptation from that used by its source is inevitably conducive to some difference in content and mood. That is to say, by encoding its source in a different form, the adaptation comes to constitute not merely an alternate way of saying the same thing but rather a *different text*—a radically separate way of conveying messages other the ones inherent in the source by virtue of its own formal distinctiveness" (Cavallaro 2010, p. 6). Relatedly, the anime adaptations of CLAMP's manga here explored are fully aware that the enjoyment supplied by adaptation at its very best requires the achievement of a delicate mix: the magic potion described by Linda Hutcheon as a blend of "repetition" and "variation" (Hutcheon, p. 4).

What is here argued, in fact, is that CLAMP's manga and the resulting anime are tied indissolubly together by the power of the line—as articulated on paper and as translated to the realm of the moving image. The technical qualities of the line—alongside the planes, figures and other geometrical and compositional elements pivotal to CLAMP's output—will be assessed in some depth later in this discussion. At this early juncture, it must first be acknowledged that those elements should not be regarded as merely technical or stylistic matters. As they infuse the images they evoke with vibrant dynamism, thus invigorating their shapes to a matchless degree, they actually stand out as the lynchpin of an entire world picture. This conceives of reality at large, in both its quotidian expressions and its numinous manifestations, as a world saturated with life or, more accurately, aliveness: a playing field of infinite vitality echoing with the lessons of indigenous mythology and lore. This point deserves closer consideration, insofar as several spiritual motifs influenced by quintessentially Eastern sources recur both in CLAMP's output and in the anime they have spawned. These include Shinto-based beliefs and customs, the teachings of *onmyoudou*, and nature-bound magic in the broad sense of the term. A particularly notable part is played by the principles of Shinto and by the shamanistic activities which these have inspired over the centuries.

Given their emphasis on the world's pervasive aliveness, all of the shows under inspection reverberate—with varying degrees of explicitness and emphasis—with animistic notions reminiscent of Shinto's perception of the universe at large as a symphony of spiritual energies. All manner of material objects, and especially natural or semi-natural entities, are regarded as the receptacles of distinct *kami* (spirits or natural forces) which are able to affect human lives in both predictable and startling ways. In the representation of the natural environment, rocks and trees, mountains and rivers, wild and domestic animals communicate this message with compelling potency. Moreover, modest domestic interiors and man-made architecture also ooze with mystical powers, not only as the settings of venerable practices of ritual prominence but also in the depiction of daily errands. In these contexts, the spirits of the departed often stand out as ubiquitous and particularly influential agencies. As Michael Ashkenazi argues, one senses that in all of these areas, there is "no effective limit to the number of *kami*," and that "no clear division" therefore obtains "between the mundane and the *kami* worlds" (Ashkenazi, p. 27).

The manga and anime under investigation mirror Shinto-based traditions in two principal ways. On the one hand, they hark back to the body of textually inscribed myths and legends which over the centuries have come to be regarded as foundational voices for the Japanese nation at large—most notably, the *Kojiki* (a.k.a. *Furukotofumi*, c. 712) and the *Nihonji* (c. 720). On the other hand, they encapsulate local tales, both recorded and fictitious, revolving around demons, goblins, ghosts, spirits, patrons, itinerant gods and saints spawned by the genius loci of each of a vast galaxy of small communities. Furthermore, some of the *kami* alluded to in CLAMP's texts are celestial and others earthly, some emulate officially documented and nationally recognized entities, and others the manifestations of contingent forces. In all forms, they serve to highlight the uniquely commodious attitude to mythology which enables the Japanese to absorb a formidable variety of mythical elements within their culture, and to integrate them into the fabric of modern everyday existence.

The contingent magnitude of the space in which CLAMP's graphic shapes come into being is unimportant compared to its resources as a signifying force. Therefore, no less significant a degree of meaning may be engendered by a humble *tatami* mat, earthenware pot or folding screen than by an imposing castle, a sprawling metropolis or an intergalactic empire. In all its expressions, CLAMP's graphic space fashions experience at both the sensory and the intellectual levels. At times, it encourages us to situate ourselves imaginatively within its compass, and interact directly with its materials and objects. At others, it seeks to involve us mentally by means of metaphors and symbols. As artworks, all of the manga and anime here examined can be seen as hypothetical or virtual places with a proclivity to encourage the seamless blend of the actual and the imaginary. When the media of manga and anime intersect with the otherworldly, an artist's opportunities to evoke a variety of speculative places in which empirical reality and imagination coalesce grows exponentially. As a corollary of this collusion, the places depicted in these works are reluctant to dish out their meanings explicitly or even visibly. In fact, and most deliberately when they merge with fantasy, they encode them cryptically in their darkest corners and most elusive interstices, as latent texts brimming with stories awaiting detection. As audiences pursue the leads at their disposal in the quest for meaning, they often find that no conclusive revelations are ultimately available and that all apparent discoveries, therefore, are only approximative and fragmentary accomplishments. Any one visible path is countered by a plethora of hidden alternative routes. Here lies the ultimate charm of CLAMP's graphic space as a reality in which the frisson of the voyage itself far exceeds the pleasures afforded by any final destinations.

An especially interesting area of study is offered by CLAMP's portrayal of the natural environment itself as a domain crisscrossed by imaginary forces. Unleashing disparate life forms that often tease or resist human understanding, the works under scrutiny bring nature and the imagination together as a means of exploding many of the myths embedded in the doctrines of anthropocentrism and anthropomorphism so dear to Western thought. Indeed, by generously accommodating a plethora of life forms that blatantly elude classification in standard scientific terms, the alternate space issuing from CLAMP's pencil throws into relief the anti-things, non-things and quasi-things which populate the gaps between any two accepted categories. In so doing, they insistently expose the intrinsic precariousness of the boundary presumed to separate presence from absence, life from death. While, as Edmund Leach points out, cultures rely on the notion of the "taboo" in order to hinder "the recognition of those parts of the continuum which separate the things" (Leach, p. 47), CLAMP's parallel realms invite us to acknowledge the life that abides on the borders as a paradoxical source of attraction and loathing at one and the same time.

This universe is so fluid and mobile as to be generally unsympathetic to the erection of strict hierarchies, categories and compartments. CLAMP's penchant for formal and thematic eclecticism emanates from a comparable impatience with rigid demarcations. Its opus is indeed consummately prismatic in both its philosophical outlook and its tangible expressions. This is typically borne out, on the generic front, by a knack of integrating seamlessly diverse mythological materials of crosscultural provenance, futuristic yarns decked with tongue-in-cheek allusions to science fiction, and the structural mainstays of the epic and the saga in the orchestration of astute political drama. At the level of imagery, this aesthetic vision is consistently abetted by the integration, alternately overt and allusive, of an exhilaratingly wide range of formal and pictorial motifs. In dramatic terms, it finds some of its most tantalizing expressions in CLAMP's worldbuilding methods, where the principles of multiplicity, multidimensionality, multiperspectivalism and transdimensional hopping repeatedly hold sway. Eclecticism is so crucial a feature of CLAMP's work as to deserve quick recapitulation in diagrammatic form:

- generic level: synthesis of crosscultural materials and forms
- imagery: amalgamation of disparate visual elements
- dramatic level: construction of multifaceted worlds

CLAMP's structural and thematic versatility finds an intriguing parallel in the group's proverbial use of crossovers, whereby characters can time and again be seen to migrate across series with often radical changes of personality, status and function. Characters, in this scenario, are approached as people — or performers — in their own right, not simply in terms of roles. Thus, just as actors may play sundry parts in different plays while remaining the same people at base, so CLAMP's crossover characters are able to embody disparate personae as they travel from one work to another without losing their fundamental integrity. As Ohkawa explains, CLAMP's crossovers are meant to operate according to the essential principle of "name recognition." This serves two purposes: "one is that readers get emotionally involved in the story quicker when a character they already know shows up, even if the plot isn't connected to the work they know the character from. The second is that it makes the characters feel more like real people — actors, if you will — than fictional characters" (cited in Smith, p. 28).

Tsubasa: RESERVoir CHRoNiCLE is especially reliant on crossovers. For audiences familiar with CLAMP's corpus, this work's intertextual nature provides a valuable opportunity to observe the group's evolution over time. This does not entail, however, that only CLAMP fans are likely to enjoy the program. In fact, its pervasive evocation of supernatural beauty, on the one hand, and human warmth, on the other, makes *Tsubasa: RESERVoir CHRoNiCLE* not only attractive but even addictive for practically any audience. CLAMP have commented thus on their decision to incorporate characters from their previous works in *Tsubasa: RESERVoir CHRoNiCLE*'s narrative tapestry: "it's actually much easier to write a whole new story with new characters. If we use popular characters from our former works, viewers can't help but see them as their previous personas, which makes it harder for us authors. Take Sakura, for example ... her cute little exclamations in *Cardcaptor Sakura* stuck in fans' minds, but we chose to leave them out of *Tsubasa* as a way of showing that she isn't the same Sakura. We also took the extra precaution of making her lose her memory at the beginning—hitting the reset button, so to speak" (CLAMP 2007a, p. 45). *Tsubasa: RESERVoir CHRoNiCLE*'s handling of crossovers will be further explored in the context of Chapter 3.

Crossovers do not always operate identically in the anime and manga versions of a story. For example, while the manga versions of *Tsubasa: RESERVoir CHRoNiCLE* and *xxxHOLiC* consistently overlap with each other in their approach to both cast and plot development, their anime adaptations steer clear of repeated crossovers, arguably for fear of alienating the less seasoned manga fans. It is also worth stressing, in this context, that CLAMP's passion for character reiteration over disparate titles should not be simply dismissed as a smart commercial ploy for it actually carries serious philosophical implications. At its deepest, it is indeed deployed as a means of reflecting on the instability and plurality of the self as an infinitely nuanced cultural construct—and particularly on its internal and often painful contradictions and rifts. The multiplicity of the self parallels the multiplicity of the world's dimensions in an inspired assertion of one of Japan's most inveterate belief: namely, the faith in the existence of a uniquely intimate bond between human beings and their environment.

While, as stated, this study hopes to contribute cogently to the field of manga and anime research, it also seeks to reach beyond the compass of manga and anime themselves to investigate the broader philosophical and social contexts which these art forms bring into play. CLAMP's output, in this respect, constitutes a multicolored lens through which those territories may be accessed and explored. In appreciating the distinctiveness of CLAMP's place in today's entertainment industry and fine arts, it is salutary to bear in mind Gian Carlo Calza's reflections on the subject of style at large. "Nowadays, the word 'style' is frequently misinterpreted," the critic maintains, "since it is used to highlight the formal, even decorative aspects of various phenomena of mass culture. This confusion has reached the point where the unfortunate term 'stylist' has been coined to refer to a person who could never exist: someone who creates style. In fact, style is the result of a complex process of personal and social transformation (and as such not attributable to a single person), one that gives rise to images capable of representing values that are profound and enduring, not ephemeral like fashion which, by definition, must constantly be changing" (Calza, pp. 8–9). This theoretical perspective is directly relevant to the attitude to creation communicated by CLAMP over the decades. Corroborating Calza's proposition, its members never claim to be inventing their worlds from scratch so as to assert their status as so-called stylists. In fact, they consistently endeavor to embrace the notion of style as a nexus of energies which inevitably transcends individual ideas, designs and techniques. Their passionately collaborative approach to the creation of manga and anime bears witness to this important aspect of their sustaining philosophy.

Ohkawa has described the four artists' typical approach to manga production in a fashion which throws the collaborative ethos into relief. However, she also makes it incontrovertibly clear that the team's division of labor is not so rigid as to stifle the free flow of the imagination. What matters most, ultimately, is not the development of specialist expertise within discrete niches but rather the cultivation of a holistic attitude to creation. This is meant to enable all four CLAMP members to work together on virtually all aspects of a title's visual and narrative identity without, in the process, having to relinquish autonomous inspiration and privacy. "I write the story and dialogue myself," Ohkawa explains. "Igarashi, Nekoi and Mokona do all the art, but they split the work up differently for each series. All four of us make contributions to each page, so it's a joint effort. But you could also say we work independently, since we have the studio partitioned off to give each of us our own space to work in" (cited in Smith, p. 28).

CLAMP's members have offered illuminating insights into their distinctive work model in several interviews, articles and books, and especially in the volume of manga illustrations titled *CLAMP North Side*, as well as in interviews conducted by Charles Solomon, Chih-Chieh Chang and Zac Bertschy on behalf of *Anime News Network*. By selectively collating the various snippets of information supplied in these sources, it is therefore possible to identify some important aspects of the collective's modus operandi which repeatedly point to its marked predilection for a resolutely non-hierarchical and fluid approach to business. First of all, the available documentary materials indicate that the four artists share a single workplace, which cuts out from their quotidian schedule any need to organize specific meetings in a formal fashion. While militating in favor of both creative efficiency and sustained application, this key aspect of CLAMP's work model is also conducive to the emergence of a salubriously relaxed atmosphere, unhampered by excessive calculation and planning. This is something from which a renowned group of *mangaka* already subject to grueling production schedules from one week to the next is bound to benefit to a considerable degree in both psychological and physical terms.

Ohkawa customarily operates in multiple capacities as the collective's director, producer and storyboarder, while also acting as its spokesperson in public situations. Once Ohkawa has formulated a promising yarn, the four members of the team get together in order to discuss the story's overarching goal and to envision the sorts of characters that would be suitable as protagonists in the light of that leading impetus. It is only after the other members of the team have had a chance to familiarize themselves with the story that Ohkawa drafts an actual outline for its development and concomitantly establishes its setting (or rather settings, given CLAMP's penchant for multiperspectivalism). The ending for each plot is usually determined in advance: this creative habit could be seen to bear an intriguing affinity with one of the key philosophical issues explored by the group throughout its career: namely, the relationship between necessity and free will. Ohkawa also designs many of the story's personae at an early stage in a project's evolution, including supporting characters bound to make frequent appearances and ancillary characters likely to be assigned fleeting participation in the action. Once a sample story and sketch has been submitted to the team's editor and received the stamp of approval, Ohkawa allocates specific roles to each of her colleagues, and then selects the graphic style or styles deemed appropriate to the story in hand on the basis of its cumulative complexity and, where relevant, its connection with CLAMP's other works. Concurrently, Ohkawa supplies her colleagues with a basic sketch for each prospective chapter which specifies the proposed amount of dialogue for each scene, the appropriate size for the panels, and the use of props in relation to the story's dynamic import and to the characters' emotions.

Although Mokona is primarily responsible for character design, while Igarashi and Nekoi focus on the background art, it is not unusual for the three artists to rearrange their roles to apportion different responsibilities to different parties according to the task before them. On occasion, conversely, they may decide to share the work entailed by both character design and background art or else have one single artist execute all the art if the story appears likely to benefit from a more particularized style. This demonstrates that CLAMP's members are no less averse to the rigid compartmentalization of creative talent than they are to hierarchical organization. It also shows that the artists are both able and willing to listen to their works (and underlying concepts) as though these were animate entities in order to recognize the distinctive needs of each, and to then assign a particular artist to a specific job in accordance with such task-related requirements. The work, in this perspective, is granted precedence over the artist. An analogously collaborative attitude underpins CLAMP's commercial decisions, so that even though it is normally up to Ohkawa to choose which projects the group should embrace or decline, it is Igarashi's job to determine the actual timetable to be followed in the execution of each project, and the exact sequence in which the group's interrelated tasks should be undertaken. Unlike many other established *mangaka*, CLAMP does not rely on assistants insofar as its members believe that the introduction of outsiders would be detrimental to the team's overall chemistry and inevitably slow them down — not to mention the fact that assistants unfamiliar with CLAMP's quotidian work model would be powerless to penetrate the "years worth of jargon" which the four artists have incrementally concocted among themselves (Bertschy 2006; Chang; CLAMP 2005f; Solomon).

As noted, a vital facet of CLAMP's characteristic modus operandi consists of the group's aversion to formal hierarchies. A direct corollary of this propensity is its conception of all artistic and all artisanal activities as equally worthy participants in a vibrant process of endless invention. In this respect, CLAMP's stance echoes the lessons of both the indigenous *Mingei* (Folk Crafts) Movement promoted in the 1920s by the philosopher Soetsu Yanagi, and its European counterpart, William Morris' Arts and Crafts Movement of the late nineteenth century. CLAMP's philosophical outlook shares with both movements the belief that artifacts should be designed to fit in with the rhythms of ordinary life, not as putative masterpieces meant to stand out as isolated and somewhat impervious entities. By channeling their rare artistic skills into the making of works intended first and foremost as forms of popular everyday entertainment, CLAMP evidently eschews the elitist tendency to insulate art from the prosaic ebb and flow of the quotidian. Beauty, for CLAMP as for Yanagi, Morris and their followers, resides primarily with hand-made works for common use, made by people working in groups, free of egocentric aspirations and materialistic goals. There are indeed plentiful indications that despite its success, CLAMP's commitment to its trade still emanates from a profound sense of dedication and responsibility which is not governed principally, or indeed at all, by status-related and financial considerations. Concurrently, CLAMP's corpus perpetuates the reverence for materials and tools which has characterized the Japanese approach to creation for time immemorial, thereby throwing into relief art's natural roots and intensely corporeal qualities. Experimenting indefatigably with adventurous mixtures of influences and motifs, CLAMP's works thus give rise to what could be termed a miniculture unto itself.

From a formal viewpoint, CLAMP's versatility is resonantly announced by its artists' ability to convey at once the gracefulness of filigree and the severity of rough-hewn rock, the genteel refinement of a *hakata* doll and the grotesque sublimity of an *oni* mask, combined with an exquisitely original integration of line, texture, color, rhythm and pattern. As anticipated in the opening segment of this discussion, CLAMP's handling of line lies at the core of its ability to engender a special visual language. In all their manifestations, of which there have been many over the decades, CLAMP's visuals draw attention to the lyrical and dramatic qualities of line, to the variable influence of force on line, to the possibility of translating the most disparate phenomena into forms of linear expression, and to the alliance of line to texture and chroma in the evocation of vividly individualized realities. One of the most compelling qualities of CLAMP's handling of the line resides with the artists' ability to engage with this elemental graphic unit in such a way as to communicate simultaneously a graceful sense of composure and an electrifying surge of dynamism. In its evocation of movement, CLAMP's artwork transcends by far the standards of the typical action adventure yarn. The sweeping curves, forceful strokes and crackling visual effects which flood virtually every page of its manga — alongside fanciful curlicues and swooshes — frequently achieve levels of stylization which border on pure abstract art. These graphic elements work most sensationally in the rendition of fire, water and lightning effects. However, it would be wrong to assume that their deployment is limited to the evocation of the more dramatic environmental features accompanying the action. In fact, CLAMP's artistic virtuosity is also dispensed with equal assiduousness on the depiction of quiet dialogical sequences punctuated by poignant character close-ups.

The coexistence of composure and dynamism in CLAMP's handling of the line carries profound philosophical implications insofar as it encapsulates a fundamental tenet of both Buddhist and Shinto thinking which John Reeve has tersely described as a collusion of "serenity and turbulence, spirituality and slaughter" (Reeve, p. 22). Mitsukuni Yoshida conveys an analogous message in a more haunting tone: "even the most glorious life will end in darkness and death; holiness and profanity, splendour and gloom form the dual basis of man's culture" (Yoshida 1980, p. 22). In both areas of human endeavor, one senses a sincere desire to approach reality as a process of unremitting flux — as impermanence (*mujou*) — and therefore as incessantly involved in assorted cycles of birth, death and rebirth. This antibinary attitude is precisely what lies at the heart of CLAMP's manipulation of the line, and specifically, its flair for investing it with a vibrant sense of animateness: the essential aesthetic quality overtly brought to dramatic fruition by the anime titles inspired by CLAMP's manga.

At the same time, the artists' ingenious association of elegantly modulated lines with bold shadowing and chiaroscuro effects enables their pencils and brushes to pursue some unprecedentedly adventurous experiments in the regions of composition and perspective. Concomitantly, CLAMP's graphic orchestration often relies to a substantial degree on vertiginously swirling or spiraling lines, as well as intricate meshes and powerful diagonals, which are capable of infusing otherwise static settings with dynamism and verve. In manga and anime, as in traditional Japanese art, the geometric lines deployed in order to animate the inert components of space are frequently further energized by their integration with the imaginary lines evoked by character interaction as a web of crisscrossing gestural and verbal exchanges, or even silent glances. As varied impressions of kinesis and stasis rhythmically alternate, the beholder's eye is encouraged to journey not only within the frame of a drawing but also beyond it. Yet, the visuals' painstaking care for details guarantees that there is always enough material for the eye to dwell upon, and thus precludes their hurried absorption. On numerous occasions, the sensation of space is more potently suggested by means of lines providing delicate intimations of motion than through stark contrasts between figure and ground. No less effective is the handling of converging or even clashing lines to suggest scenarios of strife and turmoil and so intensify the impression of menace. At its most forceful, this technique serves to put across the impression that the threat is about to break through the surface of the drawing to spread through the viewer's private space. This turns the visual plane into a door inadvertently left ajar through which dark forces may surreptitiously glide.

In its proficient handling of a manga's dynamic dimension, CLAMP brings fully to maturity the boldly experimental vision entertained by two of the greatest *mangaka* of all times: the post-war artists Osamu Tezuka and Machiko Hasegawa. As the article "History of Manga" emphasizes, "Tezuka and Hasegawa were ... both stylistic innovators. In Tezuka's 'cinematographic' technique, the panels are like a motion picture that reveals details of action bordering on slow motion as well as rapid zooms from distance to close-up shots. More critically, Tezuka synchronized the placement of panel with the reader's viewing speed to simulate moving pictures"

("History of Manga"). CLAMP's enthralling lines accommodate all of these elements, exhibiting a degree of tensile energy which imparts them with an aura of vitality even though, strictly speaking, they are motionless marks on a flat page. It is barely surprising, in the light of this remarkable capacity, that CLAMP's manga should lend themselves ideally to adaptation for the anime screen.

It is also notable, where formal play is concerned, that CLAMP's work does not only bridge the domains of manga and anime but also brings into play several other arts through the depiction of studiously detailed environments — e.g., costume design, architecture, interior design, music, cuisine and theater. CLAMP's approach to the representation of clothing undoubtedly constitutes one of the most cherished facets of the team's cachet, while sharing an essential aesthetic principle with some of Japan's most illustrious fashion designers. This, as Akiko Fukai explains, resides with the desire to establish "a new relationship between clothes and the body" which recognizes the importance of "the superfluous 'space' between the garment and the body." This interstitial site, traditionally "referred to as *ma*, is more than simply a void: it is a rich space that possesses incalculable energy" (Fukai 2010, p. 16). By playing with *ma*, CLAMP's sartorial creations depart significantly from Western conceptions of the proper relationship between the body and its garments.

In order to contextualize CLAMP's achievement, it is helpful to take into consideration some of the most significant perspectives on the emergence of manga as both an art form and a medium. Generally used to designate cartoons or comics, the term "manga" translates literally as "whimsical sketches." As Matt Thorn explains, "the word itself was popularized by the famous woodblock print artist [Katsushika] Hokusai but, contrary to a popular myth, it was not invented by him. The word is composed of two Chinese characters — the first meaning 'in spite of oneself' or 'lax' and the second meaning 'picture'— and has been used to describe various comical images for at least two centuries." A popular art form akin to manga first came into prominence "in late eighteenth-century Japan, when a growing middle class of urban merchants had developed a vibrant consumer culture.... Printed in book form using woodblock technology, *kibyoushi* ('yellow covers') were storybooks for adults in which narration and dialogue were placed in and around ink-brush illustrations, often in creative ways that consciously blurred the distinction between text and picture. (Multi-volume *kibyoushi* were known as *goukan*.) Like modern-day manga, they dealt with a variety of subjects, including humor, drama, fantasy, and even pornography" (Thorn). However, Japan's fascination with visually oriented narrative — a phenomenon which eloquently attests to the culture's ubiquitous imbrication with visuality — can be traced much further back than the eighteenth-century. There is indeed ample evidence, studiously gathered by Brigitte Koyama-Richard in the volume *Japanese Animation from Painted Scrolls to Pokémon*, that illuminated scrolls are the true ancestors of modern manga and, by extension, anime. These graphic works were distinguished by an emphatically narrative nature and were originally devoted to the representation of all sorts of "religious, literary, or historical scenes," as well as to the ideation of "a fantastical bestiary," and to the adaptation of "morality tales or stories designed for children" (Koyama-Richard, p. 12). Most crucially, from a structural point of view, the scrolls show compositional attributes of a cinematic stamp, and hence accommodate in an embryonic fashion some of the technical qualities characteristically associated with anime. The original Chinese style was in fact altered on Japanese soil through the incorporation of novel elements of indigenous conception, such as "real-life facial expressions, blocks of color as in celluloid (cels), parallel movement, effects of zoom, the portrayal of characters linked to action" (p. 13). CLAMP's marked penchant for multiperspectivalism, attested to both by the construction of its stories and by its characters' mentalities, finds a worthy antecedent in the ancient scroll's inclination to tell stories from plural angles.

It is vital to acknowledge that the history of manga encapsulates a penchant for crosscultural syncretism which can be seen to have distinguished Japanese society at large for many centuries. CLAMP's own philosophical vision participates in this cultural reality to a paradigmatic degree, consistently manifesting itself as an agile integration of diverse influences drawn from traditional and contemporary trends, on the one hand, and from milieux of both an Eastern and a Western stamp on the other. This pivotal facet of CLAMP's world picture, alluded to earlier in this discussion with reference to the group's eclectic preferences, will be investigated in detail in the work-specific analyses to follow. Where the evolution of manga is specifically concerned, the coexistence of disparate cultural forces within the fabric of Japanese society is borne out by its concurrent involvement with modern Western phenomena and traditional practices of Asian provenance. Accordingly, while some critics, commentators and historians have been eager to highlight the nature of manga as a product of Japan's exposure to American culture in the post-war period, particularly in the guise of comics, cinema and television, others have tended to prioritize manga's connections with time-honored visual and performance arts of an eminently Eastern type. In his account of the history of manga, Thorn champions the former position, arguing that "the ancestor of the modern manga ... is the European/American-style political cartoon of the latter 19th Century, and the multi-panel comic strips that flowered in American newspapers in the last years of the 19th Century and the first years of the 20th Century" (Thorn). The writings of Takashi Murakami and Takayumi Tatsumi corroborate this line of argument in their analysis of the effects of globalization and transnationalism in the dissemination of diverse aspects of popular culture virtually across the globe. The web of aesthetic and intellectual influences borne out by recent developments in the manga industry on both sides of the Pacific clearly exemplify this crosspollinating phenomenon (Murakami; Tatsumi). In addition, Sharon Kinsella's study of contemporary manga enhances the cultural scope of the inquiry in thought-provoking ways by focusing on the development of Japan's publishing industry in the post-war era and specifically on its contribution to the genesis of a consumer-oriented culture (Kinsella).

Numerous writers, conversely, have sought to draw attention to a powerful stream of continuity linking Japan's cultural and artistic traditions and the modern development of manga. Koyama-Richard's aforementioned argument regarding the relationship between manga and ancient scroll painting evidently exemplifies this approach. Another prominent voice in the same camp is Frederik L. Schodt, who argues for the existence of major, if not always direct, connections between modern manga and the aesthetic vision communicated by traditional forms such as *ukiyo-e* and *shunga* woodblock prints, and the form of itinerant theater known as *kamishibai* among several other media (Schodt). Shiro Inoue offers a particularly thought-provoking hypothesis in his assessment of manga as a blend of image-centered and word-centered elements which predate the era of American Occupation (1945–1952). In this perspective, Japan's visually oriented — or "pictocentric" — art can ultimately be regarded as a logical corollary of Japan's long-standing involvement with Chinese graphic art, whereas verbally oriented — or "logocentric" — art (e.g., the novel form) should be seen as a product of the social and economic requirements of Meiji and pre–War Japan and its nationalist agendas. The two trends, argues Inoue, have symbiotically merged in the domain of manga (Inoue 1996).

CLAMP's work is heir to both sides of the cultural equation delineated above. It is hard to imagine that anyone would wish to deny the relevance of the transnational position to CLAMP's oeuvre, given that both the imagery and plotting devices utilized by several of its most respected works often evince affinities with Western texts of both the visual and verbal kinds. Nevertheless, the group's well-documented attraction to cultural, aesthetic and philosophical concepts of incontrovertibly Eastern origin suggests that the critical position which accords priority to internal continuities might be more pertinent to the study of CLAMP's overall achievement. Even a cursory survey of the collective's output reveals the pervasive influence of home-grown traditions across both CLAMP's manga and the anime productions which these have generated. CLAMP's debut title, *RG Veda*, sets this trend with its imaginative appropriation of Hindu mythology, while *Tokyo Babylon*, the group's next big success, is permeated by a spiritualist tradition of specifically Japanese derivation. In some of its most popular titles of later years, and especially *Tsubasa: RESERVoir CHRoNiCLE* and *xxxHOLiC*, CLAMP goes even further: instead of merely adopting a body of legends or esoteric teachings drawn from an Asian context as a narrative infrastructure, it engages with the very foundations of Eastern metaphysics to explore some of the thorniest and most testing of issues.

CLAMP's philosophy, and attendant play with form, are best appreciated with reference to its manga, to the anime which those manga have inspired and to anime to which its members have contributed their designs — in other words, the visual and performance texts which provide this book's key object of study. *RG Veda*, CLAMP's first major success, already harbors many of the most salient elements of the team's epic sensibility in embryonic form. Most prominent among them, on the narrative plane, is CLAMP's flair for nuanced characterization, whereby heroes and villains alike prove capable of enlisting the audience's sympathies from an early stage, and hence maintaining its active engagement with the flow of the story in both its manifest dramatizations and its hints at peripheral side plots and implied subtexts. In the anime adaptation, the quality of character design, firmly grounded in the parent manga's drawings, abets the actors' dramatic development to a considerable degree. At the same time, even though the background art is somewhat sketchy and allusive, rather than descriptively detailed, the action staged against it derives memorable kinetic momentum and verve from the faithful transposition to the anime screen of the dynamic lines and diversified planar arrangements typical of the original manga. This is most notable in the action sequences punctuated by medieval-style martial contests, monstrous beings and portentous spells.

Revolving around six warriors brought together by the quest to overthrow an evil tyrant, the anime version of *RG Veda* focuses on a relatively small portion of the events chronicled in its manga antecedent. Since it is in the source text that the full scale of CLAMP's epic vision proclaims its special caliber, the manga version of the saga is here worth dwelling upon as a seminal moment in that vision's eminent history. The full-blown configuration of the story chronicles the exploits of the "Six Stars" in their mission, foretold by a prophecy, to bring down Taishakuten, the God of Thunder reputed to have rebelled against the Heavenly Emperor and to have killed both him and the guardian deity Ashura-ou. The quest finds inception with the awakening of Ashura-ou's genderless offspring, Ashura, by the "Guardian Warrior" Yasha, and with these two figures' ensuing efforts to gather the other four warriors mentioned in the divination. The action gains both complexity and gravity as the habitually meek and innocent Ashura reveals a destructive and blood-thirsty alter ego. This sinister presence, dormant for a long time, emerges in its full force once all six of the Stars have come together, at which point his apocalyptic aim is also disclosed: to revive the true Ashura, the god presiding over flame, blood and war who has the power to annihilate earth, heaven and hell. The saga reaches its climax with the deadly confrontation engaging Ashura's two sides and Yasha, which inaugurates the distant prospect of a new era blessed by long-awaited peace.

RG Veda, quite apart from standing out as a heroic saga of classic proportions, provides the groundwork from which one may extrapolate certain recurrent ingredients of CLAMP's philosophical perspective and of the narrative strategies utilized in order to bring that outlook to graphic fruition. Particularly worthy of notice, on this point, is CLAMP's preoccupation with certain pivotal themes and motifs, including the image of the fragmented self beset by abusive powers, the tropes of enchanted sleep and prophetic dreaming, and the concepts of fate and necessity as overarching cosmic forces. Concurrently, *RG Veda* bears witness to several of the most salient attributes of its creators' ethical stance, resolutely eschewing both the manichean polarization of humanity on the basis of stark binary oppositions between good and evil, and the tenability of neat resolutions. Accordingly, *RG Veda*'s finale puts an end to centuries of strife by positing peace as a promise to be fulfilled in a far-away future, not as a present or even imminent actuality.

Tokyo Babylon intensifies to a palpable degree the darker facets of CLAMP's vision, already alluded to in *RG Veda*, gaining urgency as the drama progresses. This work marks CLAMP's first significant intervention in the fields of the psychological mystery and the supernatural suspense thriller by chronicling the exploits of Subaru, the youngest member of a family of esteemed mystics who have guarded the country for millennia. In so doing, *Tokyo Babylon* engages with one of Japan's most captivating mystical traditions, *onmyoudou*. This term designates a blend of esoteric cosmology and natural science shaped by practices brought into Japan by Buddhist monks; by the philosophy of *yin* and *yang*; by principles akin to those promoted by contemporary *feng shui* (*fuusui* in Japanese); and by a conception of the universe as a collusion of the Five Elements — earth, fire, wind, water, and the void (*chi*, *ka*, *fuu*, *sui* and *kuu*). The activities typically pursued by *onmyoudou* include the practice of foretelling, the appeasing of evil spirits, and the control of the *shikigami*— a figure akin to the Western familiar. Even though to both many young Japanese people and the vast majority of Westerners, *onmyoudou* is only known as a versatile source of entertainment, it actually constitutes a spiritual journey designed to establish a deep sense of balance, both within the self and between the self and its environment. The figure of Abe no Seimei, invoked in anime as diverse as *Magical Shopping Arcade Abenobashi* (dir. Hiroyuki Yamaga, 2002) and *Shounen Onmyouji* (dir. Kunihiro Mori, 2006–2007), is often commended as one of the greatest *onmyoudou* mystics of all times. His legendary origin in the marriage of a fox spirit and a human, combined with his putative association with no less than twelve *shikigami*, has contributed significantly to the dissemination and maintenance of his mythical stature.

As explained in the *Onmyoudou Awakening* website, even though "the Muromachi period saw closure of the schools formally teaching *onmyoudou* and the royal affiliation with *onmyouji*," the "romantic ideal of *onmyoudou* persisted on, especially in the legends of the beloved Abe no Seimei.... It is through his adventures that many came to know about *onmyoudou* and *onmyouji*, and indeed the name Abe no Seimei is recognized by most Japanese adults and many Japanese children." In addition, while *onmyoudou* has influenced numerous activities and customs routinely undertaken by both Shinto and Buddhism, it is often outside the strictly ceremonial domain that it has survived most effectively as a magnetizing force, especially in "popular culture," where "the romantic concept of *onmyouji* lives on as youths in animated series call upon game cards that come to life and do their bidding just like an *onmyouji* would a *shikigami* in days past. So even if they have been unable to put a label upon it, they know the concept as they had been born into it" ("*Onmyoudou* Introduction"). As Arata Kanoh maintains, *onmyoudou* also proposes that when problems appear most intractable, it may still be possible to circumvent them by migrating from one world to another. The key to its spiritual perspective, in this respect, is the quintessentially epic ability to "solve all your problems by hopping from world to world" (Kanoh, p. 61). As we shall see, this playful, yet dramatically fraught, capacity is invoked by CLAMP's plots with numerous and, by and large, unpredictable variations.

Both the manga and the anime versions of *Tokyo Babylon* throw the unique powers of *onmyoudou* into relief by means of several separate adventures. In the anime adaptation, two of these are successively dramatized. In the first, Subaru is summoned to investigate a series of puzzling accidents linked with a major construction project and the corporation behind it. In the second, the action pivots on Subaru's efforts to catch a serial killer and on his concurrent involvement with a woman endowed with the ability to fathom the past. *Tokyo Babylon* also functions as a prequel to *X*, a work which will shortly be examined in some detail, by foreshadowing its contents not solely in narrative terms but also through the employment of a somberly introspective, yet energetic, mood. On the specifically aesthetic plane, this balance of thoughtfulness and vigor is mirrored by the ubiquitous use of visuals which, though dominated by dark color schemes and lighting effects, are never swallowed into an abyss of tenebrous inertia but actually exude a pulsating sense of vitality by capitalizing on the surprisingly wide range of nuances which black itself is capable of assuming. One of the series' most striking characteristics consists of its flawless synthesis of ancient spiritualist motifs and dramatic strategies typical of the present-day procedural. Relatedly, the otherworldly and the everyday seamlessly coalesce to deliver a vision whose epic feel appears to transcend time and space, yet does not fail to capture the daily rhythms of human emotions in a credible vein. Deliberate pacing assists this tonal blend to great effect, establishing throughout a tangible atmosphere of tension which neither hurls the action's build-up toward its climactic moments nor allows its tempo to decelerate to the point of stagnation. While providing a prequel to *X*, *Tokyo Babylon* also anticipates *xxxHOLiC* in its philosophical attitude by underscoring the ever-present hand of fate through its consistent reliance on chance encounters and random coincidences.

With *Magic Knight Rayearth*, CLAMP yields an unexpected interpretation of the epic mode by engaging in one of its earliest genre-bending experiments. In the manga, as indeed in the two-season TV series and its alternate retelling in the OVA version known as *Rayearth*, we witness an elegantly maintained balance of light and dark energies and corresponding plot convolutions. These attributes aptly parallel CLAMP's reliance on established formulae, on the one hand, and capacity to imbue the familiar with originality on the other. *Magic Knight Rayearth*'s narrative trigger follows quite predictably the conventions of the magical girl (*mahou shoujo*) format by focusing on three ordinary school girls — Umi, Fuu and Hikaru — as they are whisked away from their familiar world, inserted into the alternate reality of Cephiro, and enjoined to embark on the quest to become "Magic Knights" in order to save the land from the ominous forces threatening its survival. In spite of these conventional premises, the drama soon departs from its generic background to engage in an engrossing bildungsroman, enriched throughout by elaborate storytelling replete with classy surprises, an imaginative approach to the depiction of preternatural phenomena, and punctiliously detailed artwork at the interdependent levels of backgrounds, character design and mechanical design.

As the saga progresses, its murkier strands come increasingly to the fore, especially in the second part of both the manga and the anime series. The OVA further intensifies the story's somber elements on numerous occasions. Thus, the darkness which has been threatening to engulf Cephiro all along gains apocalyptic immensity, and the main characters themselves are beset by doubt, anguish and despair. However, the romantic element also progressively intensifies to enhance the text's perspective on the topoi of self-discovery and growth which constitute its very core. The overarching importance of these themes is underscored by persistent demonstrations of the need to go on learning — and remain forever open to new lessons — instead of relying complacently on existing skills and expertise. If emotional and psychological maturation is pivotal to the series' thematics, no less axial is its focus on the value of human relationships. Ultimately, the key lesson promulgated by *Magic Knight Rayearth* lies with the paramount importance of interpersonal ties and obligations: an intricately multithreaded network which it fathoms with unsentimental sensitivity to both its positive and its negative implications. This ethical principle remains crucial to CLAMP's oeuvre to this day, as paradigmatically evinced by the *Tsubasa: RESERVoir CHRoNiCLE* manga throughout its unfolding and, more specifically, as proposed in the context of the world of Infinity. When, within this story arc, Sakura insists on leaving her traveling companions behind in order to traverse dimensions on her own,

Yuuko does not hinder her. She is eager to emphasize, however, that "whether you want it or not, once you have created bonds between you and other people, those bonds will never disappear" (CLAMP 2008c, p. 49).

It is with *X* that the philosophical gravity of CLAMP's epic perspective reaches its apotheosis in a rhetorically trenchant poetry of feeling and action. In fact, few titles are in a position to confirm the group's penchant for crossing the boundary between the mundane and the sublime more eloquently than *X*. This contention is equally applicable to its manga version, its initial anime adaptation as a feature-length work and its subsequent serial reconceptualization. The work is instantly recognizable as an elegantly Gothic epic centered on a youth endowed with supernatural powers. As a psychic of matchless stature, fifteen-year-old Kamui Shirou returns to Tokyo, having left as a small kid, to honor the memory of his mother's final wish. Resolved to protect his childhood friends Fuuma and Kotori at any price, Kamui soon finds out that the mission laid before him is not simply a personal obligation but rather a quest of cosmic proportions. As Tokyo becomes the battle site of Armageddon, it is ultimately up to Kamui to decide the world's fate by choosing between the "Seven Seals" — a.k.a. "Dragons of Heaven" — and save humanity or the "Seven Angels" — a.k.a. "Dragons of Earth" — and thus trigger the human species' conclusive extinction and the cleansing of the entire planet by fire.

Though superbly drawn and lovingly detailed, *X* yields a fair amount of graphic brutality, punctuated by images of severed limbs and gushing blood. However, one does not sense any gratuitous indulgence in gruesome spectacle for its own sake. Moreover, while the series' darkness results in frequent eruptions of violence and rapidly paced action sequences, it repeatedly finds more sedate expression in scenes bathed in a nostalgic atmosphere. These seek to capture the elusive effects of recollection and premonition: topoi which rank high in CLAMP's thematic repertoire from *RG Veda* to *Tokyo Babylon*, from *Tsubasa: RESERVoir CHRoNiCLE* to *Kobato* (to cite but a handful of relevant titles). In the film, where many crucial aspects of CLAMP's cachet are lodged in a capsulated fashion, such scenes tend to record the lasting impact of childhood memories. Often enhanced by the inclusion of slow-moving or even stationary frames, they typically evince surreal and dreamlike qualities which are perfectly matched by the haunting cadences of the soundtrack. A representative case in point is the scene set in Fuuma and Kotori's garden in which their recollections of the time they shared with Kamui as children materialize in the guise of evanescent phantom images of the three characters as their younger selves. Also noteworthy, in this matter, are the frames devoted to snapshots of the three friends at a traditional festival, clothed in ceremonial garb. In addition, the visuals incorporate occasional flashbacks rendered poignantly melancholy by the reliance on overexposure and watered-down palettes. The film's opening sequence encapsulates its characteristic atmospheric mix. Focusing on Kamui's mother as she withdraws from her belly the sword which her son will be required to brandish in the decisive fight, and can only be extracted at the price of her own life, the sequence is undoubtedly perturbing in its lurid intensity. Nevertheless, it is rendered breathtakingly beautiful by the cascade of *sakura* petals accompanying the deed. Likewise explicit, yet aesthetically admirable, is the oneiric sequence in which Kamui wades through a sea of blood toward the crucified and wire-bound Kotori as her brother Fuuma, his alter ego, is eager to dismember her as though he were performing the most natural act.

In all of its incarnations, *X* accords fate the uncontested role of protagonist. Thus, as it becomes increasingly evident that the hero is fated to play a decisive part in the climactic contest whether he likes it or not, a cruel truth is concomitantly brought to the surface: Kamui has ultimately no choice but to engage in mortal combat with his childhood friend Fuuma, though he is precisely one of the two people he has undertaken to protect at any price. This unpalatable, yet ineluctable, outcome is a corollary of Fuuma's standing as Kamui's double, which makes him the only person able to equal the protagonist in every respect, and to complement each aspect of his identity in a specular fashion. The two characters' mutual inextricability entails that the moment Kamui eventually resolves to side with the Dragons of Heaven in an effort to save Kotori, who has been captured by the Dragons of Earth, Fuuma is destined to champion the conflicting side. The bond uniting the two youths is graphically emphasized by the revelation that just as Kamui's mother harbored the fatal weapon within her very body, so Kotori's body hosts a sword of comparable power for Fuuma to wield. While Kamui's mother willingly embraced her fate by wrenching out the sword with her own hand, Fuuma acquires the weapon by brute force, thus tearing his once beloved sister apart. This contrast imparts Fuuma's actions with sadistic undertones which are quite alien to the hero's own temperament. The oracles behind each warring faction, the sisters Hinoto and Kanoe, are the only characters aware of the grim fate in store for Kamui. As they vie for the youth's unconditional allegiance, they both know that finally, whichever camp Kamui decides to support, another Kamui will automatically stand up for the opposite side. Like *RG Veda*, *X* is unsympathetic to consolatory resolutions. Thus, even though Kamui defeats Fuuma in the end, his victory does not radiate any unproblematic sense of joy. In fact, the primary emotion it communicates is Kamui's stark and inconsolable recognition that much as he might have saved humanity, he has personally lost everything in the process.

CLAMP's vision takes a decisive turn in the direction of multiperspectivalism with *Cardcaptor Sakura*, where magic and textuality are presented as inextricably intertwined composite realities. The story focuses on ten-year-old Sakura Kinomoto, an ordinary elementary schoolgirl whose life becomes unexpectedly entangled with the magical realm as a result of her discovery, in her father's library, of the ancient "Book of Clow" and of the pack of likewise magical cards hosted therein. These are accidentally scattered when Sakura utters the word "windy," the name assigned to one of the cards, and thus summons an otherworldly airstream out of which a cute yellow beastie dubbed Cerberus (a.k.a. Kerberos or Kerochan) materializes. Introducing himself as the "Guardian of the Clow Cards," the beanie-like creature informs the girl that it is now her duty to recover the scattered cards as the only hope of avoiding the apocalyptic disaster which the wandering entities are likely to unleash. Sakura embarks on this taxing adventure in the company of Kero-chan himself and of her best friend Tomoyo Daidouji, who enthusiastically embraces her role as Sakura's assistant by designing magical girl costumes to suit the mood of each stage in the saga, and by videotaping Sakura's exploits for later enjoyment. One of the series' most intriguing themes is the bond which gradually—and somewhat stormily—develops between Sakura and Syaoran: a boy who is at first depicted as one of the protagonist's chief adversaries but slowly acquires the traits of a trustworthy ally.

As Carlos Ross and Christina Carpenter point out, *Cardcaptor Sakura* stands out in the recent history of manga and anime thanks to its inspired manipulation of established formulae. It thus offers "a fresh spin on the concept of magical girls. It borrows a little from every show of its kind before it, including *Sailor Moon*, but manages to come up with something unique." For one thing, even though Sakura approaches her task conscientiously, growing more competent and forceful as the saga advances, she also makes sure she enjoys the quest at every available opportunity. So does Tomoyo who, though not equipped with magical powers herself, is so unconditionally fond and protective of her friend as to participate vicariously in each of Sakura's accomplishments. Most importantly, if we focus specifically on the issue of characterization, Kero-chan "has a more fleshed-out personality than previous familiars. He doesn't exist to nag Sakura, for he feels gathering the Clow is as much his responsibility as it is hers, an attribute sorely lacking in most magical girl familiars" (Ross and Carpenter). It is also worth observing that while Sakura, Syaoran and Tomoyo are younger-looking incarnations of the personae bearing the same names in *Tsubasa: RESERVoir CHRoNiCLE*, they evince quite separate personalities and fulfill distinct roles. Sakura and Syaoran, as noted, are initially presented as antagonists—even though the boy does grant the heroine his support when it really matters—whereas in *Tsubasa: RESERVoir CHRoNiCLE*, their mutual love constitutes the multidimensional saga's very essence in both formal and psychological terms. Interspersed with challenging tests and unexpected meetings which expose the heroine to new friends and rivals at every turn, Sakura's journey incrementally acquires all of the defining landmarks of a multilayered bildungsroman. Combining the magic of CLAMP's graphic genius with an astute, challenging and judiciously paced yarn, *Cardcaptor Sakura* charts a developmental journey in which the trials and tribulations endured by the young on the path to adulthood are portrayed with both disarming frankness and an elating sense of irony.

With *Tsubasa: RESERVoir CHRoNiCLE*, CLAMP embarks on a multiperspectival project of unprecedented complexity. This stretches over not only a twenty-eight-volume manga but also a two-season TV series, the film *Tsubasa: RESERVoir CHRoNiCLE The Movie: Princess of the Birdcage Kingdom*, the three-episode OVA *Tsubasa: Tokyo Revelations* and the two-episode OVA *Tsubasa: Spring Thunder*. The saga as a whole records the adventures which befall Syaoran as he travels from world to world in the company of his beloved Sakura, the wizard Fai, and the warrior Kurogane. This transworld odyssey, which the characters undertake courtesy of Yuuko, the "Dimensional Witch," and of her mascot-like "teleportation" agent Mokona, is to retrieve Sakura's shattered memories, which have dispersed across time and space in the guise of magical feathers. (This theme echoes *Cardcaptor Sakura*'s use of the dispersed cards.) The mission, hopeless though it may look and sound, is rendered not merely desirable but absolutely necessary by the prophetic disclosure that without her mnemonic baggage, neither Sakura's body nor her soul stand a chance of protracted survival. The multidimensional perspective is complicated by the gradual revelation that Sakura herself is endowed with time- and space-defying capacities. Each of the worlds visited by the protagonists in the course of their singular quest is distinguished by very specific cultural, historical, geographical and climatic attributes. Indeed, all of those parallel dimensions are thoroughly individualized by their association with particular traditions and customs, which find apt correlatives in a wide range of vestimentary and architectural styles. The pageant of alternate realities paraded before our eyes as we journey, alongside Syaoran and his companions, from world to world also encompasses a stunning variety of genres and a related ensemble of both graphic and dramatic codes and conventions.

What renders the saga a uniquely poignant experience, thereby preventing its transdimensional flourishes from deteriorating into vapid entertainment, is the fundamentally tragic nature of the pact providing its entire action's narrative premise. As she grants the protagonists the power to world-hop in search of the scattered feathers, Yuuko sanctions that in exchange for this gift, Sakura must be forever deprived of her memories of Syaoran. This is not to say that the Dimensional Witch is something of a sadist hell-bent on imposing an arbitrary power upon the hapless humans at her mercy. In fact, Yuuko's conditions result from her pained awareness that the universe requires an underlying equilibrium to be maintained at all times, and that any gain must therefore entail a loss of comparable proportions. Yuuko's viewpoint is expounded in detail in the manga source, where she asserts that although "at first glance, the world seems to be chaotic," and "individual actions and events may seem like they're scattered and confused, the whole balances out to proceed on a certain course" (CLAMP 2008b, p. 24). A related belief, as we shall see, animates the philosophical message at the core of *xxxHOLiC*. As the saga unfolds in its various configurations, its darkness progressively thickens, to reach a disquieting culmination with the OVA *Tsubasa: Tokyo Revelations*. In this segment of the anime, as indeed in the adventures chronicled in the manga volumes not adapted to the anime format, CLAMP's appetite for multiperspectivalism gains further complexity. Personal identity itself, in these contexts, is posited as no less composite and unstable a constellation than the saga's setting. In the process, it becomes incrementally arduous to differentiate between originals and clones, benevolent agents and their iniquitous alter egos.

The major source of comfort, in this otherwise bleak scenario, is offered by the anime's repeated intimations that even though the past and its memories have been erased, as long as there is a future, new bonds and hence new memories may be positively established. Koichi Mashimo, the director of the *Tsubasa: RESERVoir CHRoNiCLE* TV series, has explicitly emphasized the paramount importance of this aspect of the saga: "when I read the original manga, I felt the message was about the importance of making new memories ... I want to make that the most important part of the anime adaptation" (Mashimo, p. 48). The suggestion that Sakura and Syaoran might gradually forge a new relationship based on mutual love and respect—and one no less valuable than the original bond—is hinted at an early stage in the first TV series by Fai's comments regarding the nature of parallel dimensions at large. Mulling over the baffling presence of ostensibly identical people in radically different worlds, the mage proposes that in "altered surroundings," humans are not likely to "act differently" but rather to "create the same friendships" and "make the same mistakes.... Where it counts, we'd end up the same, no matter what we'd done—or remembered."

With the kaleidoscopic variety of its cultural frame of reference, *Tsubasa: RESERVoir CHRoNiCLE* offers vibrant confirmation for Yoshida's assessment of the passion for multicultural syncretism which has characterized Japan for centuries. "The Japanese taste for foreign things," argues Yoshida, "helped broaden their limited horizons with tangible proof that other cultures besides their own existed. It also nurtured an openness and flexibility toward the artifacts of other cultures completely independent of the people or the historical backgrounds of the places from which they came" (Yoshida 1984, p. 40). This proclivity has also made it possible for Japanese culture to relocate and reshape its multicultural findings with unforced creativity, and without having to worry immoderately about their origins. On the whole, the imported material is approached playfully, more as a Surrealist *objet trouvé* than as an intimidating monument. The underlying philosophical message which this perspective entails—and in which *Tsubasa: RESERVoir CHRoNiCLE* indubitably participates—coincides with the intuitively discriminating spirit with which the Japanese have time and again been able to extract the structural core of the imported materials to secure its adaptability to their culture's particular requirements. Therefore, "just as when Chinese civilization was introduced centuries before," Japan can be seen to have dealt with Western sources "as a matter of *forms*, not as something so fundamental that it posed a threat to human existence or identity" (p. 111). *Tsubasa: RESERVoir CHRoNiCLE* follows this model in its simultaneously audacious and cogent synthesis of its dizzyingly disparate ingredients.

An arty cocktail of fantasy, horror, irony and dark symbolism, the *xxxHOLiC* manga has spawned an ample anime franchise which encompasses the film *xxxHOLiC the Movie: A Midsummer Night's Dream*, the two TV series *xxxHOLiC* and *xxxHOLiC: Kei* and the OVAs *xxxHOLiC: Shunmuki*, *xxxHOLiC: Rou* and *xxxHOLiC: Rou Adayume*. The story revolves around the character of Kimihiro Watanuki, a young man haunted by ghouls which nobody else can perceive. The word "haunt," in this instance, should by no means be taken as a purely figurative term. In fact, Kimihiro is afflicted by demonic agents of all sorts in a palpably physical fashion, as these resist his efforts to ignore them with insolent obstinacy. The youth, it seems, harbors an unwelcome proclivity to attract those forces magnetically in spite of his best intentions. Kimihiro turns for help to the charismatic witch Yuuko Ichihara the day he finds himself mysteriously drawn into a shop by an inscrutable power. Yuuko, we soon learn, owns the store and is committed to assisting clients who seek her help as they struggle to deal with multifarious troubles supposedly triggered by supernatural causes. Such petitioners qualify for support, however, only as long as they are prepared to pay a price equivalent to the value of the wish they pursue. Thus, the sorceress is quite prepared to help Kimihiro overcome his misfortune in exchange for his services as a chef, cleaner and shop assistant — duties which the youth punctiliously endeavors to fulfill even as they require him to negotiate relentlessly the assorted magical entities which infest Yuuko's abode and seem hell-bent on clinging onto him. The most prominent preternatural presences within Yuuko's domain are the childlike Marudashi ("Streaking") and Morodashi ("Flashing") — a.k.a. Maru and Moro. Allegedly brought into being by Yuuko herself, these characters are bound to her store and are responsible for summoning the people who beg Yuuko's assistance. Unless Maru and Moro intervene as liaising agents with the power to mediate between the ordinary human world and the enchanted reality of Yuuko's outfit, the store remains magically invisible.

A veritable incarnation of the erratic rhythms which often govern magical phenomena at large, Yuuko is highly volatile and capricious, and accordingly comes across as serious one second and girlish the next, cuttingly sarcastic at times and casually cheerful at others. Either way, she always appears to have an inexhaustible reserve of tricks up her sleeve — stratagems she is not, on the whole, readily willing to reveal to either her employees or her clients. There is little doubt, however, that deep down, she cares genuinely for the hapless Kimihiro. Alongside Watanuki and

Yuuko, a major cast member is Shizuka Doumeki, Kimihiro's classmate, who has a knack of repelling supernatural presences as expertly as the protagonist can perceive them. Although he is a generally amiable character, Kimihiro feels antipathy toward Doumeki even as he gradually befriends him, largely because he perceives him as a competitor in the quest to win the heart of the girl he fancies, Himawari Kunogi. However, Watanuki cannot deny that as a result of Doumeki's exorcistic talent, he is only really safe in the company of this unruffled, serene and constitutionally laconic youth much as he may resent him.

Central to the anime's philosophy is the idea that there is no such thing as coincidence in life since all events, even the apparently most random and unpredictable, are ultimately dictated by the principle of inevitability (*hitsuzen*). Everything that happens, in Yuuko's domain, is essentially and inexorably meant to happen. The concept of *hitsuzen* indicates that notions of inevitability and necessity do obtain in the realm of magic no less than in the sphere of ordinary human affairs but in that context, they are directed by the unfathomable rhythms of existence rather than by empirical observation and rational calculation. Across the multifaceted sequence of adventures cumulatively dramatized by the manga, the movie, the two TV series and the OVAs, disparate cases are investigated and resolved by Yuuko and her assistant with varying degrees of finality. Each episode encapsulates an ethical message, emphasizing that the steepest prices are those which people have to pay not in exchange for magical assistance but rather, more mundanely and yet more disturbingly, as a result of their indulgence in desires and habits so obsessive as to have degenerated into full-fledged diseases. By positing the supernatural realm as the cause of such addictions, the anime conveys its lesson in allegorical form instead of dishing out clear-cut morals with overtly didactic intent. Therefore, as it portrays Yuuko as a mystic therapist who can help her clients overcome their sorrows, the anime never fails to remind us that what people ultimately need to learn is how to help themselves.

Like other CLAMP series, *xxxHOLiC* grows more and more somber as its adventures unfold. Thus, as Kimihiro becomes involved in various missions with his employer, it progressively transpires that under these jobs, there lies a vicious plot which Yuuko aims to dispel by deploying the youth's abilities unbeknownst to him. At the same time, Kimihiro's tragic past is gradually brought to the surface. Indeed, the youth's fate turns out to be far more closely bound up with the preternatural realm than he might ever have suspected prior to his association with Yuuko. By recourse to this topos, the first TV series strives to chronicle its protagonist's maturation and growth even as it maintains the generic and structural qualities of the supernatural investigative thriller. The anime's darker subtexts are more starkly exposed in the second TV series, where Kimihiro becomes the victim of the wrathful Spider Spirit, whose ire he has involuntarily sparked, and loses an eye as a result. CLAMP's fascination with the trope of ocular impairment as both a narrative ruse and a symbolic motif harks back to the artists' handling of the same theme in *Tsubasa: RESERVoir CHRoNiCLE*, where Syaoran is portrayed as its victim. The connection is consolidated by the manga versions of *Tsubasa: RESERVoir CHRoNiCLE* and *xxxHOLiC* which, as noted, feature numerous crossovers which their anime adaptations understandably marginalize. A particularly important moment, in this regard, consists of the chapter in *Tsubasa: RESERVoir CHRoNiCLE* where the traveling companions are enabled to traverse dimensions by the price previously paid by Kimihiro in the form of his personal memories. The latter part of the anime also maximizes a pivotal formal attribute of the franchise as a whole, which Diane Tiu fittingly describes as follows: "all events are interconnected and ... one good turn deserves another, while grudge and sins come back to haunt. Rewards are never reaped immediately, and audiences are always treated to a pleasant surprise when Watanuki is later remembered for the good deeds he had performed in the past and is reciprocated" (Tiu).

A slice-of-life story with a mystical flavor, *Kobato* revolves around the eponymous heroine's efforts to fill a jar with all the physical and emotional pain, anxieties and worries she removes from the hearts of the people she encounters on her journey. In order to fulfill this task, however, the clumsy and ingenuous Kobato must first face a few tests herself. The reward she is promised for filling up the special vessel is to have her most cherished wish granted. The work's most intriguing character, along Kobato herself, is her sidekick: a blue dog with shark-like teeth named Ioryogi with a proclivity to chastise his young companion uncompromisingly whenever she makes a mistake — which is far from rare an occurrence. Kobato's past and background are shrouded in mystery, which sets her apart from the majority of CLAMP's other protagonists. Not all of the creatures encountered by the girl in the course of her quest are explicitly malevolent, spiteful or even unhelpful. Yet, the predicaments afflicting the lacking souls she is enjoined to return to their pristine state are unequivocally tragic even when they stem from chains of utterly mundane circumstances. In fact, they function as a compelling allegory for the state of alienation endured by people in a world where the bond between humanity and nature has been thoughtlessly eroded. The heroine's task, in this perspective, consists of restoring a fractured equilibrium upon which our very survival as a sentient species finally depends.

Kobato elliptically reflects an understanding of the relationship between human beings and their environment which has been ingrained in Japanese culture for time immemorial — and could indeed be realistically described as a mainstay of both its evolution and its progressive elaboration of a striking variety of art forms and styles. In mainstream Western thought, matter has been conventionally looked down on as a presence devoid of any spiritual value. This prejudice has served as the foundation of legion philosophical positions eager to champion the transcendence of matter in the service of the mind and the soul as humanity's supreme aim. Seeking to shape the natural world in accordance with the whims and demands of its human inhabitants, and attributing these creatures' putatively inalienable right to mastery to their possession of the faculty of reason, Western thought has insistently promoted the primacy of the Logos as the domain of neatly mapped out categories and shapes, and hence routinely discredited anything fluid, unclassifiable or amorphous as simply evil or at least sullied. The individual self, relatedly, has been typically granted precedence over the community to which it belongs, and the singular element accorded supremacy over the global ensemble. Shinto, conversely, regards the cultivation of equilibrium between human beings and their surroundings as the necessary precondition of the wholesome functioning of both singular humans and their social formations. The individual, relatedly, is perceived as indissolubly enmeshed with a vast network of other creatures entailing both actual and hypothetical interactions.

Spiritual forces traverse the entire cosmos and even the tiniest portion of the land should therefore be approached as the site of an invisible encounter between the corporeal and the spiritual, the evanescent and the eternal. In fact, even the humblest of pebbles and the faintest of ripples on the surface of a pond is saturated with potential meanings insofar as they host — less magnificently but no less tenaciously than sublime mountains, forests or waterfalls — the spiritual core which human beings themselves share with all of nature's forms, and shelter in their bodies no less than in their minds. The physical side of all experience, a dimension which has traditionally played a crucial part in Japanese art and aesthetics at large, declares its hold as a ubiquitous metaphysical principle presiding over the harmonious fusion of the material and the impalpable. At the same time, the inherent vitality of all natural forms is attested to by their physical constitution as proof of their incessant interaction with an inveterately fluid environment. An ancient pine tree, for example, will be seen to bear its history as a textual mesh inscribed by the assaults of wind, rain, hail and snow upon its gnarled branches, clinging roots and august bark, and accordingly honored not merely as a natural entity but also as a spiritual agency worthy of veneration. Likewise, a rock openly displaying the injuries of time on its surface in the guise of scratches, furrows, indentations and curls might deserve to be ceremonially surrounded by a *kumihimo*, or sacred rope, as a means of embracing the mystical energy it has stored through both its trials and its unabated resilience. CLAMP's distinctive handling of the line, particularly in its application to the execution of elaborate patterns, echoes the Shinto world picture with tactile immediacy. Corroborating this contention with understated grace, *Kobato* further embraces that same perspective with its dramatization of the heroine's efforts to restore the world's inner balance by healing its troubled souls.

The animistic ethos underpinning *Kobato* strikes its roots in Japanese mythology, where the cosmos in its entirely is conceived of as a tripartite structure encompassing the lofty celestial regions of Tamakanohara, where the supreme deities (*kunitsukami*) reside; the human domain of Nakatsukuni, where the legion spiritual energies emanating from two of those deities (one male and one female) find expression in disparate natural phenomena; and the land of Yomi, the realm of darkness beneath the earth. The word Nakatsukuni translates literally as "middle world" to point to the liminal location of the human world on the threshold where the luminous purity of Tamakanohara and the dreariness of Yomi intersect and coalesce. Although the three zones are, strictly speaking, discrete, this does not render the Japanese universe hierarchical in the Western understanding of the word. Hence, while it is generally accepted that human beings cannot aspire to divine standing, the realm of the gods is not ideated as a perfect world in the way Christianity tends to think of heaven. Most importantly, in the context of CLAMP's output, all three of the world's strata are ultimately seen to partake of one and the same spiritual essence. Related philosophical positions of an eminently animistic stamp will soon be examined in relation to *Angel Layer* and *Chobits*.

In its exploration of composite cross-generic universes, CLAMP has repeatedly focused on the concept of subjectivity as an outcome of various technologies, some of which come across as downright fictional and others as metaphorically related to real-life practices and instruments. *Angelic Layer* and *Chobits* epitomize this important facet of CLAMP's philosophical perspective. *Angelic Layer* revolves around the character of Suzuhara Misaki, her fortuitous introduction to the eponymous game and incremental involvement in its performance. The backbone of the drama consists of the chain of ludic confrontations engaging a varied array of girls and boys who purchase miniature robotic dolls dubbed "Angels," customize and adorn them in accordance with their personal tastes and dispositions, and then deploy them in conjunction with a magnetic table known as "Layer." By recourse to futuristically sophisticated technology, the human player is able to communicate his or her thoughts to the Angel and hence transmit appropriate commands. The series, in both its manga and anime configurations, takes care to throw into relief each of the main player's personality traits down to the tiniest eccentricity and to show how these translate into specific battling techniques, while also inevitably affecting the dolls' own behavior, with a refreshing mix of humor and drama. Though punctuated by narrative and performative formulae redolent by turns of the classic *mecha* show, the fighting tournament anime, and slapstick comedy, *Angelic Layer* faithfully captures the psychological acuity characteristically associated with CLAMP's output through its emphasis on the incomparable values of friendship, courage and genuine affection.

As a romantic fairy tale infused with sci fi motifs and a slice-of-life take on contemporary consumer culture, *Chobits* provides further confirmation of CLAMP's penchant for adventurous formal hybridization through its eclectic admixture of genres. Set in the not-too-distant future, *Chobits* proceeds from the narrative premise that personal computers will soon develop into "Persocoms," mobile computers with the appearance of fully sentient humans. The action finds inception with Hideki Motosuwa's accidental discovery of a discarded Persocom in the shape of an attractive girl and decision to adopt the creature as his own, even though this particular Persocom, whom he names Chi, turns out to lack the skills characteristic of other members of that technospecies. Hideki gradually finds out that no normal Persocom is able to access Chi, let alone check her technical specifications, and that this peculiarity might be attributable to her latent status as a "Chobit," an especially advanced type of Persocom endowed with independent thought. As the story progresses, the relationship between Chi and Hideki transcends by far the ordinary bond tying a computer to its user to include romantic options which the two parties, driven both together and apart by their intrinsic corporeal difference, find both tormenting and tantalizing.

Taken in tandem, *Angelic Layer* and *Chobits* offer a composite vision through their allusions to the transcultural significance of the trope of the synthetic human on the philosophical, rather than purely generic, plane. At one level, *Angelic Layer*'s depiction of its Angels and *Chobits*' portrayal of its Persocoms reflect the global popularity of creatures such as robots, androids, biomechanoids, mutants, replicants and cyborgs. At another level, their treatment of those fictional beings pays homage, albeit obliquely, to a specifically Japanese fascination with artificial human-like entities of the kind we find embedded in anime and manga. This aesthetic preference is copiously documented by figures as diverse as Astro Boy and Gundam, the Patlabor and the Evangelion Units, Gunbuster and *Ghost in the Shell*'s cyborgs, among countless others. Simultaneously, *Angelic Layer* and *Chobits* resonate with a much older expression of Japanese culture's attraction to simulated humans which dates back to the exquisite *karakuri ningyou* manufactured in the Edo period: mechanical dolls and puppets designed for a wide range of both practical and leisure-oriented functions and often invested, in accordance with native culture's animistic proclivities, with a level of animateness unfeasible for their Western counterparts.

Yet, *Angelic Layer* and *Chobits* take us even further back in time by echoing the ancient puppet arts of Japan as creative practices whish survive today in the cherished Bunraku performances which consistently attract both the indigenous population and foreign visitors in large numbers. As Jane Marie Law shows with remarkable scholarly precision in the evocatively titled volume *Puppets of Nostalgia*, much as contemporary audiences marvel at the stupendously elaborate and engrossingly romantic tales enshrined in the Bunraku tradition, Japan's puppet arts did not come into being as entirely novel phenomena in the nineteenth century, as some accounts of the rise of that theatrical vogue intimate. In fact, they strike their roots in much older activities which are intimately bound up with socioreligious values steeped in animism. The authentic origins of modern Japan's fascination with artificial humans therefore lie with the ancestral world picture promulgated by Shinto. In this respect, the universe alluded to by *Angelic Layer* and *Chobits* echoes Yoshida's inspiring portrait of the animistic ethos: "every thing and creature that exists in the earthly realm, just like all the deities of the earth that rule them ... are related by birth, so to speak. And like the *kami* that created them, all things and creatures possess a dimension of the divine ... this makes supernature a part of everyday life" (Yoshida 1985, p. 9). This atavistic conception of nature has developed over the centuries to embrace inanimate entities, following the belief that "if trees or stones possess their own anima, man-made objects made out of such materials must, too, possess that anima. Thus anima exist in all the articles and utensils of daily use. And it was these anima that in fact allowed man to live in harmony with his tools" (p. 23). Moreover, to the extent that they function as "companions of man in life and work," such objects "are often given names" and perceived as "extensions of their human users" (p. 90). Far from being dismissed as outmoded, this cultural stance still imbues people's treatment of disparate articles routinely used in the contexts of both domestic life and automated production. "In Japan," Yoshida avers, "an operator of a modern industrial robot thinks of it in much the same way as a traditional carpenter thought of his tools — as his alter ego or extension of himself" (pp. 90–91).

The domain of popular entertainment has persistently sought to communicate the animistic perspective outlined above by striving to suggest the sentient character of apparently inert man-made beings. All sorts of stories strive to remind us that dolls, too, have souls — which is why, in traditional communities, priests are asked to perform propitiatory ceremonies and exorcisms upon them when it is feared that they might harbor malevolent intentions conducive to curses. Scientific and technological developments have incrementally imparted the animistic vision with novel layers of philosophical significance and ethical complexity. Therefore, in assessing the broad cultural relevance of the figure of the synthetic human-machine hybrid, it is also important to acknowledge both Angels' and Persocoms' standing as emblems of humanity's gradual transformation in the light of its imbrication with technology. Through their imaginary creatures, *Angelic Layer* and *Chobits* reflect on the degree to which the human body itself has ineluctably altered as machines of all kinds have increasingly infiltrated its rhythms and redefined its form, not merely in their capacity as tools but also as prosthetic complements, identity markers and companions — i.e., as living entities in their own right. Concurrently, the two works urge us consider the strategies through which people attempt to resist that process of constant change or else learn to accept it and live with it.

Finally, *Angelic Layer* and *Chobits* intimate that artificial beings modeled on humans, charming though they may be, go on haunting us insofar as they prompt us to ponder two interrelated questions of vital ontological importance: whether an ostensibly lifeless object might in fact be alive;

whether, alternately, a creature which appears to be alive really is so. If a synthetic entity like an Angel or a Persocom, strictly speaking devoid of life in the biological sense of the term, is capable of manifesting full sentience, the doubt arises that humans, conversely, might be no more than machines. The conceptual affinities between *Angelic Layer* and *Chobits* delineated above are consolidated by their location in the same universe. Moreover, the two stories come momentarily together in volume 19 of the *Tsubasa: RESERVoir CHRoNiCLE* manga within the world of Infinity. Hikaru, Misaki's battle doll from *Angelic Layer*, features in the role of the cybernetic "chess piece" deployed by Sakura's opponent, Eagle, in the decisive stages of a formidable tournament run by the local mafia. Chi, for her part, makes an appearance as Sakura's means of traversing dimensions in order to travel to another world by herself in an attempt to change the future she has foreseen in a dream but concealed from her traveling companions. (Hikaru, incidentally, is herself named after one of the heroines from *Magic Knight Rayearth*.)

The technologies (in the broad sense of this term) deployed in *CLAMP School Detectives* as means of establishing specific configurations of subjectivity are of quite a different ilk. Neither mechanical nor digital, they in fact consist of the particular institutions, and attendant mores, in which the bulk of the story's numerous adventures are staged. These revolve around the tasks undertaken by three elementary students at CLAMP School — Nokoru, Suoh and Akira — following their decision to become investigators for the specific purpose of assisting ladies in trouble. Though deliberately formulaic in the rendition of several of its distinctive character traits and plot complications, *CLAMP School Detectives* is indubitably effective in the evocation of the peculiar chemistry which binds the three protagonists together from beginning to end. This enables the series to enliven its actors' more endearing connotations without these deteriorating into affected mannerisms. At the same time, even their more stilted attitudes, vapid ideals and naive preconceptions are presented in a gentle light which renders them no less charming, as underlying personality markers, than their overtly positive qualities. Sixth grader Nokoru, the youngest son of the school's founders, comes across as a perfect prodigy in every respect and serves as the prestigious school council's president. Fifth grader Suoh, the council's secretary, is not as mentally acute as Nokoru but compensates for this marginal deficiency with his impressive physical abilities. Fourth grader Akira, the treasurer, appears more ingenuous than his older associates and while this personality trait may put him at a disadvantage in the face of malicious opponents, it also imparts his portrayal with an aura of heartwarming optimism. Akira's culinary abilities are also worthy of notice and make him a partial predecessor of *xxxHOLiC*'s Watanuki.

Pivotal to the series in both spatial and thematic terms is CLAMP School's sprawling campus, a city-within-a-city accommodating distinct schools for every age group from kindergarten to college, as well as living quarters, shops, restaurants and banks. This location gives CLAMP a perfect opportunity to give their passion for multidimensional universes free rein within the boundaries of a single basic location. It thus allows the team's members to communicate at once a stupendous feel of atmospheric and stylistic variety, and a structurally satisfying impression of organizational consistency. The sense of coherence conveyed by the anime's setting is also useful as a means of counterbalancing the eminently episodic nature of its narrative, capitalizing on the dramatization of a case per installment, which could easily have induced a feeling of disjointedness or repetitiveness. The final six episodes contribute significantly to the consolidation of the drama's cumulative unity by focusing on a single case. This revolves around a transfer student and the mysterious circumstances surrounding the character's arrival on the scene, which leads to some unexpected disclosures regarding Nokoru's personal past while also lending the story as a whole a darker twist.

Mouryou no Hako harks back to *Tokyo Babylon* in its pervasive deployment of numerous motifs drawn from Japan's spiritualist lore, which enfold its plot in an overall aura of mystery-laden mysticism. The anime's very title stems from indigenous esoteric tradition insofar as the *mouryou* is a spirit reputed to devour corpses and to linger in the space between light and darkness. The word *hako*, for its part, translates as "box" and lends itself to a variety of symbolic interpretations throughout the series. In addition, an entire episode is devoted to a detailed history of Japanese goblins. Even though *Mouryou no Hako* echoes *Tokyo Babylon* through its elegant integration of motifs associated with ancient mysticism and the formulae of present-day investigative fiction, the anime's cultural and historical setting renders it more germane to CLAMP works concerned with the elaboration of varied technologies of subjectivity than to that early production. The story is indeed staged in an especially momentous phase of Japanese history where technological progress is specifically concerned, the Showa Era: a period coinciding with Japan's full-fledged entry into industrialization. *Mouryou no Hako* looks back at the Showa Era with equal doses of nostalgia and apprehension, deftly deploying its sepia-tinged backdrop and palpably immersive atmosphere to absorb us into the world of the 1950s so deeply and comprehensively as to encourage us to feel that we have actually traveled back in time to that particular phase of Japan's history. This enables us to experience its atmosphere in an almost synesthetic fashion rather than merely witness it as distanced external observers. The anime's setting comes to represent not so much a convenient spatiotemporal location but an animate character in its own right. *Mouryou no Hako* tactfully highlights the extent to which technological progress is inextricably intertwined with a pervasive sense of loss resulting from the erosion of traditional customs, values and ties, routinely exacerbated by the subject's distancing from the material substratum of existence. In this regard, the liminal zone between light and darkness traditionally associated with the mythical character of the *mouryou* could be interpreted as an allusion to the uprooted condition which human beings have to endure as a result of their loss of traditional anchors. The series objectively recognizes the Showa Era as an epoch of unprecedented openness to foreign influences, creative exuberance and heightened productivity. Nevertheless, it also persistently communicates that era's darker significance as the harbinger of a world marred by the ever-increasing alienation of the human species from nature — and hence by a flagrant betrayal of the most inveterate lesson of indigenous philosophy. At the same time, *Mouryou no Hako* exposes the ascendancy of the linguistic and rhetorical technologies which capitalize on mental conditioning so as to shape people's intellectual and emotive responses by documenting the rapid spread of a new religious cult. The spiritual dimension itself, in this respect, is portrayed as no less sick and potentially nefarious than the most blatant form of modern commodification.

In order to communicate its philosophical message in an unobtrusive yet penetrating fashion, the anime brings into play a subtle generic synthesis. The first half of the story is presented in a resolutely non-chronological order, which intentionally serves to evoke the impression that the events it recounts are quite unrelated random occurrences. In this segment of the anime, *Mouryou no Hako* focuses on two initially unconnected cases: the enigma unfolding around Kanako, the heir of a rich tycoon who is mysteriously hit by a train and then goes missing, and the serial murders and dismemberments of several young girls. This portion of the story relies primarily on the classic whodunit formula, and on related codes and conventions readily associated with various aspects of mystery, detective and crime fiction. With the second half of the show, we move into explanatory territory, as its episodes proceed, in a generally orderly fashion, to address coherently all of the mysteries and riddles cultivated in the previous installments so as to arrive at a satisfying chain of logical revelations. These are sustained by a special episode presented from the perspective of a relatively marginal character, which rounds off the drama while also offering an element of hope. Although the anime abounds with bizarre, sinister and even downright macabre moments of drama, matched by appropriately spine-chilling visual cues and symbols, it keeps its feet firmly on the ground by seeking to expose its world's endemic depravity as the supreme horror — a deeply ingrained existential malaise which is ultimately far more alarming than any amount of gory spectacle or suspense-laden action. Therefore, in spite of its mystical affiliations, *Mouryou no Hako* cannot be unproblematically equated to antiquarian entertainment of the escapist ilk.

Code Geass, an anime to which CLAMP has contributed significantly with its original character designs, explores various technologies through which subjectivity comes into being, and is thereafter fostered or thwarted by specific political dispensations, through the lens of an alternate history scenario. (Unlike other titles here examined, *Code Geass* constitutes an original anime series subsequently adapted to manga form. The CLAMP artists themselves were not directly involved in the adaptation.) This is predicated on the assumption that seven years prior to the events chronicled in the main body of the drama, Japan was occupied by the sprawling "Britannia Empire," subsumed as one of its colonies, and renamed "Area 11." So pervasive is the Empire's dominance that even Tokyo Tower, the capital's defining symbol, has been transformed into a memorial meant to celebrate the invaders' triumph. The colony enjoys an apparent state of permanent peace but this emanates from brutal military repression rather than from any genuine harmony or sense of well-being. In fact, the invaders have no regard for Japanese lives and no compunction in exterminating innocent civilians, including children, wherever they perceive potential seeds of unrest.

The anime's key characters are the valiant young men and women who dare to defy tyranny by means of clandestine rebellion. Especially notable among them are Kallen Stadtfeld, a half Japanese and half Britannian girl who works for a resistance group while posing as a meek and sickly student; Suzaku Kururugi, a low-ranking soldier in the Britannia Empire persecuted by the "Purists," a racist organization within the military who resent his Japanese lineage; and, above all, Lelouch Lamperouge, an Area 11 youth who obtains a supernatural power dubbed "Code Geass" from the Witch of Fate, C.C., which enables him to affect other people's minds, and hence resolves to deploy it to initiate a crusade under the name of "Zero" to free his homeland and its beleaguered people. The only respite from this pervasively bleak state of affairs is provided by ordinary student life on the Ashford Academy campus, the closest thing to a family which Lelouch himself has ever truly experienced. Even this atmosphere, however, is threatened by the boy's magical ability, as its use among friends is bound to carry unsavory repercussions in its wake. What is instantly obvious about both the anime's pivotal characters and other personae brought into play as supporting or peripheral presences is the extent to which the secrecy and undercover strategies to which they are forced to resort causes their whole lives to be effectively fake, simulated, even unreal. What the anime's protagonists need to develop, accordingly, is not so much refined strategic and martial skills as the courage to face the truth. Failure to do so, the drama insistently suggests, will only tear them apart. Director Goro Taniguchi has sought to elaborate this axial aspect of the anime by emphasizing the importance of inner maturation as no less worthy a goal than overt transformative action. *Code Geass* is "basically a story of two opposing approaches to acquiring freedom," Taniguchi avers, "changing things from the inside versus destroying the old to create something new" (Taniguchi, p. 36).

The axial technology exposed by *Code Geass*, in this context, is the governmental apparatus itself as a concurrently mechanized and mechanistic system which relentlessly shapes the identities of its hapless subjects by infiltrating each aspect of their existence through both coercive disciplinary measures and more furtive but no less effective psychological conditioning. Prior to Lelouch's advent on the scene, the resistance fighters were only able to operate as individual cells endowed with limited powers and therefore unable to develop systematic collaborative strategies. When "Zero" makes his appearance and the utter uniqueness of his formidable weapon begins to transpire, the rebels are for the first time supplied with the cohesive agency they need to stand up to the Empire. However, even when the young fighters do eventually find the means of waging war against their oppressors and regaining control of their country, casting off the lies, distortions and obfuscations which they have nurtured from an early age — and by which they have, in turn, been nurtured — proves far from easy. Ubiquitous mendacity is instrumental in the maintenance of the Britannia Empire itself, insofar as neither its power structures nor its ideology could subsist in the absence of the advanced technology designed by the TV producer Diethard to manipulate information and to cover up the military's genocidal activities and rampant xenophobia while demonizing so-called terrorists like Lelouch as the root of all evil.

On a more spectacular plane, the Empire's technologies of subjectivity rely extensively on a line of mass-produced weapons dubbed "Knightmare Frames," which grant it tremendous martial advantage over all other countries. Neither the Empire's sophisticated media machinery nor its *mecha* are sufficient, however, to keep at bay the threat of dissolution from within resulting from internecine power struggles and disputes regarding the line of imperial succession, alongside assorted conspiracies and assassination attempts. Moreover, the practice of assigning small portions of the Empire to prospective royal heirs as part of their education in the art of government renders the system inherently vulnerable, since the placement of all the power in the hands of a single individual inevitably entails that if the ruler's life comes to a sudden end, the government itself disintegrates. This very possibility raises its head when Clovis, the third prince of Britannia assigned to rule Area 11, is killed by Lelouch in an attack. Through dramatic twists and turns of this kind, *Code Geass* engages in some trenchant reflection on the vicissitudes of Realpolitik, intimating that the genesis and preservation of subjectivity—both human and preterhuman—are inextricable from material power structures even when these are narratively inscribed in the parallel realms of fantasy, science fiction and magic.

Homage to CLAMP (i)
From "CLAMP As I Know Them."
In *CLAMP no Kiseki Vol. 6*:

Their reading ability astounds me.... They're also proficient gamers.... Now, before I go any further, I want to assure you that I'm not just making them look good because they're my friends. I simply want to show that they're not only talented authors and artists, but also incredible people as well. The CLAMP team are also gourmets. They also love fashion and makeup.... In addition to their depth of knowledge about what might be called typical feminine pursuits, they're also quite aware of current and political events ... almost half the time I stop by, someone is facing a desk working hard. I understand that four people are working together, but it's amazing to see them work on multiple series at the same time.—Nanami Kamon (2006)

Chapter 2

EPIC REINVENTIONS

> *This might suggest that history would be the thing for an epic poet; and so it would be, if history were superior to legend in poetic reality. But, simply as substance, there is nothing to choose between them; while history has the obvious disadvantage of being commonly too strict in the manner of its events to allow of creative freedom. Its details will probably be so well known, that any modification of them will draw more attention to discrepancy with the records than to achievement thereby of poetic purpose.... Not to declare what happened, and the results of what happened, is the object of an epic; but to accept all this as the mere material in which a single artistic purpose, a unique, vital symbolism may be shaped. And if legend, after passing for innumerable years through popular imagination, still requires to be shaped at the hands of the epic poet, how much more must the crude events of history require this! For it is not in events as they happen, however notably, that man may see symbols of vital destiny, but in events as they are transformed by plastic imagination.* — Lascelles Abercrombie

The title responsible for launching CLAMP's career as an internationally renowned artistic team, *RG Veda*, was initially released in manga form from 1989 to 1996 and adapted to anime as a two-episode OVA in 1991 and 1992. *RG Veda* actually started life as a *doujinshi* and proved popular in that form even before being translated into a full-fledged commercial venture. CLAMP's debut onto the mainstream manga market was by no stretch of the imagination a smooth ride. In fact, much as the team's ascent to global fame may now seem to sport the rosy hues of a happy romance or even a fairy tale, its commercial beginnings were fraught with difficulties. This makes them less akin to a consolatory fantasy than to the kind of epic struggle which several of CLAMP's early plots endeavor to chronicle in graphic form. We should also bear in mind, on this point, that CLAMP's phenomenal success is not an outcome which all would-be *mangaka* can unquestioningly expect. In fact, as Patrick Drazen sensibly reminds us in his assessment of self-published manga, "the big comic publishers in Japan seldom go after the *dojinshi*, which sometimes build up their own fan base," even though they do keep abreast of developments in the area "as a way of assessing up-and-coming talent." However, while "it's the dream of just about every budding manga artist to land a series in a major magazine," the sobering truth is that this aspiration rarely reaches fruition. In this scenario, CLAMP's experience represents a veritably "dramatic success story," insofar as the group has gone well beyond the stage of getting a series released in a prominent publication, and hence managed "to develop their amateur work into a mainstream media empire of sorts" (Drazen, p. 353).

It was when the idea conceived by CLAMP as the foundation of an original story, complemented by a detailed abstract of its intended ambience and cast, caught the attention of an editor at Shinshokan that the artists received a commercial offer. Even then, however, they did not allow themselves to rest on their laurels since *RG Veda*, like commercial manga generally, could not be planned from the start as a protracted series and its continuation depended crucially on positive reader surveys and promising volume sales. In addition, a major hurdle which CLAMP had to confront in its glorious but not always painless progress toward commercial recognition lay with the necessity to develop a new modus operandi. To begin with, as Mokona amiably recalls, the productive rhythm imposed on her and her colleagues by their altered circumstances was nothing short of grueling: "every day was a chore ... we would draw and draw and still have more to do (laughs)! It was endless! With *doujinshi* we could set our own deadlines and extend them as much as we needed. With commercial work there are strict scheduling and deadlines that have to be met. It was hard to keep up at first." Ageha Ohkawa corroborates this view, stating that tasks which the artists "could complete in a day now would take [them] four or five days then."

As Ohkawa also observes, there are a few differences between the *doujinshi* version of *RG Veda* and the manga created for commercial publication, the most substantial consisting of the protagonist's characterization. In the self-published incarnation of the manga, the artist explains, "Mokona was drawing the character without getting a firm grasp of him, so he comes across as being a smartass ... rather than having a dualistic nature, Ashura was consistently a harsh character." This attribute of the protagonist's personality as it was initially conceived was largely a corollary of the *doujinshi*'s overall mood. Since this was generally distinguished by a greater "sense of play" in its approach to narrative construction, it tended to lack "a firm, planned structure," and its personae, accordingly, could easily come across as "inconsistent." Consequently, when the artists were faced with the prospect of publication in the commercial sector, they had no choice but to "rework the story and the characters." Moreover, "there are some episodes published in the *doujinshi* that didn't appear commercially, and vice versa." As in the case of the protagonist's initial portrayal, this is a direct corollary of fundamental divergences in the business models adopted by amateurs as opposed to commercially published artists. Thus, a major reason for which the two versions developed differently is that the creative and organizational latitude afforded by self-published and amateur works is not a luxury which commercial *mangaka* can ever hope to enjoy. As Ohkawa points out, in the context of the *doujinshi* version of *RG Veda*, it would be perfectly acceptable for the artists to "continue a certain story flow just for the fun of it, but it's necessary to have coherence and consistency in a commercial version" (interview in CLAMP 2006, p. 7). A work's positive reception in the amateur zone does not, therefore, automatically translate into a financial success.

However, few people would dispute, even in CLAMP's salad days, that the freshness of the group's approach to storytelling, allied to its outstanding artistic talent and organizational sagacity, held the potential to capture not only the attention of the contemporary manga scene but also the imagination of whole generations. The manga's editor, Miki Ishikawa, has enthusiastically asserted that just on the basis of the piece "Star Festival" (contained in the first volume of *RG Veda*), she was able to recognize almost instantly the uniqueness of CLAMP's technical dexterity and narrative ingenuity. "I was initially struck by the artwork," Ishikawa recalls. "It was visually beautiful — both dynamic and detailed.... The short story itself was about 40 pages long ... but I could see that there was a big, dramatic world there just waiting to be explored. I could tell right away that they were a phenomenal new talent." The subsequent evolution of Ishikawa's own career was profoundly affected by her encounter with CLAMP's work, insofar as "up until that point," she admits, she "was more of a reader and fan than an editor." Once *RG Veda* had entered production, it rapidly became clear that in the course of the manga's execution, CLAMP's adventurous spirit had extended to all aspects of the enterprise, and not solely to those within the zones of graphic design and narrative construction. Calligraphy, for instance, was a further area in which the artists had felt inclined to experiment with unconventional results. Ishikawa offers exemplary evidence for this proclivity: "there were technical difficulties with one of the *kanji* for Lady Kendappa's name. It's a rare *kanji* that we didn't have available in our printer, so we had to create it manually.... It's hard to imagine now that desktop publishing has advanced so much" (interview in CLAMP 2006, p. 31).

According to Ishikawa, Ashura has persistently proved to be the story's most popular character among fans. In a sense, Ashura could be said to capture CLAMP's genius in a nutshell, bearing witness to the aspect of its art which Ishikawa rightly identifies as axial to its vision. The group's distinctive "appeal," argues the eminent editor, is "the result of superior teamwork between the members of CLAMP. The fact that they can create a different mood or artistic style with each different story is great. They create something new for each project" (p. 30). Ashura's portrayal encapsulates these distinctive proclivities within a single character, insofar as it alternately blends and contrasts several different tales, moods and styles in much the same way as CLAMP's oeuvre as a whole offers a composite formation of disparate yarns and motifs. While the protagonist's privileged standing should not be dismissed, it is vital to acknowledge that all of *RG Veda*'s actors (ancillary ones included) tend to stand out as consummately heroic presences, and still deserve consideration today as unsurpassed achievements. Indeed, the series' overall character gallery, selectively adapted by the anime in accordance with its telescoped version of the story, is so ample and diverse as to rival the accomplishments of many an honorable epic saga of old.

Nevertheless, it is barely surprising that Ashura should stand out as an all-time favorite when one takes into account not only the character's captivating physical appearance, which famously exhibits the golden eyes and pointed elf-like ears typical of the Ashura tribe (of which he is the sole surviving member), but also a fraught personal history. This chronicle's most salient points consist of Ashura's three-century-long slumber under the protection of the Mahyah Forest, his awakening by Yasha, and his involvement in the epic journey meant to lead to the despot Taishakuten's conclusive overthrow. Even though Ashura appears habitually suave and kind-hearted, and capable of valuing his relationship with Yasha as the greatest of treasures, his inner self is inhabited by the God of Destruction. As the protective seals designed to keep the deity's murderous drives at bay disintegrate one by one in the course of Ashura's odyssey, the protagonist's dark side progressively surfaces in all its blood-curdling fury. The character's momentous psychological metamorphosis is punctiliously matched by no less radical a transformation of his outward appearance, achieved through stylistic adjustments in his graphic portrayal. Thus, no trace of Ashura's formerly gentle expression is to be found in the terrifying mien of his vicious doppelgänger once the latter's resurrection has reached its climactic stage.

The temporal curve traced by Ashura's personal life brings together centuries of mythology and lore in a dense web of multicultural allusions. Hence, it bears witness to a distinctively Japanese tendency to absorb the past in its disparate transnational manifestations, inspired by a predilection for ever-shifting aesthetic syntheses of indigenous and global forms, Eastern and Western trends, tradition and novelty. This perspective eschews the protectionist valorization of homogeneous cultural patterns underpinned by local priorities, fostering instead an ingenious eclecticism which enthusiastically encourages the proliferation of dualities and divergences. While it is also important to appreciate that *RG Veda*'s mythological infrastructure implicitly interweaves a number of both indigenous and foreign motifs, it is undeniable that the saga is sustained from start to finish by a mythological tradition of Eastern provenance. Even though the story harks back to Ancient Greece in its treatment of tragedy and fate, it does not, by and large, employ Western motifs as the dominant axis of its mythological infrastructure. In this respect, it appears to follow an atypical trajectory in the domain of manga and anime at large. Indeed, while series informed by various aspects of Western mythology abound, it is unusual for either manga or anime to deal with Eastern mythology as a foundational aspect of their construction. In its imaginative appropriation of Hindu mythology as enshrined in the Brahmin Scriptures, *RG Veda* constitutes a notable exception. It thus bears witness to CLAMP's proclivity to raise the bar with each new venture on which its members have embarked from an early stage in their career.

With a disarming modesty one often encounters in CLAMP interviews as a defining trait of the team's collective personality, Ohkawa has playfully explained the group's adoption of Eastern mythology as the somewhat accidental, though felicitous, offshoot of an ostensible inadequacy. "Basically, we're not very good with the Western-style fantasy genre — we have trouble remembering Western names (laughs). So we thought something with an Asian theme might be better. Since we didn't want something that had ninjas in it or anything like that, we thought mythology might be a good source." Mokona played a major part in the progressive shaping of CLAMP's mythological vision. Born in Kyoto, Japan's ancient capital and the cradle of a stupendous range of temples, Mokona was well-acquainted with the country's religious heritage and able, therefore, to fuel her personal expertise into the venture. As the artist herself points out, her ongoing interest in "Hinduism and esoteric Buddhist teachings" added further substance to the team's background resources (interview in CLAMP 2006, p. 5). It is from its quintessentially Eastern heritage that *RG Veda* draws its poignant interpretation of the metaphysical dualities of Light and Darkness, Fortitude and Action, Strength and Weakness. However, the story's ability to embody these conflicts in the personality of a single, albeit prismatic, character is a remarkable accomplishment which ought to be credited to CLAMP's own genius and sensitivity to the requirements of psychological complexity. It is also worth noting, in order to do justice to the scope of the artists' mythical purview, that many of the key characters have direct antecedents in both the *Rig Veda*, one of the sacred texts of Hinduism, and in their interpretations by Buddhist mythology. *RG Veda*'s protagonist finds close correlatives in both traditions, where Ashura (Buddhist mythology) or Asura (Hindu mythology) features as a demon addicted to warfare and devastation who challenges the heavenly gods. As the commentary accompanying *RG Veda* in the sixth volume of the *CLAMP no Kiseki* collection explains, the character's duplicity in CLAMP's story echoes the ambiguity of the original figure's designation, which can be taken to signify either "against Heaven" or "one who gives life" (in CLAMP 2006, p. 20).

This pivotal aspect of Ashura's portrayal echoes a duality intrinsic in Japanese culture which has traditionally allowed peace and turmoil, gentleness and ferocity, to coexist and blend in mutual suffusion. As mentioned in Chapter 1, this dichotomy represents a major component of indigenous aesthetics of which CLAMP's own philosophical vision assiduously partakes. In the domain of Japanese art, this concept is paradigmatically borne out by the Buddhist figure of Fudou Myou-ou (literally, "Immovable Wisdom King"), a deity invoked for spiritual protection. Traditional representations of this mythological character typically combine conflicting connotations by attesting to both his benevolent role and his forbidding strength. As John Reeve points out, "turbulence is a strong theme in religious art. As in Western art, there are also graphic depictions of hells in Buddhist art, a notion brought from China (and a useful tool for social control)." Commenting specifically on a wooden sculpture of Fudou Myou-ou dating back to the twelfth century, the critic highlights the coexistence of seemingly discordant affects as follows: "a famous Buddhist monk once said that 'a master of men must be like the two Buddhist deities

Fudou and Aizen ... [whose] weapons are not intended for slashing and shooting, but for the purpose of subjugating devils. In their hearts they are passionate and circumspect'." Thus, even though Fudou Myou-ou is accompanied by a roaring fire and endowed with "bulging eyes and fangs," it is vital to appreciate that "these ferocious aspects" are not designed to inspire simple dread so much as a sense of confidence, insofar as analogous attributes are traditionally "adopted by the guardian figures of the gates of Buddhist shrines" to signify a protective and caring disposition (Reeve, p. 126). The philosophical ambivalence just delineated reverberates throughout CLAMP's entire opus, thereby informing not only many of its most popular yarns but also the personalities of several of its most intriguing personae—from Princess Emeraude in *Magic Knight Rayearth* to Kamui in *X*, from Eriol in *Cardcaptor Sakura* to Yuuko in *Tsubasa: RESERVoir CHRoNiCLE* and *xxxHOLiC*.

In spite of its imposing chronological scope, *RG Veda* is so studiously constructed that one never loses sight of its cumulative structure as a coherent, albeit composite, whole. In reading the manga, this makes it possible to retain a solid overview of its trajectory as entire eras roll by amid ostensibly endless trials and mounting scenarios of cosmic disharmony. In watching the anime adaptation, likewise, the viewer is enabled to develop a comprehensive understanding of the saga's grand scale by the cogent framing of the limited portions of its unfolding on which the OVA concentrates with reference to the wider flow of events which surrounds them. Familiarity with the parent text will no doubt enrich the viewing experience. Yet, it is not absolutely necessary to have read the manga to form a satisfying picture of the truly epic vision entertained by CLAMP with this seminal series. Both audiences acquainted with the source text and spectators whose experience of *RG Veda* is restricted to the OVA are likely to benefit from some consideration of the overall action's key events, and especially its premises and crowning occurrences. As *RG Veda* springs into action, the ruling hand of fate comes instantly to the fore. When Lord Yasha ventures into the forest and awakens the last extant member of the formidable Ashura tribe, his actions are already tinged with the tenebrous palette of foreboding. The valiant warrior, modeled upon the Hindu god of natural spirits and associated with a clan of fierce fighters in Buddhist mythology, is indeed fully aware that the child he is stirring from his long slumber is destined to kill him in the future—though he does not yet appear to know the creature's real identity.

The ending exudes no less powerful a current of pathos—while symmetrically revisiting the destiny topos — with its dramatization of the climactic scene in which Yasha, determined to stop the God of Destruction, throws himself in front of Ashura's sword. In a stunning coup de théâtre, Ashura stabs himself instead of killing Yasha, and hence defies fate by showing that a human bond has the power to overturn the darkest of prophecies. Characteristically averse to simplistic happy endings, CLAMP gives us a finale in which a promise of future fulfillment plays a much more prominent part than tangible gratification in the here-and-now. Therefore, Taishakuten's defeat is not unequivocally followed by a celebratory mood and instant visions of planetary regeneration — as is often the case in postapocalyptic series which are granted a happy ending. In fact, Ashura is once again sealed in a deep sleep while the loyal Yasha watches over him. It will be a long time before Ashura and Yasha can be lastingly reunited thanks to the diviner Kujaku's sacrificial surrender of his life in exchange for Ashura's. It is here worth noting, for the benefit of contextual accuracy, that in one of its most memorable arcs, the multiperspectival series *Tsubasa: RESERVoir CHRoNiCLE* offers an alternate interpretation of the bond between Ashura and Yasha, positing these two figures as the avatars of a turbulent mix of heroic and romantic forces which carry equal, and frequently incompatible, weight.

From a structural point of view, *RG Veda*'s most outstanding feature is indubitably the dramatic plot reversal whereby the classic tale of good and evil, which would seem to invest the traitor and tyrant Taishakuten with the role of villain, and the Six Stars with those of heroes or saviors, is drastically called into question. A shocking twist, bound to unsettle the assumptions and values of even the most disenchanted of audiences, redefines Taishakuten as a man willing to sacrifice everything in the name of a crucial promise made to a loved one, while making the Six Stars responsible for the revival of the most lethal of all deities and hence enveloping their supposedly noble goal in a noxious vortex of destructiveness. Paradoxically, the promise made by the seemingly merciless Taishakuten to the late Lord Ashura, the protagonist's father, was precisely that he would do anything in his power to prevent the young Ashura's awakening, in the knowledge that such an event would signal the emergence of a monster. As we shall see, *Magic Knight Rayearth* also exploits a spectacular reorientation of allegiances as one of its most significant plotting strategies by proposing that its heroines' true enemy is the very person they are enjoined to protect, and not the apparent villain presumed to endanger her life. Fumiko Yamamoto has devoted an illuminating essay to CLAMP's penchant for drastic narrative reorientations. According to the critic, such reversals cannot be easily dismissed as "tricks designed purely for the sole purpose of entertaining the readers" for they actually enable CLAMP to convey a simple, yet crucially necessary, ethical message — a lesson which underpins the artists' shared vision throughout their career to date. Thus, though "these twists are often dramatic and shocking enough to make the readers doubt what they are witnessing," they also prompt a modicum of self-questioning by inviting them to "recognize the simplicity and one-dimensional aspect of their previous understanding and that the concept of good is a very fragile idea that can quickly fall apart." Accordingly, such narrative stratagems have the capacity to encourage "the readers to take a fresh look at their beliefs and to question them" (in CLAMP 2006, p. 21).

By and large, *RG Veda* tends to conform to the rules of the epic genre by focusing on a quest of cosmic magnitude and by consistently emphasizing the principles of martial prowess, fortitude and virility as pivotal to its narrative and ethical functioning. However, the series' affiliation with fantastic fiction, allied to its preference for narrative embedding, layering and looping, allied to occasional digressive curves, draws it closer to the domain of romance. According to W. P. Ker, the romance form is first and foremost the province of the fantastic, and hence the antithesis of the solid world immortalized by the epic. "Whatever Epic might mean," Ker contends, "it implies some weight and solidity; Romance means nothing, if it does not convey some notion of mystery or fantasy ... Beowulf might stand for the one side, Lancelot or Gawain for the other" (Ker, p. 14). Concomitantly, while in a properly heroic narrative, characters "always have good reasons of their own for fighting," the "wandering champions of romance" often appear to be driven by purely irrational "readiness" (pp. 15–16). Romance impishly punctures the epic's noble ideals so as to give free rein to magical occurrences, amorous exploits and childlike inquisitiveness, in the name of open-ended narrative tapestries of prismatic capriciousness. The progressive buildup of often discontinuous and even inconsistent incidents, cherished by the romance genre above all other structural considerations, blatantly defies the notion of textual construction as a quest for a privileged center of meaning, pointing instead toward a potentially unbounded horizon.

CLAMP's series, like the adventures dramatized by most medieval romances of a chivalric stamp in the West, do not usually tend to gather momentum in the service of an ostentatious climax, or an explosive manifestation of pent-up energy. In fact, they often allow themselves to wander from one provisional resolution to the next, twisting and turning at will along the way. *RG Veda* epitomizes this aesthetic predilection, and thus attests to the degree of sophistication already achieved by CLAMP at such an early stage in its career, while also figuratively laying the foundations for several works to come. In several pivotal scenes, it thereby demonstrates that any apparent resolution is merely a launchpad to yet another narrative complication. Formal patterns of reiteration, recapitulation, foreshadowing, mirroring and duplication are axial in *RG Veda*— as indeed they are in CLAMP's output at large — to the choreographing of an exuberantly multilayered textual mesh. By interweaving a heroic quest with a love story, *RG Veda* also brings to mind David Lodge's definition of the contrasting structural rhythms of the epic and the romance with reference to a specifically sexual metaphor. "Epic," like "tragedy," is held by Lodge to "move inexorably to ... an essentially *male* climax — a single, explosive discharge of accumulated tension. Romance, in contrast, is not structured this way. It has not one climax, but many, the pleasure of this text comes and comes and comes again. No sooner is one crisis in the fortunes of the hero averted than a new one presents itself; no sooner has one mystery been solved than another is raised; no sooner has one adventure been concluded than another begins. The narrative questions open and close, open and close.... Romance is a multiple orgasm" (Lodge, pp. 322–323). It should also be noted, in evaluating the distinctive nature of the relationship between Ashura and Yasha, that this could at least partly be regarded as a product of its time. As explained in the commentary on the series published in *CLAMP no Kiseki*, the appearance of "androgynous characters and unusual couplings" in the sphere of manga from the mid–1980s onward was largely a corollary of legal changes which impacted directly on the position of women in Japanese society. The abolition of "sexual discrimination in the workplace," compounded with a salutary loosening of "strict gender roles" and with the opening of the world of employment to ever-increasing numbers of women, encouraged the emergence of "new values," especially among "women in their teens and 20s," to which the popular art of manga was quick to respond (in CLAMP 2006, p. 8).

Like *RG Veda*, *Tokyo Babylon* first came into being as a *doujnshi*. As in the previous instance, the shift to commercial release inevitably entailed a few modifications necessitated by logistical considerations and the demands of greater structural coherence. Some notable differences lie in the area of characterization. Subaru and Hokuto were not subject to major alterations on the surface but underwent psychological adjustments which have palpably enriched their emotional range and intellectual acuity, while also adding pathos to their interpersonal dynamics. It is also useful to observe that in the commercial version, the girl can only perform a handful of spells even though she received *onmyoudou* training as a kid, whereas in the *doujinshi*, she could both use magic and relate to *shikigami* as all full-fledged *onmyouji* are famously wont to do. Seishiro is the character who has been affected most profoundly by *Tokyo Babylon*'s transition to the commercial domain. "In the *doujinshi*," explains Ohkawa, "there was a vet by the same name, and there was 'more to him than met the eye,' but his personality wasn't nearly as complex" (interview in CLAMP 2005c, p. 5).

The publication of the *Tokyo Babylon* manga (1990–1993) overlapped with *RG Veda*'s release to a considerable degree. With hindsight, CLAMP's members appear to harbor mixed feelings about the implications of a publication overlap requiring them to engage simultaneously in the production of two substantially different stories. Thus, while they remember quite vividly the hurdles and challenges it posed, they are also ready to recognize its energizing potentialities. Even though *South*, the magazine responsible for *Tokyo Babylon*'s commercial release, was a quarterly publication, it still required the artists to produce "about 60 pages" for "every issue," recalls Mokona. "We had to squeeze that in between *RG Veda*, which ran on a monthly schedule. That was hard." Yet, as Tsubaki Nekoi maintains, "when you're working on a series for a long time, you feel the need to do something different": in this respect, *Tokyo Babylon* is bound to have represented a welcome relief after years of steady commitment to the *RG Veda* project in its gestation and fruition stages. Ohkawa corroborates this hypothesis, stating that since "*RG Veda* was a continuous story," it was actually "refreshing to work on something with self-contained episodes." It is also crucial to recognize that even though the publication of the *Tokyo Babylon* manga intersected significantly with *RG Veda*'s release, the two series share no further elements — except, of course, their genesis in CLAMP's versatile line work. Where *RG Veda* capitalizes on ancient lore, *Tokyo Babylon* strikes its roots in present-day Japan; where *RG Veda* harks back to Hindu mythology, *Tokyo Balylon* focuses on the indigenous practice of *onmyoudou*. It is vital to remember, in this matter, that even though CLAMP was keen to invoke a time-honored esoteric tradition of undisputed distinction in the construction of *Tokyo Babylon*'s world, it nonetheless sought to highlight its topical standing. As Ohkawa maintains, neither she nor her colleagues wished "to focus just on the occult," aiming instead to "give the series a grounding in reality" (interview in CLAMP 2005c, p. 5). It is hardly surprising, given *RG Veda* and *Tokyo Babylon*'s generic and contextual divergences, that during the time of their publication, the two series managed to polarize CLAMP's fans into two distinct camps. Like *RG Veda*, however, *Tokyo Babylon* rapidly captured the attention of ample sectors of the manga world, its success paving the way to the series' adaptation to the anime format in the guise of two OVAs (1992 and 1994), and to the live-action format with a film directed by George Iida and released in 1994.

As the thirteenth head of the Sumeragi dynasty, a family with a solid reputation in the practice of *onmyoudou*, Subaru has inherited the onerous role of Japan's spiritual guardian and is therefore expected to channel his skills as a magician, medium and exorcist into the investigation of a formidable variety of puzzling occurrences. These include the case of an actress who commits suicide when her thespian aspirations are rudely shattered; that of a childhood friend who flees life's brutal truths in an alternate oneiric dimension; that of girls hell-bent on standing out as special to keep at bay the phantoms of loneliness; and that of a girl who seeks refuge in religion to escape the harsh reality of bullying. Subaru's honesty and frankness are undoubtedly his most endearing personality traits, and prove repeatedly instrumental in providing comfort for the anguished spirits he is enjoined to assist. The youth's gentle disposition is rendered all the more attractive by its juxtaposition with his status as one of the most competent *onmyouji* and martial artists in the entire history of his prestigious family — even though, it gradually transpires, he is unwittingly embroiled in some very dark secrets. In addition, Subaru's appeal is augmented by his portrayal as a down-to-earth kid who spends his ordinary moments engaged in perfectly simple activities, such as going to school while dreaming of growing up to become not a powerful magician, as one might expect, but rather a zookeeper.

Alongside the series' male lead, the other most intriguing persona is Subaru's twin sister Hokuto. A bubbly, fiercely independent and outgoing young woman, she cares deeply for her brother and often comes across as the only person who is truly capable of fathoming his emotions. Given the boy's ingrained propensity to worry about others far more than he ever thinks about himself, Hokuto provides an ironical counterbalance to her brother's natural temperament. Moreover, the girl's portrayal as a talented cook with an impressive fashion sense supplies CLAMP with some marvelous opportunities to indulge in its own passion for both the culinary and the sartorial arts. Many *Tokyo Babylon* fans have singled out Hokuto as their favorite character — so much so that the rather unpalatable destiny meted out to the girl by the series' climactic events has often aroused not merely sadness but also downright dismay. The Subaru-Hokuto pair stands out as one of the most interesting interactive dyads in the whole of CLAMP's sensitively nuanced character pantheon.

This pivotal relationship is complemented by the presence of a third major character, the tantalizingly ambivalent figure of Seishiro Sakurazuka. A kind-hearted vet on the surface, Seishiro is actually a powerful *onmyouji* in his own right, as well as the head of the Sakurazukamori: a clan whose members deploy their preternatural capacities in order to kill. The brutality inherent in this line's private ethos is epitomized by the custom whereby the Sakurazukamori can only have one member at a time, which entails that in order to rise to the rank of head, it is necessary to murder one's predecessor. Seishiro's ascent to power has therefore left a baleful pool of blood in its wake, his primary victim being none other than his own mother. Moreover, he is revealed to have made a potentially lethal bet with Subaru in his youth: an event of which the protagonist himself has no recollection but has the power to affect quite drastically both his present and his future actions. If Hokuto constitutes Subaru's counterpart at the level of outward behavior, Seishiro stands out as the protagonist's antithetical incarnation. (It is worth noting, incidentally, that Subaru's mnemonic lacuna is due to the artificial removal of the circumstances surrounding the fatal bet from his psyche: this topos foreshadows CLAMP's large-scale deployment of the theme of memory erasure in *Tsubasa RESERVoir CHRoNiCLE* and *xxxHOLiC*.)

The bulk of the story focuses on Subaru's spiritualist and investigative exploits, chronicling his quotidian efforts to honor the tradition carried by his family by solving intricate cases. As noted in the preceding chapter, the anime adaptation focuses on two discrete cases. It does not fail, however, to capture the manga's spirit with admirable faithfulness, and the observations offered in this context are therefore equally applicable to both versions of the drama. Most importantly, the manga and anime alike abide in memory as labyrinthine webs of magic and shadows, moral decadence and vapid dreams, which posits *Tokyo Babylon*'s world as a potent metaphor for contemporary global culture. The story's emphasis on its location in modern Japan thus gains precedence over its imbrication with ancient and myth-encrusted traditions. In spooling out its narrative skein, the series conforms more or less explicitly with several of the conventions typically followed by both the psychological mystery yarn and the supernatural suspense thriller. It mirrors the former genre most palpably by foregrounding the idea that the ominous atmosphere of inscrutability which pervades all of the cases which the protagonist is asked to investigate has less to do with the crimes or obsessions they entail than with the torments endured by frightened, persecuted and alienated psyches. All the people encountered by Subaru in the course of his investigations indeed share one unavoidable attribute: they are haunted by a feeling of grief so deep and incapacitating as to require the protagonist to risk his own emotional exhaustion in his efforts to offer their souls some long-awaited relief.

With the supernatural suspense thriller, *Tokyo Babylon* shares its proclivity to underscore the incidence of otherworldly elements in both mundane and extraordinary events, and to intersperse the action with generous doses of tension and uneasiness as well as ingenious plot twists. The adoption of a person endowed with psychic abilities as its hero further reinforces the series' allegiance to the supernatural thriller typology. In *Tokyo Babylon*, as in both the psychological mystery yarn and the supernatural suspense thriller, characters cannot rely unproblematically on physical strength in order to overcome their adversaries, as is frequently the case in standard action thrillers, but have to depend instead on their intellectual resources. By and large, they deploy such weapons in two major forms, either by engaging in some subtle mental match with the opponent or by striving to retain a modicum of equanimity and sanity in their own minds against the onslaughts of unreason. The feelings of trepidation and anxiety evoked by both psychological mystery yarns and supernatural suspense thrillers often derive from two or more characters' covert efforts to exploit one another's psyches, either by indulging in unsettling cat-and-mouse games or by brutally endeavoring to annihilate the enemy's mental balance altogether. The cumulative mood communicated by the series' deft generic synthesis has been tersely captured by Marc in his review of the *Tokyo Babylon* anime: "the two tales of *Tokyo Babylon* are a rich and engrossing blend of supernatural and modern investigation, something like a mystical Japanese version of the *X-Files*. Things supernatural are just a little closer to the surface than you'd expect in its vision of Japan, but not so much so that you couldn't believe it's the real world." This is primarily an outcome of CLAMP's approach to the depiction of carefully individualized personalities, which allows the personae who inhabit *Tokyo Babylon* to stand out as "solid and developed" presences, and the drama itself to preserve "a believable blend of experience with the supernatural and normal emotions" (Marc).

In assessing *Tokyo Babylon*'s generic connections, it is also worth noting that the series implicitly invokes alternate configurations of what Tzvetan Todorov has famously termed the "typology of detective fiction" (Todorov). This aspect of the series in both its manga and its anime versions is not only worthy of attention at the generic level. In fact, it also sheds light onto *Tokyo Babylon*'s social and cultural significance to the extent that it squarely situates its story in the present by underscoring its affiliation with a fundamentally modern generic field. At one level, *Tokyo Babylon* echoes the classic "whodunit" insofar as, like this subgenre of detective fiction, it develops consistently "not one but two stories: the story of the crime and the story of the investigation" (Todorov, p. 159). By relying on an essentially episodic structure and hence engaging its protagonist in a string of different cases, *Tokyo Babylon* offers multiple interpretations of both the basic concept of crime and of the investigative methods appropriate to each of its manifestations. Therefore, the series deploys the bipartite matrix described by Todorov largely as a means of promulgating a refreshingly relativistic world view in which any meaning one may choose to ascribe to a particular action or situation must be understood as inevitably partial, circumstantial and therefore rescindable. Relatedly, as Subaru progresses from one task to the next, the two basic strands postulated by Todorov proliferate into a web of multibranching narrative paths.

As a means of bringing together its different ideations of the classic whodunit, the series capitalizes on the main storytelling devices which Todorov associates with that genre: namely, "temporal inversions and individual 'points of view.'" These strategies, in underlining that "the tenor of each piece of information is determined by the person who transmits it" from his or her perspective as he or she evaluates past occurrences with the benefit of hindsight, iconoclastically declares that "the author cannot, by definition, be omniscient." Where the story of the crime is replete with literary conventions of the kind just described, the story of the investigation is seen by Todorov to rely on a relatively "neutral and plain" style so as to intimate that its function is mainly to act as a "mediator between the reader and the story of the crime" and is not, therefore, keen on ruses which might render matters "opaque." A faithful reflection of its creators' aversion to conclusive moral messages, *Tokyo Babylon* is never unequivocally transparent in style—not even in the climactic scenes in which it supplies apparent solutions and reparative consolation. Nevertheless, upon disclosing the causes of its characters' afflictions, and gradually penetrating the mysteries which shrouds its protagonist's life history, it is undeniably willing to unveil the precise import of many occluded events and cryptic details which have been merely adumbrated in the mystery-laden portions of the action.

The second category theorized by Todorov, the "thriller," is brought into play by *Tokyo Babylon* not only by virtue of its affinities with the specifically supernatural variety of this genre, as pointed out earlier. In fact, it is also invoked, in a more general sense, by the series' cultivation of the two "forms of interest" which the Structuralist critic associates with that genre: namely, "curiosity" and "suspense." The former "proceeds from effect to cause: starting from a certain effect (a corpse and certain clues) we must find its cause (the culprit and his motive)." The latter traces an inverse trajectory "from cause to effect: we are first shown the causes, the initial *données* (gangsters preparing a heist), and our interest is sustained by the expectation of what will happen, that is, certain effects (corpses, crimes, fights)" (p. 161). In *Tokyo Babylon*, curiosity is fueled by the story's insistent emphasis on the grim results of the various obsessions which haunt Subaru's patients, and attendant concern with their causes. Suspense, in turn, becomes most prominent in sequences which map out Subaru's efforts to rationalize the origins and outcomes of the psychological disturbances which he is called upon to cure without, however, relinquishing the generosity and compassion which underpin his approach to *onmyoudou* no less than magical talent. Finally, *Tokyo Babylon* could be said to mirror the third genre analyzed by Todorov in his seminal study of detective fiction, "the suspense novel": a form which integrates various facets of both the whodunit and the thriller. Like the former, the suspense novel works with riddles which convey "two stories, that of the past and that of the present." Like the latter, it seeks to kindle the audience's interest not solely in "what has happened" but also "what will happen next" (p. 164). *Tokyo Babylon* skillfully satisfies this formula insofar as it fuses the past and the present at every turn. In so doing, it seeks to preserve a delicate balance between events which have already taken place, and may in fact have been reenacted an incalculable number of times, and events which are likely to be triggered by those earlier occurrences, and likewise to go on repeating themselves ad infinitum unless the obsessive-compulsive urges at their roots are healed.

At the same time, *Tokyo Babylon* uses the dynamics of detection as a major means of drawing its readers or viewers into the story. To accomplish this goal, the series relies on four principal formal features: representation, interaction, tension, and stabilization. Representation designates the depiction of a portion of reality in a fundamentally subjective mode, be it from the protagonist's point of view or from the perspective of one of his associates or patients. Interaction results from the story's recognition of, and responses to, a potential audience — us. Tension refers to the friction generated by the narrative between our instinctive urge to see Subaru succeed in his missions, and our disappointment in the face of the obstacles put in the *onmyouji*'s way by either fate or malice. Stabilization, finally, refers to the age-old comfort which practically all stories can be seen to provide: namely, the promise that neither a character's actions nor our interpretative decisions will ever impinge negatively upon the real world.

In the face of the series' undecidables, any reader or viewer willing to plunge into the stream of the narrative in an active fashion will be faced with several interrelated tasks, each of which is connected with one of the four formal categories outlined above. Firstly, readers and viewers are expected to assess *Tokyo Babylon*'s intentional lacunae as key ingredients in the representation of a particular world with specific aesthetic and ethical priorities. Secondly, in undertaking this analytical task, they must take into account the ways in which the story encourages them to make certain interpretative choices and, concomitantly, how it takes shape in their eyes in response to those choices — that is to say, how it unfolds as a result of its interaction with an audience. The narrative, in this scenario, is conceived by CLAMP as a malleable substance, not a petrified block. Thirdly, audiences must accept that their decoding decisions are never likely to lead to certifiable answers. There will always be a tension between the solutions which they formulate and the many insoluble riddles which go on filling the air even after Subaru has successfully carried out his missions, and bravely confronted the horrific mysteries at the heart of his own existence. Fourthly, readers and viewers are given the reward of knowing that whatever answers they might believe to have reached, these will only carry conditional substance within the boundaries of the reading or viewing experience in which they have been engaged and never, therefore, foreclose renegotiation in the way real-world affairs sadly tend to do.

As the interrelated tasks outlined above are carried out, the series' narrative drift consistently encourages us to reflect on the strategies through which its diverse textual components are linked to one another in such a way that no incident can be absorbed as a complete event, insofar as disparate occurrences always intermesh, albeit elliptically, with other details, hints and clues. In this respect, the story recalls a digital hypertext: a system of language which, as George P. Landow has emphasized, seeks to capture the poststructuralist conception of language as a radically unstable and decentered constellation of signs (Landow, pp. 33–34). As a means of integrating its disparate elements, *Tokyo Babylon* relies on the sustained evocation of a palpably immersive atmosphere. This makes itself felt in two principal forms throughout the action. On the one hand, the series ushers in a type of immersion imbued with otherworldly connotations by drawing us not only into one definite time zone but rather into a potentially ceaseless cycle of recurrence of an emphatically Eastern nature. On the other hand, its deluge of enigmas, made exponentially intricate and perplexing by their presentation from disparate viewpoints, draws us intimately into the story, inviting us to take part in the detection process. At this level, we are implicitly invited to identify with the figure of the investigator, Subaru, and with the characters who are supposed to support his work, Hokuto and Seishiro, who come to constitute our intradiegetic representatives.

Taking both forms of immersion simultaneously into account, it could be argued that *Tokyo Babylon*, through its elaboration of a fluid semiotic universe capable of yoking together a prodigious variety of ingredients, stimulates the emergence of feelings of empathy and identification. This phenomenon is a corollary of the nature of the emotions evoked by Subaru's investigative assignments, which are so consummately familiar, raw and uncompromising (despite their supernatural subtexts) as to strike a powerful chord with even the most seasoned of audiences. As Ohkawa has emphasized, the artists themselves remember as one of the most affecting facets of *Tokyo Babylon*'s production the fact that they "received a lot of letters from people of all ages regarding *Tokyo Babylon*," and that this series "elicited longer letters in general than [their] other manga. Many readers wrote deep, detailed letters about how they felt, what they thought was really going on" (interview in CLAMP 2005c, p. 7).

Tackling the most ordinary of affects, and primarily sorrow, isolation and unfulfillment, *Tokyo Babylon* seeks to tackle some of the most problematic human preoccupations without ever appearing to deliver a didactic sermon or cautionary tale. We are thereby invited to engage directly, free from the cumbersome mediation of heavy-handed authorial voices, with the mysteries of hope and fear, memory and longing, kindness and strength, malice and compassion, reason and instinct — all the while pondering the possibility that even the most honest mien might amount to a deceptive mask, and the most disarming truths to an elegantly arranged bouquet of mendacity. As the article "The Essential *Tokyo Babylon*" suggests, CLAMP's handling of these seemingly unexceptional, yet extraordinarily complex, issues constitutes the series' philosophical core as well as the key to its ongoing popularity: "the way their characters resolve these tough life questions and the way their writing struggles with 'simple' words that society takes for granted is quite unique. This spirit of individuality is reflected in the quote on page 8 of book 6: 'There is no such thing as "everyone".' To many readers who feel the pressure to conform to society, CLAMP's words of support and encouragement for the individual must have been comforting. It's a message that carries over into all of their creations" (in CLAMP 2005c, p. 8). The CLAMP artists themselves have emphasized *Tokyo Babylon*'s intended ethical relevance while also explaining the practical, no less than intellectual, reasons underlying their decision. "At first, we thought we would try and make it cuter," Ohkawa recalls. "But as *South* was a seasonal (quarterly) magazine, we had a lot of pages to work with each chapter. As a result, we decided to create something with more social commentary in it. We were young, so I think we had a lot more complaints back then" (interview in CLAMP 2005c, p. 5).

It is vital to remember, in assessing the team's ethical vision for this series, that in CLAMP's world, individualism is not coterminous with either solipsism or self-centeredness. Hidekazu Katoh persuasively defends this proposition, arguing that one of the most recurrent facets of CLAMP's output consists of the "individualist philosophy" which informs several of its yarns. "Some people may confuse this individualism with selfishness, but it is not. CLAMP's brand of individualism begins by accepting that all people are different. From there, it is a clear progression that leads to the point where we are all individuals." Paradoxically, it is only by striving to achieve a modicum of self-understanding that we may eventually succeed in alleviating other people's pain — even if, as long as we turn inward in our struggle toward self-understanding, we may appear to err in the direction of sheer egocentricity. Yet, it could well be the case, as Katoh argues, that "ideal behaviors are born out of selfish ones. We can't hope to understand how other people feel, so we must do our best to understand ourselves. Those that do not look after their own self-interest cannot look out for other people. This is CLAMP's clear insight to the human heart as portrayed vividly in *Tokyo Babylon*" (in CLAMP 2005c, p. 8).

It may well be the case that in this world view, there is scarce room for altruism. Yet, this is not automatically tantamount to either condoning or glorifiying humanity's egotistical drives. Ironically, it is precisely from an honest acknowledgment of the impossibility of feeling other people's pain as though it were one's own that true compassion arises. In Subaru's experience, the ability to empathize arises from this very awareness. It is on this basis, moreover, that he progressively develops strategies through which the most malevolent of energies can be magnanimously quelled. Seishiro, conversely, seems incapable of caring about either other people or himself. In fact, his inability to care about himself, far from representing the apotheosis of altruism as one might at first assume, is also what incapacitates him from caring about others and, ultimately, enables him to take on the role of a ruthless assassin with polished aplomb. Care of the self is here posited as the precondition of the capacity to care for others. In this perspective, the cases investigated by Subaru can be regarded as discursive formulations of identity which abet self-empowerment — not in the sense that they enable the protagonist to increase his kudos or pump up his ego but rather in the sense that they provide arenas in which, by understanding himself and the scope of his skills, he concurrently enhances his capacity to understand (and care for) other human beings.

The series does not appear to presume that all readers or viewers will automatically relate to one single character as the sole or main focus of their attention but rather opens up multifarious interactive paths by recourse to an extensive cast of carefully defined personae each of whom represents, at least in principle, a possible point of special reference. The audience's opportunities for psychological immersion are thus plentiful and diverse. The mechanism of desire also plays an important part in the reception dynamics fostered by *Tokyo Babylon*, especially in the guise of a yearning to see Subaru's patients relieved of their debilitating emotive burdens. Some cases stoke this drive with marked intensity. In the manga version of the series, a good example is supplied by the case dramatized in Volume 4, "Crime," where multiple, even conflicting, desires are simultaneously stimulated by the intractably paradoxical nature of the curse at the nub of the case. In this scenario, Subaru encounters a woman hellbent on destroying the man who has murdered her daughter and on deploying, to this end, the force of the Inugami. This is a baleful spell which magnetizes the anger of animals and insects and has the power to strip its victim of all material possessions and assets. Regrettably for Subaru's patient, the Inugami hex is also renowned for its knack of cursing the person who casts it no less than its subject. Aware of the spell's double-edged nature, the *onmyouji* takes it upon himself to put an end to the woman's self-destructive ritual by invoking her daughter's spirit. While Subaru assumes that the dead girl would not wish her mother to embark on a course of action bound to destroy her in its wake, the spirit itself is in fact thirsting for revenge. This state of affairs confronts not only *Tokyo Babylon*'s protagonist but also its audience with an unnerving conundrum, as neither party is in a position to know unequivocally what to wish for. Whatever the contingent nature of our desires as readers or viewers, no obvious resolutions are readily at our disposal. We may long to see the mother's desire to avenge her daughter appeased, or else to see Subaru succeed in staying her hand: either way, we are bound to sense that the fulfillment of either of these desires will result in frustration for the unsuccessful party. No univocal form of satisfaction, therefore, can lead to conclusive resolutions, consolations or reparations.

If the desire to perceive a text as a narrative leading to a resolution is a common trait of all manner of reading and viewing experiences, it is bound to acquire additional resonance in the experience of a series that consistently invites the arrangement of its building blocks into a coherent story and yet, at the same time, blocks the path to neat solutions through its hearty appetite for enigmas. In this respect, the desire promoted by *Tokyo Babylon* could be said to be less a desire for results, plenitude or enlightenment, than a desire to engage with the story as a virtually unending process. The series makes us wish to concentrate not so much on its likely (or desirable) outcomes as on its structure, on the methods through which its narrative develops both in consonance with, and in flagrant contradiction of, the expectations it might have raised. Consequently, the situation in which we are actually invited to immerse ourselves is not some idyllic vista of unequivocal gratification but a forever provisional narrative framework — a construct governed by the ongoing performance of tentative decoding decisions. The nature of the series as a fluid constellation of meaning is thus brought into sharp focus. It would be pertinent, in this context, to speak of "structurality" in preference to "structure," since the concept of structurality expresses more faithfully than that of structure the description of *Tokyo Babylon* as a text in constant motion rather than as an ossified object. This interpretation of the concept of structurality is indebted to Jacques Derrida's writings, and particularly *Writing and Difference* (1978), where it is proposed that structures have been conventionally founded upon the existence of stable points of reference that somehow transcend the endless "play" of language. Derrida, by contrast, promulgates structurality as the mechanism that only holds systems together in a precarious and transient fashion, perpetuating their mobility and therefore fully acknowledging their self-dismantling impetus.

With *Magic Knight Rayearth*, released in manga form between 1993 and 1995 and adapted to anime in 1994–1995 as a two-season TV series and in 1997 as an OVA with the shortened title of *Rayearth*, we move into a seemingly jollier reality. The idea that three ordinary Tokyo school girls hold the fate of a legendary realm in their hands may initially seem somewhat trite and predictable, especially for seasoned anime viewers well acquainted with the magical girl formula. CLAMP's adherence to a tested template is quite understandable when we consider that the manga was first conceived when its artists were unexpectedly invited by Hedeki Yamanouchi, editor of *Nakayoshi* magazine, to work on a series for this publication. *Nakayoshi*, notably, enjoys an august reputation in the magical girl arena, having presided over the serialization of several *mahou shoujo* classics, including Naoko Takeuchi's *Sailor Moon* (1992–1997) and CLAMP's own *Cardcaptor Sakura*, the collective's next adventurous foray into the field in the immediate aftermath of *Magic Knight Rayearth*'s own release. However, *Magic Knight Rayearth* does not pander to hackneyed motifs without venturing into the as yet unexplored territories of the genre. In fact, if a *mahou shoujo* yarn was ever truly able to open the door to an enchanted world, then CLAMP's *Magic Knight Rayearth* deserves recognition as the trusty guardian of the key to that door. At the same time as it delivers a classic epic yarn centered on the tropes of the princess in distress and of her salvation by a contingent of valiant knights, *Magic Knight Rayearth* subjects the established form to radical refashioning on both the thematic and the graphic planes. In thematic terms, it incrementally reveals a proclivity to deal dispassionately with some of the darkest human drives. In purely graphic terms, the title's daring is attested to by its intrepid insertion of a prominent *mecha* element into the codes and conventions traditionally associated with the heroic saga.

In addition, *Magic Knight Rayearth* takes maximum creative advantage of one of the pivotal attributes of *shoujo* manga executed by female artists, as described in the article "*Shoujo* Manga: A Unique Genre." This particular genre is here held to rely on "a unique set of semiotic codes. Unlike comics written for men, which advance in a linear fashion from one frame to the next, *shoujo* manga employ an irregular narrative progression and make liberal use of modified frame shapes. There are frames without outlines, extremely long vertical or horizontal rectangles, portraits of the protagonists superimposed on top of several separate frames, and flowered patterns used as decorative backdrops behind the characters" ("*Shoujo Manga: A Unique Genre*"). While these formal elements are by no means limited to CLAMP's output, and its would therefore be quite preposterous to claim them as the group's exclusive prerogative, it can be realistically proposed that in CLAMP's hands, they come to unprecedented fruition. In so doing, they abet the series' experimental drive even when it departs least noticeably from standard *shoujo* fare. Thus, *Magic Knight Rayearth* could be said to have given its creators scope for innovative play at two levels, by allowing them to blend ostensibly distinct or even incongruous genres, on the one hand, and to actualize the potentialities of individual formats on the other.

Ohkawa has usefully elucidated the team's concurrently creative and pragmatic reasons for engaging in the series' distinctive discursive mix. "The editors didn't give us any direction," the artist maintains. "We wanted to take advantage of this opportunity and do something that had never been done before. At that time, there were already stories of girls in combat, but nothing that involved gigantic robots.... We figured *Nakayoshi* readers wouldn't get into something that only revolved around robots, so we added some fantasy, RPG elements into it." CLAMP's self-appointed mission soon turned out to entail some major technical challenges. Although the artists already considered themselves enthusiastic *mecha* fans in the domain of anime, they rapidly realized that "it was hard to translate giant robots to manga form," especially when it came to the evocation of their unearthly dimensions. Communicating "the scale of the robots," Nekoi explains, is "more difficult in manga compared to anime. I mean, you can't show both the people and the robots in a frame, or when they're in the robots, you can't see the characters' faces." The anime adaptation, for its part, capitalizes on the visual privileges available to its medium, providing some of the most memorable dramatic moments precisely by recourse to the sequences in which its human characters' interactions with the *mecha* are the focus of attention. Yet, CLAMP retained a healthy sense of humor in the face of these trials, missing no opportunity for fun as and when this arose. This is borne out, for instance, by the team's approach to the issue of naming, as a result of which all of the characters have been imparted with designations based on the names of cars. Ironically maintaining that she and her colleagues are "bad with fantasy names," and therefore needed to draw inspiration from existing tags, Ohkawa explains that the names allocated to cars proved ideal insofar as these are "usually easy to remember as well as sounding cool" (interview in CLAMP 2005d, p. 5).

Married to elements originating outside the boundaries of the conventional epic plot, even the more clichéd motifs pivoting on the fairytalish Princess Emeraude and the enchanted realm of Cephiro gain novel resonance and an affective appeal of timeless amplitude. At the same time, the generic mix cultivated by CLAMP in *Magic Knight Rayearth* inaugurated a substantial expansion of the group's fan base, which had hitherto consisted principally, if not exclusively, of female readers in their teens and early twenties. With the insertion of tantalizing variations into the saga's magical infrastructure, CLAMP rapidly found the support of a diversified audience. Its reputation received an additional boost with *Magic Knight Rayearth*'s adaptation into anime format by enlisting male teenagers and youths into the ranks of the group's aficionados. It is worth pointing out, in considering the story's migration from the manga world to the screen, that the first season remains by and large loyal to the first arc of the manga, except for the inclusion of the original character Inouva and of a chain of subplots, whereas the second season departs more radically from the parent text. The most remarkable difference, in this respect, consists of the ideation of two new personae indigenous solely to the world of the anime, Nova and Lady Debonair, who are said to have emanated from the deep grief experienced by Hikaru and the people of Cephiro respectively in the aftermath of Princess Emeraude's demise. The OVA version of the epic marks a more drastic departure from the source. While the characters remain the same, their relationships undergo significant reconceptualization, as do many of the settings and events.

In all its configurations, the anime invites us to engage with its heroines' epic quest as an allegory of ever-mounting momentum, and to empathize with their psychological dilemmas—no less than with their achievements—from the instant they are summoned to Cephiro to the very end. To encourage its audience's affective and intellectual involvement in the three protagonists' mission, *Magic Knight Rayearth* consistently emphasizes that task's subjection to the unbending law of necessity. The principle of *hitsuzen*, discussed in Chapter 1 and to be revisited in Chapter 3, clearly plays a major—though implied—role in dictating the action's tempo and momentum. Therefore, once Umi, Hikaru and Fuu have taken on their roles as Magic Knights and embraced the duty to rescue Princess Emeraude, the "Pillar" of Cephiro and hence the agent upon whom the land's safety depends, from the clutches of the vicious Zagato, they cannot hope to return to their homeland until their quest has reached its completion. Zagato is eventually vanquished as a result of the Magic Knights' acquisition of the power to don their respective "Mashin," the legendary guardians of Cephiro who take the forms of a dragon, a four-winged giant bird and a wolf with a fiery mane. However, not even this triumph paves the way to a rosy resolution. In fact, fresh challenges of a genuinely tragic scale await the Magic Knights, since Zagato's defeat does not prove conducive to Princess Emeraude's well-being but rather to the ineluctability of her annihilation. It would appear that in CLAMP's irreverent reversal of the classic chivalric formula, damsels in distress are there to be destroyed rather than married off to a strapping prince. The girls' return to Tokyo, in this scenario, can hardly be regarded as an unproblematic blessing. This sinister twist imperils again Cephiro's survival, requiring the Magic Knights to intervene once more in the tangled skein of the land's history, confront a slew of unscrupulous foes, and finally face the thorny issue of whether to bravely replace Cephiro's lost Pillar with a new one or, more courageously still, endeavor to abolish the Pillar system altogether.

The incorporation of the ludic factor deserves special consideration as a reflection of the distinctive context in which *Magic Knight Rayearth* came into existence. It is indeed perfectly consonant with the climate of the early 1990s, when role-playing games such as the Japanese productions *Dragon Warrior* (a.k.a. *Dragon Quest*) and *Final Fantasy* were enjoying immense prominence on the pop cultural scene. In this type of game, the player is typically cast as the story's protagonist, and is hence required to interact with various characters and their worlds while confronting numerous challenges and unraveling assorted riddles in the process. The RPG's distinctive gameplay does not normally incorporate conspicuous action elements and is therefore allowed to develop at a deliberate pace. As a result, the player is free to dwell on its intricate and highly detailed graphics, and thus enjoy the game's imaginary universe as a text and as an artifact of autonomous aesthetic caliber. This is a luxury which standard action adventure packages predicated on rapid-fire rhythms and intensely dynamic sequences, as well as strict time constraints, do not generally afford. Therefore, the RPG model has proved popular even among people who are not habitually adept to gaming. The fairly straightforward point-and-click interface they characteristically adopt has further enhanced the appeal of RPGs among disparate audiences. An early form of adventure RPG is the Text Adventure game: an exercise in interactive fiction (IF) pivoting on mystery-laden treasure hunts, and keen to juggle with storytelling methods capable of maximizing audience engagement. The Text Adventure game itself was substantially dependent on written language but the development of increasingly refined technologies for the creation of CGI created scope for the development of a further ludic type, the Graphical Adventure. Visuals thus rapidly began to match and even replace the text-heavy blocks of narrative which had characterized the earlier form, by and by establishing their artistic standing as major components of the gaming experience and as pivotal to the construction of a particular game world. The Graphical Adventure package also allowed players to interact with the graphics by means of icons and buttons. A subsequent development was the Dialogue game, where the player advanced through a narrative not by accomplishing predetermined tasks but by virtue of verbal skills demonstrated in the course of conversations with virtual characters. An even more recent offshoot of the original form consists of LAPR games: i.e., live-action role-playing games.

Dennis Waskul and Matt Lust's observations on players' attitudes to rules in the domain of fantasy RPGs are especially pertinent to CLAMP's series. "In role-playing games, players use a complex system of rules to craft fantasy personas in a fantastic universe of make-believe," the critics maintain. "In practice, however, these rules are less regulatory and more a set of conventions and guidelines that provide a structure for exquisite detail. In other words, players use 'rules' as gaming resources rather than gaming limitations.... Rather than being bound by rules, role-playing games are structured by conventions that loosely define basic persona traits and qualities of a make-believe world that participants play at and game with.... Participants create fantasy personas from basic attributes generated by random dice rolls that players interpret by assigning their personas varying levels of strength, intelligence, wisdom, dexterity, constitution, and charisma — allowing them to create imaginary personal characteristics that are best suited for the kind of fantasy persona they would like to play" (Waskul and Lust, pp. 340–341). James Carse promulgates an analogous argument in suggesting that the most competent RPG players operate on the assumption that "there are no rules that require [them] to obey the rules" (Carse, p. 10). Gary Allen Fine further corroborates the same basic hypothesis: "one of the cardinal 'metarules' of FRP [fantasy role-playing] gaming," argues the scholar, "is that there are no 'rules'; the rulebooks are only guidelines" (Fine, p. 115).

In reflecting the basic mechanisms which regulate the internal functionings of the typical RPG, *Magic Knight Rayearth* emphasizes that the three heroines are aware throughout that they are performing predefined roles even as they begin to care for the fate of the land to which they have been forcibly transposed, and for the friends they make along the way. This element of self-consciousness is heightened by occasional suggestions that the girls, and Hikaru in particular, cherish the idea that they have become fantasy personae. Any such positive attitudes are brutally contested by the tragic climax of the first story arc, which results in the Magic Knights' performance of an act which has been predetermined on their behalf and they would never have elected to carry out of their own accord. At this point, it becomes painfully obvious that the girls have no more control over the scenario in which they have been inserted than players of an RPG operating in accordance with a strictly preestablished system. Umi, Hikaru and Fuu, it thus emerges, have only been playing arranged parts all along, and never been truly granted any self-determination or decisional power. The divergences in both tone and ethos evinced by *Magic Knight Rayearth*'s two parts can be assessed with reference to the significance of rules and rule-bound behavior within the RPG's formal parameters, as described by the critics cited above. Thus, it could be argued that in the first part, the heroines are not consciously aware that they are playing a game, even though they enjoy the thought that they have become fantasy characters. Most crucially, they do not seem to know that they are playing according to predetermined rules, and are consequently powerless to manipulate the rules in accordance with their own principles and goals.

In the second part, conversely, the Magic Knights appear to have grasped their epic mission's ludic nature, understood that the quest is governed by arbitrary rules, and that it is ultimately up to them to decide whether to abide by such rules or else bend them in light of their objectives. In addressing these issues, *Magic Knight Rayearth* deploys its ludic components as a means of reminding us, in a tactful yet unequivocal fashion, that the performance of role-playing is by no stretch of the imagination limited to the domain of games. In fact, as Katoh pertinently observes, "many of us live our lives trapped in a real world RPG. Those who are unaware of the connection between the world and themselves are similar to characters in an RPG.... So how do we leave this role-playing construct and lead our lives without regret? In order to do that, we must be aware of our relationship with our surroundings, and understand our role in it.... It's about having awareness of our world and ourselves. That's the first step in breaking out of a role-playing existence" (in CLAMP 2005d, p. 15). The importance of the bond between humans and their environment, deeply ingrained in Japanese culture for centuries, is here affectingly upheld. In underscoring the protagonists' resolution to take not only Cephiro's fate but also their personal destinies as Magic Knights into their own hands, *Magic Knight Rayearth* articulates a moral message akin to Katoh's: in CLAMP's reimagined epic, as in the scholar's analysis, awareness is instrumental in the individual's self-emancipation from the deceptions and snares of an unexamined existence.

At the same time, *Magic Knight Rayearth* emulates the RPG's distinctive creative stance as a form of interactive fiction. Just as that type of game characteristically invites its players to participate in the production of the text as integrated agents, so CLAMP's series calls upon its readers and viewers to contribute actively to is overall semiosis or meaning-making process. Like the most accomplished adventure RPGs, *Magic Knight Rayearth* indicates that it is only through an actively engaged viewer, reader or player that the storytelling potentialities of a visual or written text are truly actualized. It thus calls into question conventional notions of authorship by enthroning the receiver as instrumental in the genesis of narration and meaning. At the same time, it encourages its audience to piece together plural storylines without dishing out easy answers to their underlying moral dilemmas. In placing the reader or viewer in a subtly grained imaginary setting, in which he or she is expected to use both text-analysis capacities and puzzle-solving skills, *Magic Knight Rayearth* offers an innovative way of delivering and receiving the narrative experience. In exploring the series' imaginary environment in order to discover its guiding rules, while simultaneously endeavoring to interpret its events, the reader or viewer is indeed invited to navigate the text in an attitude of continuous and mindful alertness. In this respect, *Magic Knight Rayearth* could be seen as an example of the kind of narrative discourse which Espen J. Aarseth has described as "ergodic literature." The term derives from the Greek "*ergon*" ("work") + "*hodos*" ("path") and succinctly connotes a type of literature in which "nontrivial effort is required to allow the reader to traverse the text" (Aarseth, p. 1).

It should also be borne in mind, in the present context, that the quasi-medieval flavor of several aspects of *Magic Knight Rayearth*'s terminology, landscape, architecture and costumes is largely a corollary of its aesthetic affiliation with the RPG form. In the classic RPG, characters, settings, trials and magical skills inspired by medieval mythology and lore have played a prominent part virtually from inception, with the groundbreaking creation *Dungeons and Dragons*, commonly credited with marking the inception of the modern RPG and RPG industry, in the vanguard. The aforementioned *Dragon Quest* itself is based on the quintessentially medieval yarn pivoting on the rescue of a persecuted damsel and the slaying of a dragon. Thus, in evaluating *Magic Knight Rayearth*'s debt to the RPG mode, it is important to acknowledge the anime's imbrication with the aesthetic of "neomediaevalism," a concept introduced by Umberto Eco in his essay "Dreaming the Middle Ages" (Eco). In its broadest sense, the term designates the revamping of medieval material in both scholarly circles and the realm of popular entertainment as a receptacle of themes and motifs applicable to a broad range of historical situations and philosophical debates. For Eco, the contemporary fascination with the Middle Ages is by no means governed exclusively by fantasy. In fact, it entails a recognition, albeit unconscious, of that epoch as the point of inception of many key systems and discourses which still underpin both Western and Westernized cultures, including modern languages, nation states and capitalism. Moreover, the collusion of medieval tradition and popular fantasy offered by *Magic Knight Rayearth* mirrors a ubiquitous attraction to medieval themes not just in popular culture at large but in the domain of games in particular. The pervasiveness of the neomedieval vogue in the field, which often stretches to quite unexpected milieux and groups, is vividly captured by Eddo Stern's portrayal of the crowd attending the *39th Annual Renaissance Pleasure Faire* (San Bernardino, California, 2001): "the creatively anachronistic Renfaire crowd is comprised of a colorful band of jolly Anglophiles, mediaevalists, woodworkers, elves, druids and wizards selling handmade crafts, performing jousts, drinking mead and offering an all out sun-beaten Californian version of new-age virtual reality" (Stern, p. 258).

In the gaming world, medieval ingredients of Celtic and Gothic provenance frequently blend with images drawn from Tolkien, Wagner and, of course, the realm of Camelot and its mythical leader, Arthur, to conjure up mock-historical and magic-infused realities. According to Stern, in order to grasp the reasons for the huge popularity of medieval (as well as quasi-medieval and pseudo-medieval) topoi, it is necessary to acknowledge the relationship between "magic and technology" as both a historical event and a philosophical concept. The bond originates in a curious "mix of power, religion, science and art" (p. 259). Nowadays, Stern maintains, "technology operates to realize what was previously in the hypothetical realm of magic. There is definitely some connection in the way both magic and technology create a sense of wonder as they seem to expand upon the notions of what is or has been feasible in the realm of the real." Appropriately, Stern cites A. C. Clarke's famous line — "any sufficiently advanced technology is indistinguishable from magic" — to substantiate his hypothesis (p. 260). Therefore, in assessing the revival of medieval themes and imagery in a work like *Magic Knight Rayearth*, it is useful to remember that fantasy-driven popular entertainment is not the only goal at stake. In fact, even the passion for nostalgic antiquarian flourishes can helpfully remind us of the pertinence of magical epics to the here-and-now no less than to bygone eras.

By delivering a complex narrative while emulating the conventions of a ludic form, *Magic Knight Rayearth* is implicated simultaneously with two discrete disciplines: i.e., narratology — the study of narrative structures and of related writing and reading techniques — and ludology — the study of games as dramatic constructs of a particular kind. In assessing the relationship between gameplay and storytelling, several theorists have contended that RPGs accommodate particularly powerful storytelling tendencies, and that these often gain precedence over their action-driven components. Daniel Mackay expounds this proposition by throwing into relief the fundamental differences between games with an emphasis on action and RPGs of the fantasy variety. Many popular games in the former category, according to the critic, capitalize on fighting skills or the accrual of points and prizes by means of dynamic pursuits. Fantasy RPGs, by contrast, are closer to an interactive improvisational performance in which players adopt a wide range of character roles, and are largely free to establish imaginative identities for their personae within relatively commodious pre-designed scenarios. Consequently, they are granted the right to weave multifarious narrative tapestries, which those predesigned scenarios partly restrict but also inspire at every turn. These textual formations are finally responsible for investing the game with a recognizable identity at the artistic, structural, social and broadly cultural levels (Mackay).

Satu Heliö's writings have been especially influential in documenting the essential nature of the RPG as a very distinctive ludic typology governed by "strong narrative aspirations." Heliö persuasively maintains that even though there may not be an "actual story" at the heart of the game itself, in the sense of an autonomous narrative with a clearly identifiable beginning, middle and end, "there are events, characters and structures of narrativity giving the players the basis for interpreting it *as* narrative." To this extent, the game can be said to strive toward the status of a story by stimulating "the 'narrative desire' to make pieces we interpret to relate to each other fit in" (Heliö, p. 68). Extending Heliö's argument, it could be proposed while the game as such does not host a self-standing narrative in the conventional sense of the term, its arcs and multibranching developments are capable of articulating a story as long as a player is willing to interact with them, and to string their elements together through step-by-step decisions. The game might not be a story but it does feature all of the raw materials of an embryonic or hypothetical narrative which holds the potential to come fruition as a result of external contributions, and is therefore open to interpretation in eminently narrative terms.

This point is worthy of special emphasis, in the present context, insofar as it could be realistically argued that the aspect of both the adventure and the fantasy RPG which *Magic Knight Rayearth* most consistently honors is precisely its narrative thrust. It is indeed through its basic narrative premises that the series declares its allegiance to that ludic typology. The summoning of the Magic Knights by preternatural means to an otherworldly domain in which they must confront a series of monsters and formidable antagonists, gaining the assistance of a few helpers on the way, is in itself so typical a feature of adventure and fantasy RPGs as to verge on the status of a cliché. However, *Magic Knight Rayearth* does not stay satisfied for long with the gifts of established formulae. In the case of the anime adaptation, specifically, the show's narrative leanings are borne out most effectively — and imaginatively — when it transcends convention, and concentrates on bringing the parent text's linear energy to dramatic fruition by capitalizing at every available opportunity on the narrative integration of its pivotal themes and its character dynamics. To achieve this effect, secondary and supporting actors are assiduously brought into play alongside the protagonists themselves, with an emphasis on their ongoing contribution to both the show's pivotal subject matter and its ancillary motifs. It is to this strategy that *Magic Knight Rayearth* ultimately owes its capacity to engender in equal measures an atmosphere of ubiquitous enchantment and a sustained sense of structural coherence. The anime throws the organic interdependence of its characters and themes into sharp relief from an early stage with the sequences in which a seemingly mundane occurrence, a trip to Tokyo Tower, abruptly morphs into a momentous event with far-reaching cosmic repercussions. It is at this very point that Umi, Hikaru and Fuu are encircled by a magical glow and transposed to the land bound to stage their chivalric exploits amid countless threats.

As the epic unfolds over the two TV series and, with some substantial narrative reorientations, in the subsequent OVA release, the girls' distinctive personality traits increasingly blend with the ethical import of the drama's axial themes. Paramount among them are importance of loyalty, determination and sheer kindness. While learning to appreciate the incomparable worth of these interrelated moral principles and to translate their abstract import into tangible choices, the heroines must also negotiate many unsavory truths and hostile realities. Most crucially, they must accept that nurturing and destructive energies coexist at all times, as do, ultimately, life and death themselves. Unsurprisingly, when they discover that the protective roles they have adopted and cherished in the name of a redemptive mission have actually been designed to induce them to undertake a lethal mission, their entire value system receives the severest of blows. However, it is precisely in the wake of this bleak epiphany that Umi, Hikaru and Fuu finally develop the ability to make a radically positive input into the reshaping of Cephiro's history—a contribution which is triggered neither by preternatural visions nor by magical agents but entirely by their own will power. It is therefore vital to appreciate that despite its adherence to the RPG formula, *Magic Knight Rayearth* is not merely a manga or anime version of a role-playing game. In fact, its reconceptualization of the epic mode shatters the stereotypical ludic impetus associated with that form by proposing that the three heroines' assumption of their heroic roles is motivated essentially by their desire to return home to Tokyo. The RPG's conventions are questioned even more drastically by the girls' decision, following Princess Emeraude's horrific end, that if they were ever to reenter the alternate world of Cephiro, they would do so in their own terms and to carry out the deeds they personally believe to be right instead of fulfilling slavishly somebody else's game plan.

In looking at CLAMP's approach to characterization, it is worth noting that the portrayal not only of a character's physical attributes but also of its often complex psychology plays a comparably important part in the architectonics of RPGs. In this context, characterization is instrumental in supplying the player with emotive and visual stimuli capable of generating a truly absorbing immersive experience. This contention has been eloquently advanced by Petri Lankoski and Satu Heliö, who argue that "an important tool for setting up motivations and goals for the player are well-defined characters with distinct natures and needs. Those will create the basis of conflict in the game" (Lankoski and Heliö, p. 311). In addition, "consistency in character motivations and game structure is prerequisite for players to perceive a game as logically whole" (pp. 312–313). Embracing an analogous position, *Magic Knight Rayearth* unfailingly relies on inspiring characters with clearly identifiable drives and objectives, and this technique is largely responsible for imparting the franchise in its entirety with unique affective richness. CLAMP seems well aware that a great deal of character interpretation is likely to take place at a subliminal level, yet be able to influence the audience's attitude toward not only an individual character per se but also the story as a whole. This is because it is inevitably bound to impact to a significant degree on the sorts of interpretations the audience might be inclined to formulate at any given juncture. The characters' aspirations could therefore be said to shape, albeit implicitly, the audience's own aims.

Ironically, *Magic Knight Rayearth* delivers some of its most remarkable character portraits when it does not go out of its way to come up with innovative designs but rather strives to communicate diversity and novelty through judicious modulations of existing codes, conventions and popular typologies. In this regard, its aesthetic is fully consonant with the preference for recurrent stylized motifs which has distinguished Japanese art in all its forms for time immemorial. As this study repeatedly intimates, CLAMP has consistently shown itself able to enhance character appeal by situating its personae in worlds brimming with environmental, architectural and sartorial details. In both its manga and anime incarnations, *Magic Knight Rayearth* reinforces this proclivity by yielding a plethora of vibrant backgrounds abetted by dramatic lighting effects. Such settings resonantly demonstrate that the CLAMP artists do not hesitate to channel their creative efforts into the execution of aspects of a work which might not have any obvious or momentous influence on the plot but will implicitly sustain its import in a symbolic fashion. At the same time, they focus on settings which are capable of enriching their characters' personalities, distinctive expressions, movements and quirks. Hence, CLAMP's members appear determined to put no less effort into the depiction of sceneries, props and accessories than in the portrayal of humans and other animate creatures. As a lynchpin of the group's graphic and philosophical vision, this objective transcends by far any apparent dependence on established generic formulae derived from the *mahou shoujo* and *mecha* genres or from the domain of gaming.

In the area of characterization, *Magic Knight Rayearth* also bears eloquent witness to CLAMP's belief in the emphatically relational nature of human identity by yielding a whole gallery of character portraits based primarily on the interplay of affinities and divergences. Especially notable among the main actors are Cephiro's Pillar, Princess Emeraude, and her wayward assistant Zagato, the childlike (though 745-year-old) wizard Clef and the armor maker Presea, Ferio the valiant prince and Mokona the toy-like guide (and, as it transpires, the creator of the universe itself). It is with its depiction of the three heroines themselves, however, that CLAMP's genius as a creator of psychologically nuanced and vibrant personalities shines forth in its full colors. Most importantly, the girls complement one another harmoniously from the very start, and as their relationships evolve in the course of the saga, increasingly collude as interdependent facets of a composite personality ensemble. This idea is reinforced by the nature of the supernatural skills they acquire during their sojourn in Cephiro: in keeping with their names' original meanings, Hikaru, Umi and Fuu come to specialize in the interrelated arts of Fire, Water and Wind Magic respectively. Hikaru stands out as a candid tomboy, as well as a proficient kendo practitioner with a knack of communicating with non-human species. This enables her to connect with Mokona and to translate the creature's messages for the benefit of her friends. Having been made mature well beyond her years by the tragic events crowning the story's first arc, Hikaru develops the power to become Cephiro's new Pillar. Fuu, an exceptionally intelligent girl with an impressive storehouse of knowledge at her disposal, combines a sharp mind with a disarmingly sweet smile while also excelling at archery. Umi, the gorgeous model from a rich family, never shows any sign of the kind of haughtiness one could easily expect to see in a girl with her credentials. Though exceptionally sensitive to other people's feelings, she ironically appears oblivious to those of the boy who loves her. The mixture of innocence and competence which all three of the protagonists evince, in different areas and to various degrees, is largely responsible for imparting *Magic Knight Rayearth* with affective density in spite of its sporadic concessions to generic stereotypes.

Magic Knight Rayearth's serious tenor is effectively confirmed by its finale, which steers clear of facile resolutions of a providential or miraculous stamp in favor of an open-ended ethical message eager to underscore the ascendancy of eminently human qualities — above all, perseverance, sympathy and selfless courage. It is barely surprising, in the light of CLAMP's audacious formal experiments, that *Magic Knight Rayearth* should have met with considerably mixed responses within the ranks of both weathered CLAMP fans and casual consumers ever since its initial release. Yet, there can be little doubt that this title has made a groundbreaking contribution to the intertwined histories of manga and anime by flouting the standards of the typical epic adventure aimed at the younger strata of the public. In the process, it has managed to address with unsentimental lucidity, though not without color and wit, the gravest of topoi: namely, the fraught relationship between humanity and the cosmos.

The epoch-making CLAMP manga released under the title of *X/1999* between 1992 and 2002 received adaptation to the anime format both as a movie and as a TV series, released in 1996 and 2001–2002 respectively. In addition, the *X* saga bears witness to CLAMP's penchant for multimedia experimentation through the OVA *X—X2 Double X* (1993). A condensed prequel to the film version of *X*, this consists of four music videos. The first three pieces bring together a series of stills of CLAMP's pre-1994 artwork for *X/1999* and do not contain any real plot. The fourth video articulates an embryonic yarn, introducing some of the main characters and then rapidly whipping through the first few *X/1999* manga chapters (corresponding to the first three installments of the TV series), whose events are supposed to occur prior to those dramatized in the movie.

The theatrical and serial versions of the anime offer complementary interpretations of the same basic epic, putting to maximum advantage the distinctive attributes of their respective formats. Therefore, the film capitalizes on its relatively limited compass to deliver a poignantly capsulated version of the saga, revealing certain key aspects of its characters' personalities and aims in an allusive or symbolic guise rather than through extensive description. This allows it to focus on the story's essentials and thus bring out its epic significance in a dramatically impactful mode. Relatedly, the movie concentrates on the roles played by Kamui, Kotori, and Fuuma in deciding humanity's fate, thus highlighting the human component of the drama while demoting the Dragons of Heaven and the Dragons of Earth to the category of marginal personae. Readers of the original manga may at times feel that this abridged version of the story fails to situate the characters' choices and deeds in their proper context. Nevertheless, the movie has been profusely commended for its oneiric and even surreal atmosphere, arresting imagery and galvanizing action sequences. The TV series, conversely, can afford to dwell at some length (though not exactly at a leisurely pace) on character portrayal. This enables it to introduce its personae's principal attributes gradually over a number of episodes. At times, it endeavors to reinforce particular facets of their psychological and emotive makeup which it deems essential to their being, while at others it amends or even subverts previously established impressions to expose hidden components of their mentalities or else depict a dramatic reorientation in their goals. The epic's essence per se, meanwhile, is deliberately distributed over the program's entire duration, which entails more detailed presentation than one encounters in the film version but also, on occasion, a marginal dilution of its dramatic force.

Having already commented in some depth on the *X* movie's most salient attributes in the course of the preceding chapter, the TV series would seem to deserve some attention at this juncture. This version of the saga chronicles the running battle destined to seal humanity's fate in which the Dragons of Heaven and the Dragons of Earth vie for supremacy, advancing deliberately — yet inexorably — toward the climactic fight between the two factions' leaders. While this brief summary might indicate that the show follows the standard action-driven pattern characteristic of *shounen* anime and manga, *X* actually disrupts the established formula quite radically. In this regard, it evinces no less hearty an appetite for rule-bending and generic reconceptualization than *Magic Knight Rayearth* did in the field of RPG-influenced series. *X* parts company with the *shounen* mode most decisively through its avoidance of any cathartic climaxes, delivering a finale which, though pervaded by impeccably animated action, offers neither neat resolutions nor consolatory relief. Its world view, accordingly, remains undilutedly dreary, its goals grave, and its storytelling style so viscerally brutal as to verge on the sadistic.

X vaunts a stunning multitude of characters, the vast majority of whom are sensitively portrayed down to the minutest detail of their often contorted personalities. This proposition applies to *X* in all of its media incarnations but is especially true of the parent manga and of the anime series. In both instances, one soon realizes that the protagonists and supporting personae alike have been carefully individualized with reference to a broad range of backgrounds and to unique capacities of both human and superhuman caliber. As a result, the seven Dragons of Heaven enjoined to protect Kamui and the seven Dragons of Earth meant to combat them come across as some of the most engaging warriors ever committed to either the manga page or the anime screen. The sheer size and diversity of the saga's character ensemble posed substantial challenges for CLAMP during the production of the original manga, insofar as the task of imparting each character with the visual individuality they needed while juggling with no less than fourteen main characters and a plethora of secondary presences often felt nothing short of titanic. "We'd stay up all night, then sleep, then stay up all night, then sleep," recalls Satsuki Igarashi in an interview addressing the team's hardships in creating the series. "There were times when we could only sleep every other day" (interview in CLAMP 2007e, p. 5). However, the actual magnitude of the task can only be appreciated when one considers that in the year *X/1999* started its run, several other CLAMP manga were already being serialized (including *RG Veda, Tokyo Babylon, CLAMP School Detectives* and *Duklyon: Clamp School Defenders*), and that the following year, *Magic Knight Rayearth* would also make its debut.

In dramatizing the struggle between the Dragons of Earth and the Dragons of Heaven, here outlined in the context of Chapter 1, *X* in all of its formal configurations is very much a product of its epoch. As Fumiko Yamamoto observes in his essay on CLAMP's "Construction of Armageddon," the manga's full title itself, *X/1999*, encapsulates this idea: "when *X* started its run in 1992, the signs of the times indeed seemed to make it worthy to be called the end of the millennium. The prophecies of Nostradamus, the alignment of the planets, the daily occurrences of violent crimes.... Beginning under these circumstances, *X* captured the readers' hearts and gained popularity in the blink of an eye." According to the critic, what renders this saga special, compared with other works likewise dealing with the end of the millennium, is the stark nature of the two options posited by CLAMP's story as possible scenarios for the end of the world: the destruction of humankind as a means of saving the Earth or the destruction of the Earth as a means of saving humankind. Thus, "whatever painful, frightening images of Armageddon may have been depicted in other works, reading (or watching) them doesn't bring us ... close to such grave alternatives.... But in *X*, we're pressed to choose which side of these two no-win alternatives to stand on ... *X* attempts to build a tense relationship with the reader, and perhaps the uneasiness of not having an answer, of not being able to see the future ... became the dividing line between *X* and the numerous other works about the end of the millennium"(CLAMP 2007e, P. 11).

At the same time, *X*'s topical relevance should not obliviate the fact that one of the main reasons for which it remains memorable among both weathered and occasional anime audiences is its treatment of issues of veritably timeless appeal. First and foremost among these topics is the philosophical conundrum surrounding the irreconcilable dicta of determinism and free will. The clash between collective priorities and personal desires is thus consistently thrown into relief as the actors strive to negotiate the tangled thread of destiny in a desperate — and, by and large, vain — attempt to fulfill foreordained duties without sacrificing individual dreams altogether. The pivotal conflict underpinning the anime's metaphysical stance is encapsulated by the divergent views regarding the future — and, by implication, the world's fate — voiced by Kakyou and by Kotori when the dreamseer traverses the dream experienced by the girl at the precise time of her death. While Kotori, with her parting words, states that "the future isn't decided," Kakyou maintains that "there is only one future." Although the drama oscillates between these two positions at several key junctures, the prevailing atmosphere is one of dire inevitability. To reinforce the notion that its characters' destinies are predetermined, *X* frequently foregrounds the ascendancy of random chance on all human affairs, and its power to impact momentously on trivial matters and heroic deeds alike. Thus, as heroes and villains on both sides clash or collude in shifting constellations, the only constant lies with the sense of sheer inscrutability surrounding all these various encounters. Time and again, its characters renounce happiness, reason and life itself in a heroic effort to change their destinies. Yet fate, the epic ultimately intimates, may only be affected at the expense of appalling sacrifices. Relatedly, the action points unremittingly to the virtual impossibility of autonomous choice. This is most painfully conveyed by its intimation that no matter which destiny Kamui had opted for, Kotori's death would have been equally inescapable. At the same time, Kamui is incrementally enjoined to accept that no choice he makes will ever be unequivocally untarnished by the stains of loss, sorrow and sin.

When the original CLAMP manga entered the laborious process of adaptation as an anime series, the challenges faced by the saga's creators reproposed themselves with something of a vengeance. In the hands of less capable directors, *X*'s enormous cast would have burdened its flow to breaking point. However, anime veteran Yoshiaki Kawajiri, the TV series' director, was able to deploy an ingenious strategy in order to circumvent this potential obstacle. This consisted of the release of the OVA *X: An Omen* in anticipation of the series' premiere in 2001. The OVA recounts the story of the forthcoming battles in which the fate of the Earth will be decided through the prophecies of the charismatic dreamgazer Kakyou Kuzuki as he recalls the life and death of a young woman whom he encountered in dreams. Though ostensibly created for the purely commercial purpose of drumming up interest in the forthcoming TV series, the OVA actually serves an important dramatic function as a means of stirring the audience's interest in an exceptionally large cast of characters without having to resort to protracted (and feasibly tedious) expository sequences. To this extent, it still holds unquestionable value today, retaining the potential to appeal to diverse audiences as an anime accomplishment of autonomous aesthetic worth.

> Homage to CLAMP (ii)
> From "CLAMP The Courier of Dreams."
> In *CLAMP no Kiseki Vol. 1*:
>
> *It seems like the members of CLAMP prefer to come up with something original every time. We cannot ignore their Asian heritage when talking about this subject. Many fans probably learned about Hindu Mythology after they started reading* RG Veda. *As a creator, it's a thrill to take an obscure subject, put your spin on it, and present it to your readers.... A worthy creator will always challenge himself or herself to something new rather than rehashing the same formula over and over. If you look at it differently, CLAMP has proven themselves to be a pioneer by constantly challenging themselves to new frontiers with every project.* —Yoshiki Tanaka (2005)

Chapter 3

TRANSWORLD MIGRATIONS

A Level 3 parallel universe is a consequence of the many worlds interpretation (MWI) from quantum physics in which every single quantum possibility inherent in the quantum wavefunction becomes a real possibility in some reality... you're continually in contact with Level 3 universes — every moment of your life, every decision you make, is causing a split of your "now" self into an infinite number of future selves, all of which are unaware of each other.... A Level 4 parallel universe is the strangest place (and most controversial prediction) of all, because it would follow fundamentally different mathematical laws of nature than our universe. In short, any universe that physicists can get to work out on paper would exist, based on the mathematical democracy principle: *Any universe that is mathematically possible has equal possibility of actually existing.* — "The Theory of Parallel Universes"

Originally released in manga form between 1996 and 2000, *Cardcaptor Sakura* partakes at once of the fantasy adventure atmosphere characteristic of *Magic Knight Rayearth* and the flair for psychologically nuanced characterization which sustains the *X* saga in all of its incarnations, interspersing its protagonist's exploits with esoteric allusions redolent of *Tokyo Babylon* and heroic flourishes worthy of *RG Veda*. The fantasy adventure mood is palpably conveyed by the structural motif of the staged quest on which *Cardcaptor Sakura* evidently revolves, and derives both emotional depth and dramatic impactfulness from the diversified cast of characters involved in the mission alongside its charismatic heroine. The mystery element, which pivots on the enigmatic character of an exchange student from England, courses the story in a predominantly unobtrusive fashion but proves instrumental in determining its eventual outcome and thereby establishing the protagonist's true worth on both the human and the supernatural fronts. It is through its intimations that its heroine's quest ultimately carries metaphysical implications of cosmic amplitude that *Cardcaptor Sakura* declares its ambitious aims even as it stays true to a generic mode capable of satisfying the younger members of its audience. Many people still regard *Cardcaptor Sakura* as CLAMP's finest production to date, and even those who have come to cherish a later series as their favorite would readily concede that this was the title which declared CLAMP's standing as one of the most admired and influential creators in the manga galaxy.

The diverse elements delineated above reverberate throughout the entire franchise, to bring together into one harmonious whole the exceptionally protracted TV series *Cardcaptor Sakura* (1998–2000), the films *Cardcaptor Sakura: The Movie* (1999) and *Cardcaptor Sakura Movie 2: The Sealed Card* (2000), and the OVA *Cardcaptor Sakura Video Diary* (2000). The structural agent chiefly responsible for accomplishing this stirring tonal synthesis is *Cardcaptor Sakura*'s intelligent handling of the theme of multiperspectivalism. This is inaugurated by the protagonist's accidental discovery of the mystic volume known as Clow Book, and the resulting dispersal of the magical cards it hosts (the Clow Cards), as well as the awakening of the tome's guardian, Cerberus (a.k.a. Kero-chan). Since disaster will befall the planet unless the scattered cards are found, the unremittingly bouncy Sakura Kinomoto feels she has no choice but to embark on the retrieval mission. This exposes her to a series of largely unpredictable experiences, each of which opens up a novel perspective and fresh opportunities for self-discovery and growth. However, Sakura soon discovers that the recovery of the missing Clow Cards does not mark the end of her odyssey: in fact, she must pass one further test, the so-called "Final Trial," if she is to prevent the cards from unleashing a lethal curse whereby all of the people who have been somehow involved with the Clow Cards will be doomed to lose their memories of the people they love most deeply. This topos, as we shall see, will be developed by CLAMP to great dramatic effect in *Tsubasa: RESERVoir CHRoNiCLE*. Sakura's magical powers and esoteric awareness progressively grow with each new challenge she faces, while her emotions concurrently develop, and she is therefore exposed to quite a different bundle of riddles and trials: those inherent in the mystery of human love.

In examining the thematic and formal influences underlying *Cardcaptor Sakura*, the *mahou shoujo* formula instantly springs to mind. This genre vaunts a long and colorful history in the interrelated realms of anime and manga. Ushered in by *Sally the Witch* in 1966, it proved instantly popular among young girls and rapidly found further articulation in legion series well into the 1970s and 1980s. Some of the more renowned productions include *The Secret Akko* (1969), *Chappy the Witch* (1972), *Magical Girl Meg* (1974–1975), *Magical Princess Minky Momo* (1982–1983) and *Magical Angel Creamy Mami* (1983). It was *Sailor Moon*, released in 1992, that radically reconceptualized the genre by combining the established magical girl formula with the figure of the fighting heroine. *Cardcaptor Sakura* evinces the salient attributes of both modalities but it is ultimately its defiance of conventions, more than its preparedness to stay true to their original spirit, that imparts the whole franchise with unforgettable vigor. Moreover, *Cardcaptor Sakura* does not rely mechanically on magical tricks and theatrical effects in order to communicate the otherworldly flavor of its multiperspectival exploration. In fact, even though the series often capitalizes on vibrant action sequences, it does not derive poignancy from these high-octane moments so much as from the ever-present sense of mystery lurking in the background, and from its introduction of unforeseen conspiracies and traps.

Ageha Ohkawa has commented thus on the team's own attitude to the *mahou shoujo* typology: "at first we were going to make her a witch. But the more we thought about is, the more we wanted to do something unique with the 'magic' part of the story. We wanted her to be something more original than just a witch with a magic wand. That's when we came up with the 'Cardcaptor' concept" (interview in CLAMP 2005a, p. 5). Furthermore, CLAMP's members made no self-conscious effort to engage with the *mahou shoujo* genre when they received *Nakayoshi* magazine's request for a new series, just as *Magic Knight Rayearth* was drawing toward a close. "None of us had really paid attention to series where the character was a magical girl," Ohkawa maintains. "We've seen maybe one or two episodes on TV." To reinforce her distance from the *mahou shoujo* genre, the artist also claims to have been mainly a fan of "detective stories" as a child. The actual reason for resolving to experiment with the magical girl formula, therefore, was not that CLAMP was familiar with its ingredients but rather that "it was more of a challenge" than other genres in which the artists were already proficient. "We wanted to see how it would turn out. We included all the basics.... However, fans that are into that genre tell me that *Cardcaptor Sakura* stands out in the genre because it's somewhat atypical" (p. 7).

While there can be little doubt that this is indeed the case, it is also important to acknowledge CLAMP's rather unusual treatment of the theme of love. As Saiga Kiyoshi observes in an essay devoted to CLAMP's handling of this important topos, "by all appearances, *Cardcaptor Sakura* is fundamentally a series created for the grade school girls who read *Nakayoshi*. It's evident in the straightforward love story between Sakura and Syaoran (which is rare for a CLAMP book).... But this is by no means the only form of love that is portrayed in the series. Scattered throughout the series are many other relationships that might be difficult for a grade-school audience to understand. I think it adds an essence of 'CLAMP' to the series. I would almost say that that's what makes this a CLAMP manga." Tomoyo's connection with the protagonist is a resplendent case in point, insofar as it transcends the conventional *shoujo* manga definition of friendship among school girls in its almost disturbing selflessness. "The idea that there are no borders with love," Kiyoshi continues, "that love comes in many different forms, is a favorite theme of CLAMP" (in CLAMP 2005a, p. 17). This impression fully vindicates Ohkawa's intention to portray Sakura as "accepting of love in all its different forms," and hence open to "advice from a lot of people," which entailed CLAMP's presentation of "as many different types of relationships as possible" (interview in CLAMP 2005b, p. 5).

The anime's treatment of the romantic liaison laboriously unfolding between Sakura and Syaoran over several episodes, though supposedly consonant with its *shoujo* substratum, attests to CLAMP's imaginatively commodious take on human relationships. By the time the TV series reaches its closing installment, not even the most cynical spectator will be likely to doubt the depth and authenticity of those characters' mutual affection. Yet, the drama does not indulge either in soppy confessions or promises of future bliss, choosing instead to bring out the more comical side of the relationship in a tactfully affectionate fashion. The result is a gem of emotional irony: while Sakura is able to negotiate her final test with relative aplomb, thus managing to break the spell which has caused the entire city to fall into a state of deep slumber courtesy of Eriol, she still finds it arduous to voice her emotions regarding matters of the heart. As Zac Bertschy amusingly points out, in this regard, "waking up the entire city proves to be an easy task compared to admitting her feelings for Shaoran Li, who winds up on the slow boat back to Hong Kong when his mother finds out that his Card-acquiring job in Japan is at an end" (Bertschy 2004).

No less typical of CLAMP's ethical outlook at its rosiest than the choreographing of the love dimension is the heroine's favorite line, which resonates throughout *Cardcaptor Sakura* with the spell-binding force of a magical refrain: "I'm sure you'll be all right." These few words are actually pregnant with meaning, their central message being one about the power of love, resilience and hope. The magical girl genre typically relies on spectacular transformation scenes in which their protagonists morph into significantly more mature, as well as infinitely more powerful, female types. Sakura, by contrast, remains a child at all times. With this drastic departure from one of the *mahou shoujo*'s most fundamental tropes, CLAMP emphasizes the degree to which their protagonist's eventual triumph is the product not so much of preternatural skills as of pluck, honesty, kind-heartedness and, above all else, an unwaveringly optimistic attitude. Thus, while other CLAMP series typically intermingle their more positive lessons with sobering reminders of the inevitability of sorrow and loss, *Cardcaptor Sakura* offers the rare jewel of a series with an elatingly happy resolution.

The "Cardcaptor" element itself has precious little to do with the *mahou shoujo* as it actually belongs to the long-established history and lore surrounding playing cards in general and the Tarot deck in particular. The CLAMP artists were well aware of the nascent popularity of diverse dim Collectible Card Games (often tied in with manga and anime productions) but it was from the much older tradition of the Tarot that they drew inspiration for the design of *Cardcaptor Sakura*'s cards — and specifically, according to Ohkawa, from a "foreign Tarot card design ... filled with a lot of details" (interview in CLAMP 2005a, p. 5). All of *Cardcaptor Sakura*'s magical cards echo the Tarot system at a number of interrelated planes. In specifically graphic terms, they are most redolent of the Tarot deck's sixteen Court Cards (which form the Minor Arcana alongside the forty cards numbered one to ten in each of four suits). The younger and more vivacious characters are comparable to Knaves, the more martial or athletic to Knights, and the older and graver to Kings and Queens. In iconographic terms, *Cardcaptor Sakura*'s cards emulate the Tarot's intricate and multilayered symbolism by recourse to their own impressive range of cryptic signs. At times, such signs turn out to be significant if assessed in conjunction with specific narrative developments. At others, they are playfully and deliberately nonsensical and thrown into the mix for the sake of ornamentation alone. The *Cardcaptor Sakura* cards do not always bring overtly into play the Tarot system's dense web of symbolic references. They do, however, consistently incorporate many of the pivotal meanings embedded in that time-honored structure of signification in an implicit or allusive fashion.

The various realities explored by Sakura and her associates in the hunt for the hidden cards, in particular, can be seen to pay tangential homage to the elaborate esoteric code that has accompanied the Tarot tradition over the centuries. This has occasioned the gradual emergence of correspondences among the Tarot suits themselves, the elements (and related alchemical spirits), and the signs of the Zodiac, thus integrating some of the most ancient esoteric systems ever chronicled in either history or legend. The principal correspondences here entailed are delineated below.

Tarot Suit:	Wand			
Element:	Elemental:	Star Signs:	Cardinal Point:	Meaning:
Fire	Salamander	Leo, Aries Sagittarius	South	Animation Growth Energy
Tarot Suit:	Cup			
Element:	Elemental:	Star Signs:	Cardinal Point:	Meaning:
Water	Undine	Pisces Cancer Scorpio	West	Feeling Unconscious Femininity
Tarot Suit:	Sword			
Element:	Elemental:	Star Signs:	Cardinal Point:	Meaning:
Air	Sylph	Gemini Libra Aquarius	North	Strife Aggression Courage
Tarot Suit:	Pentacle			
Element:	Elemental:	Star Signs:	Cardinal Point:	Meaning:
Earth	Gnome	Taurus Virgo Capricorn	East	Wealth Business Enterprise

Most vitally, *Cardcaptor Sakura*'s cards obliquely allude to the Tarot's Major Arcana: the twenty-two allegorical pictures believed to depict the ceaseless flow of multifarious energies, both spiritual and corporeal, which shape all life and govern human destinies. Traditionally, different Tarot packs adopting diverse dimensions and designs have shared one fundamental attribute: their emblematic status as visual exemplifications of various stages of human existence which encompass not only the past as it was really experienced and the present as it is being experienced but also all the possible or potential pasts and presents one could have lived or be living.

More importantly still, the Tarot system is inextricably intertwined with the topos of fate—a subject which is never too far from CLAMP's vision and pencils, and is unquestionably axial to *Cardcaptor Sakura*'s unfolding. The Tarot is indeed held capable of hosting an archetypal and unconscious grasp of the future, and hence of the myriad hypothetical experiences which that dimension always accommodates. The connection between *Cardcaptor Sakura*'s cards and the Major Arcana is not, by and large, made explicit by either the CLAMP artists themselves or the story's personae. Nor is it openly acknowledged or cited in the action as such. Nevertheless, it does make itself felt at a subliminal level insofar as the series' emphasis on the concept of fate finds an ideal correlative in the very essence of the Tarot tradition as a philosophy of fate. The Major Arcana, specifically, could be regarded as symbolic equivalents of the characters' intersecting destinies and attendant multiperspectival explorations. At the same time, *Cardcaptor Sakura* obliquely echoes the Tarot discourse as a storytelling experience which links the past, the present and the future by bringing into play disparate facets of the Questioner's psychological and emotional baggage. In the logic of CLAMP's story, such a narrative should never be thought of as a preordained event, wholly dominated by an inflexible fate, since human courage, generosity and potential for free choice never quite lose their hold on the action.

It is with *Tsubasa: RESERVoir CHRoNiCLE* that CLAMP's passion for multiperspectival travel — both literal and figurative — takes a veritable leap into the artistic stratosphere to deliver an ensemble of parallel worlds worthy of quantum theory at its most audaciously visionary, and hence gives rise to a metauniverse of unrivaled richness. As the four principal characters undertake their epic quest, driven by different goals yet bound by a shared destiny, the past and the future intermingle in a kaleidoscopic present comprising a galaxy of parallel dimensions. Across all of these worlds, history merges with legend, while magic colludes with disarmingly real human emotions. The present analysis is not primarily concerned with exploring the defining features of the saga's individual worlds. In fact, it is far more interested in identifying the strategies deployed by the artists in order to constellate those disparate dimensions within a coherent structure of meaning and action. Indeed, it is from an understanding of those structural mainstays that the quality of CLAMP's multiperspectival ethos is best developed. The ensuing paragraphs propose that *Tsubasa: RESERVoir CHRoNiCLE* relies on three fundamental principles to hold its composite reality together: the establishment of a dense metaphysical mesh in which time, destiny, chance and free will alternately collide and intertwine; the use of stylistic, generic and thematic contrasts between different dimensions, intended to emphasize each world's distinctiveness in relational, rather than bluntly individual, terms; the cinematographical weaving of flashbacks meant to impart present occurrences with levels of significance stretching beyond the contingent flow of events. All three strategies enable CLAMP to highlight the incidence of continual, though often barely perceptible, change by focusing on the characters' emotional growth alongside material transformations in their historical, geographical, cultural and ideological circumstances. The discussion addresses these three areas with specific reference to the two seasons of the TV series *Tsubasa: RESERVoir CHRoNiCLE*, aired in 2005–2006, and then moves on to consider salient aspects of the saga which have unfolded outside the remit of the TV series—i.e., in the original video animations *Tokyo Revelations* (2007–2008) and *Tsubasa: Spring Thunder* (2009), the film *Tsubasa: RESERVoir CHRoNiCLE the Movie: The Princess of the Birdcage Kingdom* (2005), and the volumes of the parent manga which have not been adapted to the screen.

Tsubasa: RESERVoir CHRoNiCLE dives straight into the deepest waters of its multiperspectival epic with its inaugural installment, where we are instantly introduced to the young protagonists: Princess Sakura of Clow and the archaeologist Syaoran. Sakura, we soon learn, possesses an uncanny gift of world-changing proportions. Just as her hitherto unsuspected power is about to awaken, spectral wings sprout from her back as a corporeal expression of her memories. At the same time, the girl's body begins to fuse with a symbol inscribed within the ruins which Syaoran is excavating. This chain of otherworldly phenomena is witnessed by magical means by enigmatic agencies keen to appropriate Sakura's power in order to achieve uncontrasted mastery over time and space. Syaoran strives to remove Sakura from this inauspicious setting by wrenching her body away from the emblem which seeks greedily to absorb her but in the process, the ghostly wings are destroyed, alongside her heart and soul, while her memories are sent adrift in the guise of floating feathers. According to the royal priest and soothsayer Yukito, this baleful occurrence condemns Sakura to certain death: "a body with no heart," he ominously intones, "is just an empty shell. Without those memories, the princess will die."

It gradually transpires that the cause of Sakura's misfortune is the arch-villain extraordinaire Fei Wong Reed, whose ultimate aim is the reactivation of a quiescent transdimensional power. The roles played by the princess and the ruins within this grandiose plan remain unexplained until the saga is well under way. Deploying a band of ruthless warriors as his emissaries in order to initiate Sakura's metamorphosis, Fei Wong Reed operates from a secret location known simply as the "Secret Base." We also learn that the villain's headquarters accommodate a glowing liquid chamber wherein a youth with Syaoran's appearance floats unconscious. The TV series periodically returns to this image, especially to mark moments in which Syaoran is the victim of inner turmoil. However, its true meaning is only clarified in the three-part OVA series *Tsubasa: Tokyo Revelations*, to be accorded additional layers of both dramatic and symbolic significance in the final volumes of the manga which have not found adaptation to the anime screen to date. The far-reaching malevolence of Fei Wong's schemes is reinforced by the incremental revelation that the feathers hosting Sakura's memories, harmless as long as they are solely in her possession, hold devastating potentialities once they are appropriated by unscrupulous agents keen on advancing their personal, and normally iniquitous, quests.

When the protagonists turn to the Dimensional Witch Yuuko for help, another major aspect of the story's metaphysical fabric comes into prominence. We thus learn that within its distinctive world view, any gain must entail a loss of comparable proportions if the cosmos' underlying equilibrium is to be preserved at all times. Hence, when they are granted by Yuuko the faculty to world-hop in search of the wandering feathers, the protagonists must also accept that in exchange for this gift, Sakura will be deprived forever of her memories of Syaoran. Sakura and Syaoran's traveling companions, Kurogane and Fai, must also pay steep prices for that same gift: the ninja is required to relinquish his trusted sword, a weapon of mythical reputation, and accept that he is destined to become weaker every time he kills, while the mage must surrender the tattoo on his back which enables him to regulate his magic, which is practically tantamount to foregoing magic altogether insofar as Fai is not prepared to trifle with its potentially deadly force. As the full significance of the possessions which the two characters have had to relinquish progressively emerges, it also becomes evident that in spite of their manifest differences, the grim warrior and the suave wizard share a common legacy of sorrow and strife. It is this emotional and psychological substratum that enables them to empathize instinctively with Syaoran and Sakura's plight throughout the adventure's laborious unfolding.

Relatedly, the saga's metaverse affords no leeway for random chance. This position, already mentioned in the context of Chapter 1, is known as *hitsuzen*, and is instantly posited as integral to *Tsubasa*'s entire plot in all its elaborate ramifications. The doctrine of *hitsuzen* is paradigmatically championed by Yuuko, who holds that although "at first glance, the world seems to be chaotic," and "individual actions and events may seem like they're scattered and confused, the whole balances out to proceed on a certain course" (CLAMP 2008b, p. 24). Syaoran has been encouraged since childhood to embrace this credo, and accordingly asserts in unequivocal terms that "there is no coincidence ... the only thing is *hitsuzen*" (CLAMP 2009c, p. 140). This philosophical perspective, as we shall see, is also pivotal to the *xxxHOLiC* franchise. Yuuko's assertions are overtly echoed by the character of the old sage met by the protagonists in the arc where they journey aboard a hi-tech bus through desert in pursuit of a feather fortuitously stuck to a trailer moving swiftly ahead of them, with a gang of motorcycled robbers at their heels. "They do say there must be some sort of tie when sleeves touch," the old man maintains. "There is an invisible link between all encounters. It's not a coincidence on how we all met here. Perhaps it may be a meeting where we are supposed to do something. There's no such thing as coincidences in this world. There is only inevitability."

As helpfully elucidated in the relevant article supplied by the website *On Philosophy*, "events that fall under the domain of *hitsuzen* happen in accordance with some scheme, plan, or design.... Events that fall under *hitsuzen* can be understood as connected to other events within that scheme, and thus signify the scheme and its ends as a whole." The diametrical opposite of *hitsuzen*, in this philosophical perspective, is the concept of "*guzen*." This designates events which "occur by happenstance and aren't part of some larger scheme. Thus events that fall in the domain of *guzen* are meaningless, in the sense that that they are unconnected to other events and thus signify nothing beyond themselves, certainly not some larger scheme or goal." Therefore, while *hitsuzen* "manifests teleology, i.e. goals or ends," *guzen* simply "does not" ("*Guzen* and *Hitsuzen*"). Assessed in a broad philosophical context, the principle of *hitsuzen* (and, by implication, its antithesis) can be seen to bear important connections with a whole nexus of debates surrounding the notions of fate, destiny and free will. In this scenario, fate designates the cosmic force endowed with the power to preordain future events and to impart them with the qualities of apparent inevitability and finality. Countless traditions and cultures have regarded fate as the creation of preternatural agents tirelessly engaged in spinning the threads of individual human destinies into the expansive tapestries which ultimately form the histories of entire worlds. In the context of traditions inspired by the teachings of Buddhism and Shinto, the principle that all life forms are inextricably interconnected provides the underpinning of a complex metaphysical vision of the cosmos at large as something of a gigantic spider web. A distinction must be drawn, at this point, between the concept of fate and the notion of destiny. Indeed, whereas fate is supposedly impervious to human intervention, destiny may allow for the individual's participation in its making as a relatively independent force endowed with a modicum of free will.

In its articulation of a multiperspectival narrative in which the unfolding of both individual and collective destinies is influenced by mystical forces, *Tsubasa: RESERVoir CHRoNiCLE* experiments with diverse interpretations of the idea of destiny. On numerous occasions, the saga appears to work on the assumption that destiny is fixed and ineluctable. In the light of this interpretation, the protagonists' concurrently physical and spiritual journeys appear rigidly predetermined. At times, this position veers toward fatalism, the philosophical doctrine according to which no human choice can influence the future for good or ill regardless of its intentions. Any action or decision performed by the individual is, in this world view, simply pointless. (Fatalism results from a radical interpretation of the concept of fate outlined earlier.) Alternatively, dogmatic fatalism may be supplanted by determinism, a position which maintains, like fatalism, that the future is tied to necessity, yet also proposes that people's contingent actions have the power to affect how that future will come about. In a fatalistic perspective, people's experiences are planned occurrences in which they have no decisive part; in a deterministic one, by contrast, they are seen to issue from those individuals' fundamental dispositions. In some cases, libertarianism also comes into play as an option, and it is therefore suggested that the future can never be considered settled as long as human beings can be thought of as fundamentally free.

This may be the case even if their freedom is not a given on which they can unproblematically depend but rather a capacity they must be willing to appropriate and demonstrate at a considerable price. Sakura and Syaoran's ability to forge a new relationship and new memories to replace what they have lost at the hands of fate can be seen as the fruit of just such an effort. It is an expression of their abiding freedom, yet it entails a great deal of hard work and suffering. A further example of the same basic approach to the concept of freedom is provided by CLAMP's seminal achievement, *RG Veda*. Although the fabric of the entire epic appears to be subject to the rule of a tyrannical fate, Ashura and Yasha are able to establish and honor their bond in defiance of that power — and hence to reverse the course of events spun by inscrutable forces on both their and their land's behalf. Without an underlying consciousness of their freedom, these characters would simply have lacked the strength to survive the long centuries of strife which their odyssey entails.

In a universe governed by formal logic, the approaches to fate and destiny delineated above would be considered incompatible with one another, and an ethos presuming to favor their coexistence, therefore, would be dismissed as incongruous, erratic or even downright ridiculous. Nevertheless, as repeatedly suggested in the course of this study, CLAMP's vision is not normally constrained by the rules of formal (let alone binary) logic. Hence, it allows for the possibility of a multiperspectival philosophy — which is quite consonant with its conception of a multiperspectival reality — and boldly proposes that human beings might well be both the prisoners and the makers of their destinies at one and the same time. Most importantly, it intimates that even when the destiny of a character (or group of interdependent characters) appears to be so ineluctably sealed as to bar any hopes of reorientation, it may prove possible to interfere with the world's spatial and temporal coordinates just enough to open up new ways of looking at the world. It is crucial to underline, in this context, that CLAMP posit such a strategy as a means of creating an alternative *perspective*, not an alternative *reality* as such. In fact, the artists are keen to stress that if by defying space and time thanks to Yuuko the travelers were to bring about new worlds from scratch, their actions might be conducive to happiness but this achievement would only be the unreliable bliss notoriously promised by utopias: an escape into a pseudo-reality from which no lessons could be learned and through which no self-understanding could be achieved. By meddling with space and time just enough to tilt their axes and bring about subtle shifts of perspective, conversely, those characters establish fresh viewpoints from which the world can be assessed and interacted with. This approach can induce them to look at both themselves and their ordeals differently and, in ideal circumstances, to learn something from theirs experiences. Besides, CLAMP emphasizes that while its characters may be aware from the start of their connections with supernatural forces and destinies, they still have to learn at their own cost how to identify and bear the onus implied by their roles through tortuous journeys of self-exploration. Thus, even though *Tsubasa*'s protagonists initially appear caught in destinies which they cannot hope either to transcend or to elude, they incrementally develop a capacity to break through their fatal cages through resilience, courage, and a love deeper than the even most extraordinary multiperspectival ocean.

Throughout the *Tsubasa* franchise, the ascendancy of chance is playfully intensified by the limitations of the agent with whom Yuuko entrusts the protagonists in order to abet their interdimensional odyssey: Mokona Modoki, a marginally rabbit-like creature exuding all of the most endearing attributes of the playful end of CLAMP's design spectrum. Able to convey several people across world boundaries an indefinite number of times, Mokona also functions as a competent feather detector and translation device, which allows the travelers to understand each other even though they come from vastly different cultures and speak disparate languages. Despite these impressive abilities, however, Mokona is only able to traverse dimensions and has no real control over the choice of destination. The protagonists' itinerary, therefore, is wholly at the mercy of fate.

It is worth emphasizing, at this juncture, that even though it is by no means exceptional for an anime series to be orchestrated in terms of relatively discrete arcs, the narrative organization evinced by *Tsubasa: RESERVoir CHRoNiCLE* is refreshingly inventive. Tasha Robinson corroborates this point, maintaining that "it's good that the series doesn't follow a predictable pattern of one feather or one new dimension per episode, which would get dull fast — instead, it takes the time to focus on and develop the first world the stars visit, with worthwhile results.... That unhurried vibe stretches into the direction, as well, with long lyrical sequences simply depicting Sakura flying, or Syaoran contemplating his memories of her" (Robinson 2007). In addition, the series abounds with panned stills and methodically prolonged sequences — recurrent characteristics of director Koichi Mashimo's typical style — which contribute vitally to the consolidation of its deliberately unhurried rhythm. The unassuming tone conveyed by such techniques is aptly echoed by the depiction of the central visual motif: i.e., the scattered feathers into which the heroine's memories have been transformed. Indeed, the image of the wandering plume brings to mind something quintessentially fragile, incomplete and unanchored, and could therefore be said to reflect a preference for the beauty radiating from imperfection: a concept accorded great prominence in the context of traditional Japanese aesthetics.

The multiple worlds visited by the travelers are stunningly diversified, and inspired by both settings and characters drawn from previous CLAMP productions. Among the numerous personae imported from earlier CLAMP manga and reproposed in *Tsubasa*, the most prominent are Sakura, Syaoran, Princess Tomoyo, Touya and Yukito, who have all been borrowed from *Cardcaptor Sakura*, Ashura from *RG Veda*, Kamui and Fuuma from *X/1999*, Mokona and Princess Emeraude from *Magic Knight Rayearth*, Chi from *Chobits*, and Yuuko from *xxxHOLiC*. With the exception of Yuuko the Dimensional Witch, the recycled characters portrayed in *Tsubasa* are not really the same as their precursors in prior titles but pristine configurations of those people who preserve their names and faces but not their narrative and figurative import. Alongside these crossovers, we encounter several other characters created expressly for *Tsubasa* who likewise appear in different roles within disparate worlds. CLAMP's fascination with split, multiple and ramifying subjectivities reaches an apotheosis with this device. Recurrent characters are at one point described by Syaoran as "parallels with the same appearance" who "seem to have the same essence" though "their lives and memories are different."

Both established and budding CLAMP fans may sample the group's passion for crossover characters by focusing on *Tsubasa: RESERVoir CHRoNiCLE* as a series which relies to a stupendous extent on the occurrence of personae previously encountered in other CLAMP works. This series' tendency to capitalize more pervasively than many others on crossover characters should not be dismissed as a purely utilitarian move on CLAMP's part: i.e., a strategy designed to minimize the team's creative input in the conception of novel personae. Nor can it be attributed exclusively to the artists' desire to take maximum advantage of their regular readers' attachment to certain characters by regaling the pages of the new work with familiar faces. In fact, the pervasive use of crossovers throughout practically all of *Tsubasa: RESERVoir CHRoNiCLE*'s arcs is a perfectly logical corollary of the series' metaphysical preoccupations, intended to bring into sharp focus the latent interconnections of all lives and all worlds across a limitless cosmos. The list of crossovers presented below, partially indebted to the article "Crossover Universe" for corroborative evidence, offers an illustrative overview of the range of crossovers delivered by the *Tsubasa: RESERVoir CHRoNiCLE* manga in just a diminutive portion of its principal arcs.

- Clow Country, alternate timeline
  Touya (*Cardcaptor Sakura*)
  Yukito (*Cardcaptor Sakura*)
  Fujitaka (*Cardcaptor Sakura*)
  Clow Reed (*Cardcaptor Sakura*)
- Clow Country, original timeline
  Syaoran Li, Sakura's mother (*Cardcaptor Sakura*)
  Sakura Kinomoto, Syaoran's mother (*Cardcaptor Sakura*)
  Nadeshiko (*Cardcaptor Sakura*)

- Clow Country Final Arc
  Yuko Ichihara (*xxxHOLiC*)
  Kimihiro Watanuki (*xxxHOLiC*)
  Yue and Keroberos (*Cardcaptor Sakura*)
  Clow Reed (*Cardcaptor Sakura*)
  Sakura Kinomoto (*Cardcaptor Sakura*)
- Celes Country
  Chi (a.k.a. Elda) (*Chobits*)
  Ashura-oh (*RG Veda*)
  Miyuki-chan (*Miyuki-chan in Wonderland and CLAMP School Detectives*)
- Japan (Modern Day)
  Yuuko Ichihara (*xxxHOLiC*)
  Watanuki Kimihiro (*xxxHOLiC*)
  Marudashi (*xxxHOLiC*)
  Morodashi (*xxxHOLiC*)
  Mokona Modoki (a.k.a. Mokona) (*Magic Knight Rayearth*)
- Hanshin Republic
  Sorata Arisugawa (*X*)
  Arashi Arisugawa (*X*)
  Kudan (a.k.a. The Rune Gods) (*Magic Knight Rayearth*)
  Shougo Asagi (*X*)
  Masayoshi Saitou (*Clamp School Detectives*)
  Masayoshi's Kudan (a.k.a. Sang Yung) (*Magic Knight Rayearth*)
  Tomoyo Daidouji (*Cardcaptor Sakura*)
  Toya Kinomoto (*Cardcaptor Sakura*)
  Yukito Tsukishiro (*Cardcaptor Sakura*)
  Primera (*Magic Knight Rayearth*)
  Miyuki-chan (*Miyuki-chan in Wonderland*)
- Koryo Country (Nayutaya in the anime version)
  Chun'yan (a.k.a. Chun-hyang) (*Legend of Chun Hyang*)
  Hyantan (*Legend of Chun Hyang*)
  Chun'yan's mother (*Legend of Chun Hyang*)
  The Kiishimu (*Magic Knight Rayearth*)
  The Amen'osa (*Clamp School Detectives*)
  Miyuki-chan (*Miyuki-chan in Wonderland*)
- Jade Country
  Princess Emeraude (*Magic Knight Rayearth*)
  Miyuki-chan (*Miyuki-chan in Wonderland*)

- Outo Country
  Minoru's maid persocoms (*Chobits*)
  Blanche (*Angelic Layer*)
  Yuzuriha Nekoi (*X*)
  Inuki (*X*)
  Kusanagi Shiyuu (*X*)
  Ryuuou (*RG Veda*)
  Souma (*RG Veda*)
  Eri [Eri Chusonji] (*Duklyon: Clamp School Defenders*)
  Kentarou [Kentarou Higashikunimaru] (*Duklyon: Clamp School Defenders*)
  Takeshi [Takeshi Shukaido] (*Duklyon: Clamp School Defenders*)
  Caldina (a.k.a. Gardina) (*Magic Knight Rayearth*)
  Fusion of Rayearth, Selece, and Windam (*Magic Knight Rayearth*)
  Oruha (a.k.a. Ora) (*Clover*)
  Misaki Suzuhara (*Angelic Layer*)
  Oujiro Mihara (*Angelic Layer*)
  Tamayo Kizaki (*Angelic Layer, Kobato*)
  Karura-oh and Garuda (*RG Veda*)
  Qiang Ang (a.k.a. Chanan) (*Magic Knight Rayearth*)
  Sang Yung (a.k.a. Sanyun) (*Magic Knight Rayearth*)
  Utako Ohkawa (*Man of Many Faces*, CLAMP *School Detectives* and *Duklyon: Clamp School Defenders*)
  Makoto Ohkawa (*CLAMP School Detectives*)
  Hinata Asahi (*Suki, Lawful Drug, Kobato*)
  Shirou Asou (*Suki, Lawful Drug, Kobato*)
  Seiichirou Aoki (*X*)
  Koutarou Kobayashi (*Angelic Layer*)
  Vayu and his sword (*RG Veda*)
  Varna and his sword (*RG Veda*)
  Sumomo (*Chobits*)
  Kotoko (*Chobits*)
  Miyuki-chan (*Miyuki-chan in Wonderland*)
  Seishirou Sakurazuka (*Tokyo Babylon, X*)
  Chitose Hibiya (*Chobits*)
  Touya (*Cardcaptor Sakura*)
  Yukito (*Cardcaptor Sakura*)

Although the anime version of the saga is necessarily selective, its conscientious treatment of the range of settings it adapts from its source does full justice to the parent manga's fundamental creative vision. The stupendous diversity of the worlds nested within the anime's diegesis is vividly proclaimed not only by the variety of adventures staged therein but also, on a more immediate sensory plane, by their visual definers. It would indeed be hard to deny that the highlight of CLAMP's art for this title lies precisely in its ingenious manipulation of style as a means of evoking the flavor and mood of each new dimension with palpable immediacy. Accordingly, each of *Tsubasa*'s realms is scrupulously individuated in terms of both its natural scenery and its architectural preferences. In addition, the atmosphere of each location is matched by distinctive costumes, accessories, and both magical and everyday objects linked with time-honored rituals and customs. Thus, Clow, Sakura's homeland, is instantly identifiable as a desert encircling for miles a city placed on a lush oasis. At the same time, however, its sweeping towers, ornate hallways, secret gardens and shrines embody the essence of legend with arresting charisma. The clothes favored by Clow's inhabitants mirror the country's twofold identity. Pragmatically tailored in accordance with Clow's climate and desert-swamped situation, they feature ample hooded cloaks meant to protect their wearers from frequent sandstorms. Yet, they also emanate a bewitchingly exotic aura redolent of the *Arabian Nights*. The dynamic effects unleashed by these garments, with their profusion of folds, creases, rucks and rimples, are extremely varied and visually fascinating. Fai's country, Seresu (also often transcribed as Celes), stands out as a forbiddingly glacial land with medieval European undertones. The garments worn in the icy world of Celes are principally distinguished by heavy fur-lined coats. Kurogane's own place of origin is recognizable as feudal Japan. The costumes associated with Kurogane's ancient Japan are congruous with Japanese fashions of the feudal era, yet enhanced by original details ideated purposely for *Tsubasa*'s metaverse.

Even a rapid panoramic survey of some of the worlds visited by the protagonists in the course of their odyssey will instantly attest to their kaleidoscopic range, further reinforcing the penchant for multiperspectivalism already conveyed by the key characters' own countries. With the Hanshin Republic, *Tsubasa: RESERVoir CHRoNiCLE* depicts a consummately animistic world. Each of the inhabitants of this tiger-shaped island indeed possesses an animal spirit (*kudan*): a presence which should not be regarded merely as a person's accessory or even as a companion as it actually constitutes a fundamental aspect of his or her being. No human identity, it is here intimated, could even begin to subsist in the absence of its animal double. The Hanshin costumes have a casually contemporary feel. Intriguingly, the local street gangs favor looks designed to foreground their subcultural identities, such as biker goggles and large gloves or accessories inspired by Punk and Mohawk vogues. The country of Nayutaya (Koryo in the original manga) is a feudal nation in which Syaoran and his companions make it their moral duty to unite an oppressed people and incite them to overthrow their despotic rulers. This arc's central character, Chu'nyan, is especially notable as a paradigmatic example of CLAMP's attraction to free-spirited and plucky girls whose generosity of spirit renders them mature beyond their years without, however, numbing their exuberance and enthusiasm. This character is quite explicitly modeled on the protagonist of the manga *Legend of Chun Hyang*, released from 1992 to 1994. The Nayutaya clothes are emphatically old-fashioned and often influenced by traditional Korean garb, especially the *hanbok*. Layered attire and umbrella-like straw hats of feudal provenance also make prominent appearances.

The picturesque world of Jade transposes us to a radically different atmosphere, providing the saga with the opportunity to weave a dystopian fairytale centered on the charismatic figure of the royal specter Princess Emeraude. From a stylistic point of view, this facet of *Tsubasa* is rendered most captivating by the presentation of the legend by recourse to voiceovers accompanying still images which resemble stained-glass panels exuding an aura of timeless wonder. Additionally, the visuals' debt to the Gothic style fittingly complements the haunting topos at the heart of the Jade arc as a whole. In Jade, the characters wear garments inspired by diverse phases of European fashion with a preference for Restoration and Victorian motifs. Many fans — and not only those with a taste for ghost stories or Gothic-tinged fairy tales — would readily agree that the character of Princess Emeraude stands out as one of CLAMP's most charismatic personae ever. Her portrayal in the context of the *Tsubasa* series, while directly echoing the character's presentation in *Magic Knight Rayearth*, is also redolent of the female figure central to *Shirahime-Syo: Snow Goddess Tales*: a manga anthology published in 1992 and as yet untranslated into anime. The first collection of short stories drawn by CLAMP in one single stint, *Shirahime-Syo* offers an intensely personal interpretation of the mythos of the Snow Goddess, or Snow Woman (*Yuki Onna*), fragrant with melancholy, gravity and longing — i.e., affects which also imbue Princess Emeraude's ordeal over many centuries of loneliness and sorrow, as depicted in *Tsubasa*. The anthology's pervasive atmosphere is stunningly underscored by the employment of monochrome illustrations, redolent of traditional Chinese ink drawings.

In Outo, the travelers discover a tournament-driven dimension governed by the codes and conventions of the RPG genre, here discussed in the context of Chapter 2 vis-à-vis *Magic Knight Rayearth*. Outo's citizens, accordingly, are demon-hunters who progressively ascend the country's martial hierarchy by vanquishing monsters which have been rigorously classified according to their strength, and thus gaining points with each defeat. The illusory nature of Outo is exposed through the disclosure that its world is inextricable from the Country of Edonis and its popular amusement venue, Fairy Park, which harbors egg-shaped capsules by means of which its visitors can access the virtual reality of Outo. In Outo, the costumes combine traditional Japanese elements and twentieth-century Western vogues, recalling the climate of Japan's Taisho Era (1912–1926): a period of cultural transition in which indigenous traditions were confronted by the challenges of Western modernity. The anime plays with retro-chic sci fi in its depiction of the Piffle World, a nostalgically pseudo-futuristic setting evincing many of the architectural and dynamic motifs conventionally associated with sci-fi anime and cinema at large, such as aerial traffic lanes and vertiginously proportioned high rises. In the parent manga, this dimension receives a pointedly airy and fluffy look from its brightly lit and almost shadowless settings, and from its graceful meshes of line work. The "Dragon Fly Race," a local tournament in which the protagonists compete in the hope of recovering an errant feather, enables CLAMP to give full rein to its passion for spirals, twirls and swooshing arcs. It is also noteworthy that CLAMP's avoidance of overtly futuristic vogues in the rendition of Piffle World's architectural and sartorial styles is bolstered by its association with outfits which echo the Jazz Age as envisioned by F. S. Fitzgerald, with a few concessions to contemporary sports gear and to the magical girl subgenre.

With Shara Country, the anime experiments with the extension of the structuring principle of contrast by exploring the internal tensions besetting this world from within rather than focusing purely on its difference from other realities previously visited by its protagonists. This dimension is initially distinguished by a hearty appetite for playfulness, which manifests itself primarily through the representation of the hilarious incidents resulting from Sakura's and Syaoran's involvement with an itinerant circus and its all-female "Suzuran troupe." The anime will later enthrone the carnivalesque mode sampled by these events as an unmatched dramatic force with the protagonists' transition to a dimension in which they appear as infantilized caricatures of their former selves (*chibi*), drawn by a Princess Emeraude lookalike with the assistance of a pencil powered by one of Sakura's feathers. With the Shara arc itself, however, *Tsubasa* veers away from its initial comic mood to deliver what in fact abides in memory as one of its most complex and pathos-laden segments. This atmosphere results to a considerable extent from the anime's experimentation not solely with spatial migration but also with time travel. Thus, the protagonists find themselves inexplicably transposed to the legendary land of Shura and its ceaseless conflict with the land of Yama — that is to say, to Shara's ancient past as inscribed in indigenous lore. The dark mythological tapestry woven in this arc delivers some of the anime's most stunning visuals.

As a dyad of interdependent dimensions, Shara and Shura offer a lavish gallery of costumes, ranging from the blatantly theatrical clothes typical of the Suzuran troupe (and temporarily appropriated by Sakura and Syaoran themselves) to the myth-infused garb of the ancient realm which stages Ashura's and Yasha's epic confrontation. In addition, the CLAMP artists' skills as costume designers come gloriously to the fore in the representation of flowing robes, cloaks and veils. It is with the portions of the saga staged in Shara and Shura that the anime also provides one of the most satisfying examples of CLAMP's talent in the areas of set design and interior design, thereby offering some of the most astounding visuals at the levels of both background art and dynamic effects. These unleash a remarkable range of contexts, ranging from brightly colored urban scenes to murky battlefields, from luxuriant royal gardens exalted by the blissful sound of waterfalls to ominous night skies dominated by a blood-red moon. The sumptuous interiors of Ashura's palace are most memorable in their punctilious depiction of a plethora of furnishings, accessories and ornaments oozing with pictorial and textural sensuousness. In its pursuit of multiperspectivalism, *Tsubasa* leaves no generic stone unturned, endeavoring at once to interrogate the conventions inherent in each of the categories it draws on, and to enable their disparate languages to collude in a novel graphic constellation.

Moving on to the saga's handling of flashbacks, it should first be noted that many of the most significant of these dramatic occurrences are a direct corollary of the price which Sakura and Syaoran are required by Yuuko to pay in return for her provision of world-hopping means — i.e., the princess' loss of all recollections of her once beloved friend. In some of the most memorable flashbacks, Sakura manages to recapture some happy childhood moments following the absorption of a recovered feather. On such occasions, she is able to visualize quite clearly all of the people present in those contexts except for Syaoran, who only ever features as an absence: a vacant space, a pathos-laden lacuna in otherwise richly detailed and chromatically varied settings. Thus, the recollection of a cheerful birthday party, for example, will only ever feature Syaoran as an empty chair; a photograph portraying him in the company of his adoptive father, the archeologist Fujitaka, as a papery blank. The most genuinely affecting aspect of those scenes lies with Sakura's pained awareness that no matter how hard she tries, the true source of the happiness enshrined in those precious moments is fated to remain inscrutable and invisible. At times, especially as the saga advances and various submerged or dormant facets of Sakura's original personality are gradually restored, the girl seems to sense subliminally the existence of a connection between Syaoran and her own identity crisis. A touching instance is the sequence in which she engages in a telepathic exchange with the giant fish, which in itself confirms the princess' possession of unearthly powers. In response to the creature's encouragement to explain what has brought her to this world, she indeed states: "I am here because he [i.e., Syaoran] brought me. And I seek to know who I am." Scenes such as this intimate that the bond between Sakura and Syaoran is everlasting and hence capable of defying the strictures of both memory and its evaporation.

Sakura hopes in vain that one day she might be able to recall the identity of the person once so important to her. Syaoran, in turn, appears to have resigned himself to the idea that Sakura is simply powerless to remember him, and therefore looks vaguely surprised whenever she voices concern about his safety. Nevertheless, neither Sakura's lingering optimism nor her champion's pragmatism ever threatens to spoil the soothing beauty of their relationship. The wistful mood pervading this liaison from start to finish finds a worthy antecedent of a much more modest scale in the manga *Wish* (1996–1998): a touching love story revolving around the innocent angel Kohaku and the reserved surgeon Shuichiro, and somewhat unpredictably culminating in tragedy. The CLAMP artists were well aware that the story's graceful mood, abetted by Tsubaki Nekoi's distinctively delicate graphic style, had contributed significantly to the steady increase in the manga's popularity during its run. Nevertheless, their proverbial aversion to banal happy endings finally won the day. According to Ohkawa, established CLAMP fans were by no means taken by surprise by this narrative outcome — if anything, it is far more likely that they would have found the gentle and fanciful atmosphere infusing the bulk of the manga a bit unusual. Asked what she considered most memorable about their readers' reactions, Ohkawa has observed: "it was an unusually cute story, so everyone was kind of curious. However, it didn't remain that way, so fans were like 'we knew it!'" (CLAMP 2007d, p. 19). *Wish*'s melancholy finale, specifically, foreshadows *Tsubasa*'s drama by exposing the inevitability of irretrievable loss. In 1997, *Wish* reached the screen in the form of a short music video portraying the manga's chief characters in a predominantly mellow and magical tone, and with minimum dependence on plot elements.

Tsubasa's retrospective leanings gain considerable momentum from its revelation of an important portion of Syaoran's hazy background. We are thus informed by means of flashbacks that upon meeting Sakura, the boy had no recollection of any occurrences predating his adoption by Fujitaka. In these scenes, the girl endeavors to comfort him by suggesting that they "make a lot of new memories instead," and further proposing that insofar as Syaoran cannot recall the date of his own birthday, he might as well share hers. This ensures that they will always be able to celebrate the anniversary together. Given Sakura's current ordeal, this flashback yields a painfully ironical reversal of roles. The most disturbing flashback is the one, offered in the context of the Outo arc, in which Sakura marginally overcomes her amnesia, and begins to suspect that she might have known her protector prior to her memory-dissolving mishap and that she and this unnamed person might even have come to know each other as children. Nonetheless, she has no means of establishing the veracity of this impression. Just as she hesitantly considers that Syaoran is "someone very important" to her, she is assaulted by a hallucination in which a fuzzy image of the cloaked Syaoran from the Clow days spirals backward against the background of a cut-out of Sakura's head flooded with psychedelic effects, as if her remembrance of the boy were being sucked into a black hole. A shot of the Dimensional Witch with an enigmatic smirk on her mien makes a brief appearance at this point to remind us of the rigorous terms binding the protagonists to the law of cosmic balance. It is as though Sakura's dormant, yet eternal, affection for Syaoran were struggling to break through an impervious barrier, only to be repressed by the unrescindable authority of those conditions. Fai somberly comments on the situation as follows: "even when [Sakura] regains feathers that carry memories of [Syaoran], he'll be immediately removed. Like a story written on paper filled with holes because every mention of him has been cut out."

Closely related to the saga's handling of flashbacks are its recurrent reflections on the vicissitudes of memory as a palimpsest of impressions endowed with not only mental but also densely corporeal significance. The Shara/Shura arc plays an especially significant part in foregrounding CLAMP's dedication to the portrayal of the material dimension of experience, instead of focusing solely on its conceptual import, by throwing into relief the corporeality of memory. This is attested to by the scenes in which Sakura strives to relieve Syaoran's physical pain. In one of these, she touches a wound he has received in order to help it heal by injecting her feelings into it. This "treatment," as her father Clow Reed would term this kind of gesture in Sakura's childhood, intimates that the girl harbors dormant feelings for Syaoran which her body remembers even though her conscious memory has no direct access to that affective pool. In another related scene, Sakura kisses Syaoran's left eye, which immediately begins to hurt following a shot of the Syaoran held at the Secret Base and Fei Wong's remarks concerning the likelihood of this creature's impending awakening. Mokona explains that Sakura has been unconsciously steered by remembrances encoded in her material frame: "that kiss just now may be a memory from your body. Yuuko said so. That there are two types of memories. The heart's memories and the body's memories. The heart is very important but the body is too. 'At times the heart may forget but the body will remember' is what she said.... Your wanting to kiss his aching eye was because even though you forgot due to losing your feathers, your body probably remembered. So until all your feathers come back, your body's memories will help you out."

Tsubasa's exploration of the physical manifestations of memory reaches its apotheosis in the final arc of the TV series' second season. This is set in the Country of Tao, a world modeled on the traditional East where everyone is endowed with special powers. This is due to the realm being enveloped by *senriki* (literally, the "power of the hermit"), which affects not only Tao's original inhabitants but also visitors to the land. *Senriki* manifests itself in variable degrees, enabling some people just to influence ordinary objects telekinetically and others even to fly. It is in this dimension that Sakura experiences the nefariousness which her memory feathers are capable of unleashing in all its horror as she witnesses the dismal fate of Tao's monarch, King Chaos. Utterly obsessed with the princess, and resolved to take her as his companion at any price, the character's very essence ultimately turns out to consist of a bundle of Sakura's feathers which "began to develop a mind of their own somewhere along the way." The reason behind Chaos' fixation with Sakura is that he is actually a part of her — and, most crucially, of her mnemonic legacy. Having revealed this perturbing truth to the princess herself by recourse to a vision in the course of his climactic fight, Chaos begs her to free him from his curse.

The open-endedness of the TV series is vital to the entire saga's structure as it sanctions that the protagonists' pilgrimage is destined to continue not only beyond the close of the program but, feasibly, ad infinitum. In order to fathom *Tsubasa*'s multiverse in its genuine magnitude, it is therefore necessary to turn to its articulation outside the boundaries of the TV series per se — namely, in the original video animations, the movie and the manga. Unsurprisingly, several facets of the manga behind the *Tsubasa* saga are not overtly dramatized in any component of the anime. This is a logical corollary of its breadth: the publication ran from May 2003 to October 2009, thus reaching a total of 28 volumes and accruing no less than 233 chapters. The ensuing paragraphs assess the first OVA's contribution to the saga as a whole by focusing on some of its key moments alongside the corresponding portions of the source text.

The OVA *Tsubasa: Tokyo Revelations* is considerably darker and bloodier than the TV show. In fact, it is often so unsentimental and raw as to threaten to dissolve altogether the tender fantasy element which courses the TV series even in its gloomier moments. Where the TV series' prevalent atmosphere is nostalgic, the OVA's verges on the tragic. This is borne out by practically all aspects of the production: its acting style and dialogue, which steer clear of any concessions to either humor or romance; its locations, where a ubiquitously postapocalyptic mood dominates the action; and its character dynamics, through which the positive bond forged by the protagonists in the context of the TV series is exposed to some serious threats. At the purely visual level, it is hard to imagine a dimension more starkly removed from the snow-clad elegance of Jade or the airy playfulness of Piffle World than the Country of Tokyo, where the OVA is set. The vast white expanses seen in those earlier domains are gone, brutally replaced by tenebrous skies, deep shadows, accentuated silhouettes and the darkest blood conceivable. In the manga version of the Tokyo arc, these same elements are also consistently deployed, their dramatic thrust reinforced by some impeccably executed impact sequences with a marked cinematic feel.

The prevalent image associated with the OVA's interpretation of Tokyo is that of a desolate metropolis which is being slowly consumed by highly corrosive rain. The only two aquatic reservoirs as yet uncontaminated are controlled by warring clans and their formidable leaders: Kamui and Fuuma. These characters could be regarded as reincarnations of *X*'s protagonists with substantially altered roles. While Syaoran, Fai and Kurogane do their best to adapt to this unfriendly environment, which is reputed to host two of Sakura's precious feathers, the princess herself remains unconscious for a long time, and it gradually emerges that her body and soul have parted company. While Sakura's body lies comatose as nothing more than an inanimate vessel, her soul rests in a cocoon-like luminous globe as it is visited by cryptic visions and dreams. The theme of the split self thus comes rapidly to prominence in the OVA. As argued later in some detail, this motif plays an unprecedentedly crucial role in the latter arcs of the parent manga, accruing complexity and momentum as the saga draws toward its close.

One of the most tantalizing topoi developed by the source text which the TV series only hints at is the relationship between the active Syaoran and his quiescent lookalike, who is imprisoned, as noted, within Fei Wong' Secret Base. The Piffle arc and the Shara/Shura arc drop discreet allusions to the boy's divided identity but do not explicitly invite reflection on this theme's broader implications in either structural or psychological terms. To do so would be quite inappropriate to the tone, rhythm and scope adopted by the TV series and would, therefore, simply spoil its formal coherence. We do not necessarily have to turn to the manga itself for the purpose of grasping the exact nature of the relationship between the two Syaorans, as this is actually elucidated in the OVA as the Syaoran thus far held captive by Fei Wong makes his sensational appearance on the scene at long last. Having awakened and managed to break free, Syaoran begs Yuuko to convey him to the location of his "right eye," which he is resolved to recover at any price. This is a wish which the Dimensional Witch is prepared to grant without hesitation, reckoning that the boy has already paid the necessary price in the guise of his "connections," his "freedom" and his "time" (CLAMP 2007b, p. 155). It is with the appearance in Tokyo of the hitherto inactive Syaoran that the story finally explains the shocking truth behind the two Syaorans' relationship. It is hence revealed that the youth we have known all along as Sakura's protector and as a tenacious feather hunter is a clone deriving from the Syaoran who has just awakened, who is in fact the original boy.

Needless to say, Fei Wong's vicious hand lies behind the character's splitting and replication, the villain's possession of two Syaorans being instrumental in the advancement of his dark agenda. Whereas the clone was not originally in possession of any autonomous magical abilities, the original was a proficient wizard worthy of his ancestor Clow Reed, whose talent Fei Wong strives to control and possibly harness to his own shady ends. In an effort to curb his artificer's wicked intentions, the original Syaoran bestowed his left eye and half of his heart to the clone so as to impart the artificial being with a human essence while also gaining the power to witness everything which the clone himself would experience. In the process, the clone also absorbed some preternatural faculties, situated in the original's right eye. Fei Wong's initial intention in response to his prisoner's infraction was to remove the magical eye but, having rapidly realized that the clone would perish were he to do so, he decided to send "the image in the path that would unerringly lead him to a meeting with the princess and to the ruins that would be the key to everything" (CLAMP 2008a, p. 65). Following the villain's disclosure, the scene focuses on the Dimensional Witch, who explains that as a result of surrendering his left eye, the original Syaoran's magical power was "cut in half." All he could do, as long as he lacked the strength to "break the confinements ... constructed for him" was to wait patiently and silently (p. 68). With the original Syaoran's awakening, the magic embedded in the clone swiftly begins to weaken, and the heart bestowed upon him by the original automatically returns to its owner. Much of the pathos which pervades *Tsubasa: Tokyo Revelations* issues from its portrayal of the clone's precipitous descent into mechanistic brutality once he has been divested of both his legitimacy as Sakura's loyal protector and of his magic endowments. Fai insists that even though the Syaoran with whom he has gradually become acquainted is an artificial being, he is still "a good kid" (p. 55) and is therefore determined to help him recognize and preserve his human dimension. Even a "false soul," argues the wizard, is "a true soul" to the person who harbors it (p. 74). Moreover, the heart the clone has developed over the journey is undisputedly his own in Fai's perception: "it's something you and Sakura-chan, and all the people who love you made together" (p. 78).

However, the clone proves utterly unresponsive to this passionate plea, making it clear that his sole concern now lies with the retrieval of the portentous feathers — i.e., the task for which he was initially conceived. "I will obtain what I need to get her feathers back," he coldly declares. "And I will remove anyone in my way" (p. 109). Hence, he unscrupulously proceeds to gouge out and absorb one of the mage's preternatural eyes in a desperate attempt to replace his lost powers. The original Syaoran is likewise unsuccessful in his efforts to help his double acknowledge that even though the heart he gave him at the time of his creation must now be returned to its natural owner, he has acquired a heart and emotions of his own over time. Most crucially, the original contends, the heart which has come to care so deeply for Sakura as not to hesitate to confront deadly challenges for her sake is the clone's own heart. Since the synthetic entity, in response, seems only keen on vanquishing his alter ego at any price, the original Syaoran is left with no choice but to destroy the clone. It is Sakura, awake at last, who stops him just in the nick of time: the princess, we soon realize, is not readily willing to accept that the youth she has come to know and love in the course of her transworld migrations is not an actual human and is, in fact, so merciless as to deserve execution.

In the arc following the adventures set in Tokyo, which takes us to the world of Infinity and its live-action chess tournament, the manga throws into relief the inner torment suffered by Sakura in the aftermath of *her* Syaoran's replacement by the original. This aspect of the girl's development is most touchingly exposed by the sequence in which she dolefully confesses to Fai that although she is well aware that the recently introduced version of Syaoran "may be the basis" for the boy she is "familiar with," she still senses in her "head that they're two different people." Sakura's inner conflict is fittingly echoed by the original Syaoran's painful knowledge that no matter what he does or say, "to the princess, Syaoran will always be *that* Syaoran. The shoulder she leans on is not mine" (p. 108). Sakura's choice of words in referring to the youth she cares for is worthy of notice as evidence of CLAMP's sensitive handling of dialogue as a means of throwing into relief a character's psychological vicissitudes. Indeed, when Sakura describes the version of Syaoran she loves as someone she is "familiar with," instead of spelling out what she actually feels for him, the characteristically reserved side of her personality is tactfully thrown into relief. The scene also echoes a key moment from the saga's first chapter: just before entering the ruins bound to destroy her memory and endanger her very being, Sakura informs Syaoran that there is something she wishes to tell him, adding that she will wait until "next time"—without even vaguely suspecting, of course, that there will never be a real "next time" for the two of them together as they are there and then. Sakura's bashful behavior also recalls the attitude evinced by her predecessor Sakura Kinomoto from *Cardcaptor Sakura* at the end of the TV series, where voicing her feelings for her Syaoran proves far more onerous a task than pulling off an impressive magical feat.

The OVA's closing segment brings together all of the most salient ingredients of *Tsubasa*'s metaphysical vision, as Yuuko discloses that Fei Wong's decision to cause Sakura's feathers to scatter across innumerable worlds stemmed from his conviction that the phenomenon would force the princess to "travel across many universes looking for [her] memories" and to "commit all of those dimensions to memory." It is especially worth noting, in this regard, that the villain is said not to be "interested in the memories contained within Princess Sakura's mind. But the memories contained in a vessel called her 'body'" (p. 8), insofar as these are the ultimate tools necessary to the realization of his own sinister plan. The physical dimension of a person's mnemonic storage is again highlighted as it was in the Shara/Shura arc. At a later point in the manga, Yuuko reinforces this message by stating that "though the heart may forget," "the body will remember" (CLAMP 2009b, p. 43). We thus learn that Fei Wong, having kidnapped the original Syaoran (who suspected the villain's iniquitous scheme) and manufactured a duplicate that would make the recovery of Sakura's feathers his raison d'être, also murdered Kurogane's mother and destroyed his country in the knowledge that these calamities would eventually induce the ninja to embark on an inexorable voyage. It was to enable the princess to traverse myriad dimensions and collect her lost memories that the companions were drawn together as partners in her journey. A similar message is later communicated by Fei Wong himself in the scene where he predicts Fai's peregrinations across time and space with Sakura and her cohort, and states that the princess' "long journey" is "required" for his "wish to come to fruition." Sakura, he adds, "must add the physical memories of many different worlds to her body" in order "to activate a ruin that sits in the Kingdom of Clow" whence he seeks to draw supreme power (CLAMP 2009a, p. 9).

In the story arc situated in the world of Infinity, CLAMP engages in one of its most inspiring, as well as graphically trenchant, interpretations of the theme of the divided self. This mirrors the events dramatized in the Tokyo arc by proposing an analogous split between Sakura's body and soul. When Sakura's soul journeys to the World of Dreams in search of Syaoran the clone, CLAMP regales us with an intriguing crossover by depicting the princess' meeting with Kimihiro Watanuki, *xxxHOLiC*'s male lead. As we shall see, this same character will play a pivotal role in *Tsubasa*'s tortuous progression toward its climax. Furthermore, CLAMP's articulation of the topos of divided identities by means of Sakura's soul-body split finds a parallel in Fai's occluded history, which is finally — and sensationally — disclosed in volumes 20 and 21 of the source text as the wizard returns to his homeland with Kurogane, Mokona and the original Syaoran in the hope of locating Sakura's body after its separation from her soul. It is here that we discover, with some of the most disturbing and starkly realistic visuals accompanying the verbal text, that Fai was born one of identical twins. Insofar as the birth of twins was deemed an evil omen in his country's lore, it was decreed that one of the unfortunate children must be destroyed. This horrific decision led to the death of the original Fai and to his brother Yuui's assumption of the departed twin's name. At the same time, the survivor became the victim of two of Fei Wong's vicious curses and was condemned to journey across worlds to virtual infinity as his sole means, supposedly, of reviving the lost twin.

It is through these disquieting revelations that we also learn that behind Fai's jovial façade lies an abysmal legacy of horror and guilt. In addition, this portion of the saga's background history enables CLAMP to reinforce in the starkest of terms a key component of *Tsubasa*'s overarching metaphysical vision: namely, the ineluctable convergence of a tangle of individual destinies bound by a shared obligation to traverse innumerable dimensions. Taken as a metaphor, this topos alludes to the comprehensive world picture, discussed earlier, in which all the strands of a seemingly sprawling tapestry prove subtly, though cryptically, interwoven, and random chance turns out to encapsulate a hidden design, a pattern. On the graphic plane, this motif finds a direct correlative in CLAMP's stylistic preference for the elaboration of highly wrought patterns which faithfully abide by the indigenous aesthetic principle known as *kazari*: a delight in ornamentation which does not relegate the decorative dimension of art to the periphery of creativity but actually celebrates it as no less worthy an enterprise than representational painting or sculpture.

As the *Tsubasa* manga laboriously advances toward its multilayered finale, CLAMP's passion for plural and divided subjectivities escalates. An especially poignant moment coincides with the sequence in which Sakura is lethally assaulted by the Syaoran clone, whereupon her soul disintegrates and she confesses that she, too, is a clone — an *image*, in the manga's parlance, designed to replicate the original Princess of Clow. For many *Tsubasa* aficionados, it is nothing short of shocking suddenly to find out that the girl they have been following from world to world after her traumatic memory loss is actually a synthetic replica of the real Princess of Clow.

Her instinctive attachment to the Syaoran clone may partly spring from a subliminal recognition of her constitutional affinity with that creature. This plot twist gives rise to quite a heady scenario, which induces us to ponder a whole series of successive transformations in the saga's portrayal of its protagonists' identities and relationships. These encompass four alternate pairings: ostensibly real Syaoran/ostensibly real Sakura; clone Syaoran/ostensibly real Sakura; real Syaoran/ostensibly real Sakura; real Syaoran/clone Sakura. (The disclosure concerning Sakura's identity is anticipated in *Tsubasa: Tokyo Revelations* by the aforementioned splitting of the character into an inert body and a conscious soul.) Following Sakura's confession, her body is conveyed to Fei Wong, who deems it vital to the advancement of his scheme insofar as it constitutes the utterly unique repository of several magical feathers—and, more crucially, of the multidimensional memories they carry in a tangibly material guise. The villain himself explains the reasoning behind Sakura's cloning in the context of a major flashback to the saga's initial incident: "the one on the journey," he announces, "will be the image. So even if the image were to die ... we only need to bring the body to the Kingdom of Clow. I will change her memories into feathers ... and scatter them throughout the universes. The other image [i.e., Syaoran's clone] will believe that this is the only way to save the princess ... and chase through the worlds to find her feathers" (CLAMP 2009b, p. 79).

Yuuko reckons that Sakura understood that she was an artificial being after ingesting the feather recovered in Tokyo. At the time, as intimated, the girl's personality evidently altered to a palpable extent but her companions assumed that this was due to her inability (or unwillingness) to accept the original Syaoran as a replacement for the boy she cherished. The "truth," the witch avers, "was that she had come to the realization that she was an image herself" and that the "real Sakura was in some other place" (pp. 114–115). In revealing that *Tsubasa*'s heroine is a clone, CLAMP is not merely reiterating the dramatic formula already deployed in the characterization of the male lead. In fact, the artists are keen to emphasize that Syaoran's and Sakura's "images" (p. 118) are inherently different. Syaoran's body came into existence as an artificial copy of the original Syaoran but was then endowed with the original's soul, and therefore harbored an authentically human element of great importance. In Sakura's case, by contrast, both the body and the soul are entirely artificial. Fei Wong's retention of the original Sakura's entire being in both its physical and its spiritual manifestations entails that he will always be in a position to create an extra Sakura clone whenever the need might arise.

As anticipated, Watanuki from *xxxHOLiC* plays a key role in the climactic moments of the *Tsubasa* manga, making it possible for the original Syaoran, Kurogane and Fai to travel to the Kingdom of Clow, where the Secret Base is situated within a zone known as a "time removed" (p. 141), having already paid the price for this wish by forfeiting his own memories. At this stage, Yuuko describes Watanuki as "someone who is closer to Syaoran than any other" (p. 135). The significance of the action's transposition to that peculiar portion of time-space cannot be overestimated for it is at this particular juncture in the saga as a whole that CLAMP chooses to amplify its cosmic vision to as yet unparalleled extremes. The multiperspectivalism studiously cultivated by the artists throughout the manga's progression is unexpectedly complicated by its integration with additional spatiotemporal tropes of metaphysical gravity. These are given form by recourse to a series of momentous revelations. Firstly, we discover that this "world cut off from time" (CLAMP 2009c, p. 20) is trapped in an inescapable cycle of endless repetition — an almost parodic interpretation (some would feasibly term it a perversion) of the Buddhist concept of Eternal Recurrence — which condemns people to perform the same identical actions over and over in a state aptly described by Kurogane as "a living death" (p. 95). The uncompromisingly tragic tone which the saga has been steadily acquiring since the Tokyo arc reaches its peak when it becomes evident that the travelers' arrival in this dimension has caused the cyclical events to come to a halt. This does not free their enactors, however. In fact, insofar as these people's very "existence" is "ensured" by the "lack of forward movement" (p. 82), when they are deprived of repetition, "their equilibrium is destroyed" (p. 83). Thus, their lives abruptly end, graphically sealed by CLAMP's pens with amorphous pools of mud. It is in the wake of these baleful occurrences that the action returns to the adventure's pivotal site in a physical sense rather than in the form of flashbacks. We thus revisit the ruins wherein Sakura's — and, of course, Syaoran's — ordeal began.

This momentous spatiotemporal shift is matched by a pointedly dramatic flashback, which proposes that Syaoran's mother foresaw her son's journey to an alien dimension in which he would meet a person who had been expecting him. In the wake of this prophetic vision, Syaoran obtained from Yuuko the power to reside for exactly one week in the Kingdom of Clow, where he met Sakura. At the end of his sojourn, Fei Wong placed a curse on Sakura which would by and by devour her life. Loath to be separated forever from his new and treasured friend, Syaoran accepted Yuuko's offer to be allowed to travel once more to Clow without, this time around, the chance to return to his homeland. As Fei Wong's lethal curse was about to take effect, the boy entered a further agreement with the Dimensional Witch, gaining the ability to turn back the time in order to save Sakura by relinquishing his own freedom as the necessary price required by the law of cosmic balance. He thus became Fei Wong's prisoner, while *xxxHOLiC*'s Watanuki took on his role in his original world, and stoically awaited the moment when he could go in search of Sakura. It is also noteworthy, in this context, that the close bond connecting Syaoran and Watanuki's destinies, and concomitantly cementing the formal interdependence of the *Tsubasa* and *xxxHOLiC* franchises, constitutes the focal concern of the OVA *xxxHOLiC: Shunmuki*, where Watanuki pursues some bizarre dreams which eventually link up with a mystery involving Syaoran, thereby exposing Watanuki's own significance in the worlds of both series.

With the return to the present, the manga plunges into a flurry of convulsive action, culminating with Fei Wong's attempt to kill the original Syaoran, which fortuitously results in the clone's destruction instead, and the fusion of Sakura's soul with the body held by the villain since the climax of the Infinity arc, which finally supplies him with the most potent of weapons. Complementing the narrative convolutions just witnessed, Yuuko delivers a veritable coup de théâtre by presenting the company with a glass tube accommodating two more Sakura and Syaoran lookalikes, said to have issued from the witch's reconstruction of the previously shattered clones. As synthetic humans, these creatures cannot, after all, truly perish despite appearances. The hope, in this bleak scenario, is that the freshly introduced duplicates will be able to reverse the damage inflicted by Fei Wong on the protagonists for the sole purpose of appeasing his own fathomless greed. At this juncture, Yuuko's actions clearly indicate that the enchantress considers herself to be no less beholden to the rule of cosmic equilibrium than the petitioners seeking her assistance. Thus, she does not take the new clones' efforts for granted but actually compensates them to the best of her abilities by conveying them to a new dimension, where they later have a son who turns out to be the original Syaoran.

What follows, as the manga winds up its disparate strands, is a vertiginous swirl of plot twists, reversals and reorientations which eloquently demonstrate that CLAMP's appetite for multiperspectival storytelling has not abated in the course of *Tsubasa*'s six-year run. At the graphic level, the action's intensity is accentuated by the generous use of raw penstrokes, ink and screentone stretched to their extremes, and gravity-defying perspectives. Concurrently, its tempo is sustained by the flawless manipulation of pace by means of panel placement. The one-page and two-page spreads, in particular, pause the action at vital points to allow for a few moments of quiet reflection. Given the profusion of shockers and novel plot details regaled by the manga's climactic chapters, this opportunity is especially precious. As the action glides toward its dénouement, diverse incarnations of the protagonists' originals and clones engage in the weaving of an intricate quadrille. In full consonance with CLAMP's aversion to neat — let alone moralistic — resolutions, *Tsubasa* thus delivers a bittersweet finale in which Syaoran and Sakura must part once more, their sole comfort being the undying hope that they will meet again. In addition, the manga's ending anticipates the thematic and ethical preoccupations to be explored in depth in this book's following chapter, where the analysis focuses on technologies of subjectivity. Indeed, in revealing that her "true name" is "Tsubasa" (CLAMP 2010, pp. 261–263), Sakura intimates that her identity is inextricably intertwined with the esoteric apparatus in which the saga's multiperspectival universe finds inception and to which it inexorably returns. She thus also points, in an oblique fashion, to the self's imbrication with technology — in particular, with the technologies sustaining the space-time continuum by means of which both individual lives and collective histories are incessantly made and unmade.

As previously observed, the *Tsubasa* TV series is also complemented by the film *Tsubasa: RESERVoir CHRoNiCLE The Movie: Princess of the Birdcage Kingdom* and by the additional two-episode OVA *Tsubasa: Spring Thunder*. The film maximizes *Tsubasa*'s dynamic thrust, exuding vitality, exuberance and passion at every turn of its thirty-minute jaunt. At times, the action's tempo is so snappy as to leave out any explicit linkages between scenes or pauses allowing character development to stand out. This is a wholly logical strategy when one considers that most of the film's viewers are likely to be already familiar with the saga to some degree. It would be quite absurd, after all, to presume to familiarize oneself with *Tsubasa*'s multiperspectival cosmos by recourse to this morsel of narratively condensed, albeit visually tasty, CLAMP drama. Director Itsuro Kawasaki could barely have ideated a companion to the *Tsubasa* TV series more drastically different from *Tsubasa: Tokyo Revelations* in both style and mood than this film. Where the OVA, as argued, amplifies the saga's darker components to perturbing extremes, *Princess of the Birdcage Kingdom* intersperses the pivotal adventure it dramatizes with frequent sorties into romance, comedy and martial spectacle, thus mellowing the story's potentially ominous subtexts.

Exploiting the power of one of Sakura's feathers as his weapon, the titular realm's ruler has entrapped the land within a magical birdcage barrier and rendered his subjects utterly powerless by capturing the bird spirits with whom each of them is associated. The despot's ultimate aim is to plunge the realm into eternal darkness so as to achieve unchallenged dominance. The most grievously affected victim of the villain's vicious scheme is his niece Princess Tomoyo, who has been robbed not only of her avian companion but also of her voice. Tomoyo is meant to serve as the ultimate "sacrifice" through which the tyrant may gain the cooperation of the murky powers capable of bringing his perverse desire to fruition. The princess is clandestinely sheltered by a young boy, Koruri, who turns to Syaoran and Sakura for help in the protection of the wretched princess. With typical generosity, the protagonists do not hesitate to fuel all of their enthusiasm into the mission, meanwhile suspending the duties entailed by their personal quest.

The character of Tomoyo also features prominently in the OVA *Tsubasa: Spring Thunder*, an anime version of the manga's Nihon arc, with the closing portion of the Celes arc as its prologue. In this anime, we are transported to Kurogane's legend-soaked homeland in the company of the warrior himself, Fai and the original Syaoran, while Princess Sakura floats in the World of Dreams. Insofar as there is a substantial gap between the events depicted in *Tsubasa: Tokyo Revelations* and the action dramatized by *Tsubasa: Spring Thunder*, there is a chance that spectators who are not acquainted with the manga and have not, therefore, traveled through Infinity before reaching Celes and Nihon, will feel somewhat disoriented. While this may be considered a shortcoming in purely cinematic terms, it undeniably carries emotive weight as few affects could be more appropriate than the feeling of disorientation to describe the *Tsubasa* franchise in its entirety. To see this feeling engendered not only in the saga's personae but also in its audience prompts recognition of the animators' ingenious approach to the translation of the parent manga into an OVA. Like *Tokyo Revelations*, *Spring Thunder* does not demur from exposing the darker facets of the source text without any hint of sentimentality or mawkishness. The action dramatized in the second OVA opens in the immediate aftermath of Kurogane's killing of King Ashura, Celes' monarch, and resulting activation of a curse placed upon Fai by Fei Wong Reed. Since the company is now trapped in Celes and cannot rely on the enfeebled wizard's lingering power in order to transit to another dimension, Kurogane resorts to self-mutilation, sacrificing an arm in return for the necessary magic and thus enabling the travelers' move to Nihon Country, his own original land. True to her legendary generosity, Princess Tomoyo willingly relinquishes her dream-seeing talent to pay Yuuko for the provision of an artificial arm for the ninja, while Fai contributes his residual magic to the cost. This segment of *Spring Thunder* also takes us to the World of Dreams, where the original Syaoran ends up after retrieving a memory feather, there to meet not only Sakura, as one might expect, but also Watanuki and his duplicate. The OVA exploits to considerable dramatic effect the climactic moments of this story arc in the dramatization of what many readers of the original manga still regard as the entire publication's most sensational portion: i.e., the scenes in which Sakura declares that she, too, is a clone, before dissolving into a deluge of *sakura* petals. It is in the wake of this momentous disclosure that the OVA, like the manga itself, reveals that Fei Wong secretly resides in Clow Country, and that Watanuki, Syaoran's alter ego, has made the travelers' transition to that dimension possible by surrendering his own memories to the Dimensional Witch — and, by implication, to the inflexible dictates of *hitsuzen*.

It should also be observed, in this context, that the world-hopping mechanism so integral to *Tsubasa: RESERVoir CHRoNiCLE* in both visual and dramatic terms finds some engaging comic antecedents. A humorous interpretation of the theme of multiple worlds is supplied by *Sweet Valerian* (2004), a series of five-minute vignette-like installments for which CLAMP has supplied the character designs. This unusual series chronicles the adventures of three young girls, Kanoko, Kate and Pop, as they negotiate the coexistence of two conflicting worlds within the town of Asialand, where they live: i.e., the city's ordinary and peaceful façade, on the one hand, and its hidden reality as a space under the constant threat of attack by evil monsters on the other. An analogously comic title of greater breadth and complexity is the manga series *Miyuki-chan in Wonderland* (1993–1995), adapted to OVA format in 2001. A slapstick comedy punctuated with downright farcical gags, this pivots on the character of a school girl afflicted by a bizarre tendency to wander accidentally into peculiar worlds. These disclose a series of scenarios, each replete with laughably ominous adversaries, based on parodic distortions of Lewis Carroll's Alice books or else issuing purely from CLAMP's imagination. Accordingly, the hapless girl is confronted by twin warriors, by a short-tempered queen, by her own double and by the weird pieces populating a giant chess board, is dragged into a mirror, gets lost inside a TV set, must negotiate an RPG virtual reality, and even finds herself immersed in the world of *X*— to cite just a few instances of Miyuki-chan's insane journeys. In addition, *Miyuki-chan in Wonderland* abounds with jocularly affectionate allusions to legion anime and video games, which renders it especially pleasurable for devotees of these forms — and particularly those with a penchant for the "I spy" approach to in-joke recognition.

What remains most memorable to this day about Miyuki-chan's zany exploits is neither their narrative content nor their taste for spoofs. In fact, it consists of the sheer sense of creative enjoyment which its adventures unremittingly exude even as they verge on the inane. Hence, what one feels most palpably, as the OVA progresses, is the pleasure which the CLAMP artists would have derived from drawing the original series, and from devising strategies which would allow them to sublimate their personal predilections and tastes to the production of shareable entertainment. Even the story's least savory visual flourishes appear quite justifiable when assessed in the light of this proposition. Thus, as noted in "The Essential *Miyuki-chan in Wonderland*," an essay included in the ninth volume of *CLAMP no Kiseki*, "although there are many characters who wear fetish-type costumes or openly wear lingerie, it doesn't seem strange or indecent. Might it not be that CLAMP, while thinking of their male readers, avoided getting too close to them and purely enjoyed figuring out what kind of character would look attractive in what kind of costume — almost like playing dress-up with dolls?" (in CLAMP 2007e, p. 14).

Notably, CLAMP's fascination with multiperspectivalism has also served as a concurrently aesthetic and commercial means of consolidating the collective's iconic status in the germane domains of anime and manga. This contention is vibrantly borne out by the two video collections *CLAMP in Wonderland* (1994) and *CLAMP in Wonderland 2* (2007). The first set consists of a seven-minute music video showcasing salient characters and motifs from some of the most popular series released by the group up to 1994, the date of the anthology's release. These encompass *X*, *Miyuki-chan in Wonderland*, *Shirahime-Syo: Snow Goddess Tales* and *Magic Knight Rayearth*. The second anthology covers in an analogous fashion CLAMP's subsequent productions, including *Cardcaptor Sakura*, *Angelic Layer*, *Clover*, *Tsubasa: RESERVoir CHRoNiCLE*, *xxxHOLiC*, *Legal Drug* and *Kobato*.

Like *Cardcaptor Sakura* and *Tsubasa: RESERVoir CHRoNiCLE* before it, the *xxxHOLiC* franchise consists of a richly diversified range of media and products. Alongside the parent manga, released between 2003 and 2011, these encompass the film *xxxHOLiC the Movie: A Midsummer Night's Dream* (2005), the TV series *xxxHOLiC* (2006) and *xxxHOLiC: Kei* (2008), and the OVAs *xxxHOLiC: Shunmuki* (2009), *xxxHOLiC: Rou* (2010) and *xxxHOLiC: Rou Adayume* (OVA, 2011). As stressed in the foregoing analysis, *Tsubasa: RESERVoir CHRoNiCLE* frequently intersects with *xxxHOLiC* in both thematic and structural terms. In fact, the two series were conceived as mutually crisscrossing projects from the very start. Crossovers, as also noted, have been a distinctive aspect of CLAMP's signature from an early stage in the team's career, and its characters have accordingly breached the boundaries of their worlds to appear in other dimensions with palpable gusto. However, this is the first time — not only in CLAMP's career but in the history of manga at large — that two works of substantial breadth have been so intimately intertwined as to virtually merge into a single, intricately multilayered, metaverse. Taken in tandem, therefore, *Tsubasa: RESERVoir CHRoNiCLE* and *xxxHOLiC* represent an unprecedented expansion of CLAMP's multiperspectival vision.

The simultaneous serialization of two intersecting works of such caliber cannot be regarded merely as a clever storytelling ruse but actually marks the birth of a novel technique for constructing an extensive cosmos comprising a potentially limitless quantity of multiple worlds. Indeed, while the number of such worlds might seem calculable to the extent that they issue mainly from CLAMP's other works, their effective amount becomes immeasurable the moment one realizes that in traversing one another, they concurrently develop the power to engender new and unforeseen realities. While *Tsubasa: RESERVoir CHRoNiCLE* and *xxxHOLiC* may be independently enjoyed as autonomous accomplishments, they have even more to offer if they are read (and viewed) in conjunction, insofar as this brings out their full worth as complementary creations. In addition, certain aspects of their individual plots acquire unsuspected meanings when they are assessed not solely in relation to the main story to which they belong but also to the complementary narrative. For instance, in reading or watching *Tsubasa: RESERVoir CHRoNiCLE* on its own, we recognize the enormity of the sacrifice performed by Syaoran in exchange for the ability to go feather-hunting across dimensions, and this is likely to leave its mark on our memory as the crux of his relationship with Sakura. However, if we read or watch the *Tsubasa* saga in conjunction with the *xxxHOLiC* manga, we also come to appreciate more fully the nature and implications of Sakura's own sacrifice.

Commenting on the genesis of *Tsubasa: RESERVoir CHRoNiCLE* and *xxxHOLiC* as twin series united by myriad parallelisms, correspondences and convergences, Ohkawa has stated: "our works that take place in the modern day, except for some special cases among our works, are all connected, but the fantasy series and parallel world ones like *Miyuki-chan in Wonderland* weren't especially connected. So we wanted to create a CLAMP work that included all of those as well. Also, we wanted to try writing two stories at the same time that were linked to each other." The matchlessly charismatic character of the Dimensional Witch operated as a cohesive agent, in this context, as a figure "who grasped all the worlds in CLAMP's works." An almost inexhaustible source of both creative and organizational challenges, this venture often entailed the performance of some tricky balancing acts. The two series' "linked content," in particular, required CLAMP to concentrate indefatigably on the issue of "delicate fine-tuning" when it came to deciding, week after week, which series they "should draw first — *xxxHOLiC* (released on Mondays) or *Tsubasa* (released on Wednesdays)" (interview in CLAMP 2008d, p. 5). This quotation, incidentally, provides us with a succinct insight into the murderous schedule governing the lives of successful *mangaka*.

Even in isolation, the reality depicted in *xxxHOLiC* is redolent of quantum cosmology in its repeated allusions to the concept of a consummately composite universe pervaded by the impression that other worlds always coexist with the world one happens to inhabit. "Before those who know, the world is not only one," Yuuko gnomically announces in the manga's first volume (CLAMP 2004, p. 108). Instead of indulging in simplistic quasi-scientific speculations, *xxxHOLiC* capitalizes on CLAMP's flair for blending esoteric and everyday events with seamless grace by translating its cosmic vision into an engaging case-based mystery drama. The cases themselves are both varied and carefully individuated, their subject matter ranging from internet dependence to superstitious dread, from haunting phenomena to the affairs of rain sprites. On numerous occasions, Kimihiro Watanuki takes it upon himself to follow subjects tormented by apparently supernatural troubles in an effort to ascertain the actual causes of their ordeals. At times, he tends to adopt the role of an impassive observer; at others, he intervenes directly into the action in order to guard the vulnerable and comfort the misguided. Some of the most poignant moments coincide with Watanuki's own exposure to preternatural occurrences — a potentially calamitous occurrence, given the youth's inveterate proclivity to perceive all manner of non-human entities, even when he does not explicitly fall prey to their inscrutable schemes. The various cases enlisting Watanuki's services are formally enchained by the ethical message which courses through *xxxHOLiC*'s fabric.

As anticipated in this study's opening chapter, all of the problems which lead Yuuko's prospective clients to her store stem from one common root: their subjugation to habits and yearnings which have escalated to the status of pathological addictions. Virtually each installment intimates that the prices which the afflicted subjects must pay, as their compulsions are quotidianly renewed by the tyranny of desire, are not simply those demanded by Yuuko in exchange for her magical backing. In fact, what they are repeatedly forced to surrender — not by the Dimensional Witch herself but by their own addictions — is nothing other than their intrinsic humanity. The demons at stake, relatedly, are not otherworldly entities or energies in the literal sense of the term, for they are ultimately shown to emanate from all-too-human urges — just as the prices involved in this hazardous game, as noted, are themselves of an eminently human nature. However, by immersing its characters' prosaic experiences in the eerie atmosphere of the supernatural thriller, *xxxHOLiC* is able to defamiliarize its central message and actively engage the audience in the interpretation of both its moral weight and its aesthetic individuality.

The axial significance of the addiction topos has been explicitly foregrounded by Ohkawa in her elucidation of the process leading to the choice of the series' unusual title and tenor. "At first, we thought about 'Addict,' meaning '-holic,'" the artist has noted, "but that's not a very well-known term in Japan. 'Holic' is used in common words like workaholic, so people are familiar with it. That's why we decided on 'xxxHOLiC.' We used a social pathology theme with *Tokyo Babylon*, so this time we thought we'd do something more occult" (interview in CLAMP 2008d, p. 5).

Like *Tsubasa*, *xxxHOLiC* accords conceptual prominence to the doctrine of *hitsuzen*, emphasizing the sheer sense of inexorability surrounding both Yuuko and Watanuki's encounter and the vertiginous chain of events unfolding in its wake, from the very moment the Dimensional Witch is intuitively able to guess the youth's entire life history after obtaining just his name and date of birth. Beside *hitsuzen*, other aspects of Yuuko's ethos are invoked as a means of providing the series with a solid philosophical infrastructure. Especially prominent among them is the conundrum surrounding the uneasy relationship between addiction and desire. Thus, the series repeatedly intimates that unless the various characters who turn to Yuuko for help in their efforts to overcome powerfully addictive drives face up to their true desires, they will remain forever powerless to break free of those obsessions. The urge to cultivate an addiction issues from the afflicted individuals' determination to comply with its irrational authority, and this resolve becomes akin to a promise which they make to themselves and on which their very identities seem to depend. Yet, the identities thus established are ineluctably specious insofar as they are erected in accordance with utterly arbitrary rules which the individuals involved have uncritically embraced and, by and by, elevated to the status of transcendental truths. They are not, in essence, any more credible or reliable than the dogmas underpinning the oppressive systems of belief on which political and religious ideologies have routinely thriven for time immemorial.

In order to dismantle the addictions which haunt them, Yuuko's clients must learn how to question the rules which govern their functioning and, in so doing, serve to perpetuate their hold. This, in turn, involves an honest examination of the desires from which addictive urges stem, and of the ethical defensibility of the promises they make to themselves when they commit themselves to indulging those passions at any price. Sooner or later, all of the affected characters will arrive at the same unsavory realization: i.e., the desires they have been pursuing are not their *true* desires. When these are honestly acknowledged, the epiphany may initially occasion excruciating pain. Yet, Yuuko makes it incontrovertibly clear that a desire from the heart holds the power to defy not only reason and logic but the law of gravity itself, even though the magnitude of that desire ineluctably entails a sacrifice of corresponding proportions—as both *Tsubasa* and *xxxHOLiC* eloquently reveal. If the ability to face up to one's true desires depends on magic, then this is not the magic dispensed by potions or spells, enchanted circles or amulets. In fact, it is a magic worked by the individuals themselves through and upon themselves: in other words, it is the hard-won magic of self-understanding. A genuinely well-meaning witch, in this scenario, may act as a facilitating agent but never aspire to place herself in the spurious position of a dea ex machina.

Art and design play a critical role in imparting the entire franchise with a sense of wonder which is immediately recognizable as bearing CLAMP's signature. Emblematic instances are offered by the episode depicting the annual festival known as the "Monster Procession," and the one dramatizing Watanuki's journey into a jar of purified water. Another indubitable asset consists of *xxxHOLiC*'s generic suppleness—a logical outcome of its assiduous employment of quirky personae and a flexible mood which allows it to oscillate at will between quasi-realistic human drama and the folk tale, zany comedy and the procedural. Some episodes focus exclusively on the psychological issues triggering the assorted afflictions of Yuuko's clients, steering clear of narrative tangents and ornamental digressions of any kind. An apposite illustrative instance of this trend is the installment centered on a girl who compulsively sabotages her own life in order to preempt success and happiness: a trenchant anatomy of the unfathomable mystery enfolding warped human motivations. There are also episodes which go for the diametrically opposite approach, choosing to prioritize character portrayal virtually to the exclusion of plot. A case in point is the snowball fight installment, which is intentionally designed to keep the plot element down to the bare minimum in order to give the audience an opportunity to grasp the characters' hidden personalities by observing their symbolic expression through the medium of snow sculpture.

The most remarkable facet of the style adopted by the *xxxHOLiC* franchise in its entirety consists of its character design, where CLAMP intensifies to stylized extremes its proverbial passion for overly elongated physiques, which results in the depiction of characters with spindly limbs and almost preposterously extended necks. While this preference for intentional exaggeration may initially prove disconcerting for audiences as yet unfamiliar with CLAMP's output, it holds the potential to draw the audience intimately into the series' distinctive world in the space of just a few chapters or episodes, simply by virtue of its visual idiosyncrasies. Moreover, all of the pivotal and supporting personae are thoroughly individuated at the levels of both somatic features and sartorial accessories. Marginal characters and extras, by contrast, are left blank and almost amorphous, which reduces them to the status of spectral presences devoid of any obvious substance or weight. This technique serves to strengthen the key characters' significance throughout the unfolding of the drama. At the same time, it alerts us to the status of invisibility as a potentially ubiquitous phenomenon which cannot be safely relegated to the domain of magic but is in fact capable of puncturing the actual world at all times — most disturbingly, in the guise of depersonalized throngs of humans so addicted to their solipsistic passions and so enslaved to consumerist promises of fulfillment as to have become blind to both one another and themselves. The emptiness and pointlessness of the material world are thus tersely communicated. On the stylistic plane, *xxxHOLiC*'s recurrent visual effects are also worthy of notice: the plumes of smoke billowing around Yuuko, and enhancing her enigmatic aura with almost hypnotic allure, are arguably one of the most memorable touches in CLAMP's entire repertoire. Furthermore, the group's art makes generous use of lacelike decoration, often redolent of filigree, and of various aesthetic elements typically associated with the achievements of Art Nouveau, such as sinuous and whiplash lines and gracefully stylized organic forms, alongside starker graphics characteristic of Art Deco, such as sweeping curves and multifaceted, trapezoidal and zigzagged patterns.

The formal multiperspectivalism afforded by *Tsubasa: RESERVoir CHRoNiCLE*'s engagement with a phantasmagoric variety of worlds is revamped by CLAMP in the context of *xxxHOLiC* with the chronicling of Watanuki and Yuuko's disparate adventures. Although these do not necessarily take us into alternate dimensions in quite the same literal fashion as *Tsubasa: RESERVoir CHRoNiCLE*'s travels do, they could nonetheless be said to constitute a galaxy of parallel realities in an allegorical guise. The genres invoked by *xxxHOLiC*, in the process, are wonderfully wide-ranging—at times, they are juxtaposed so that they vie with one another for supremacy over the flow of the action in the interests of dramatic tension; at others, they are integrated so as to communicate a vision of simultaneously metaphysical and topical relevance. In the depiction of supernatural phenomena, both the manga and the anime versions of *xxxHOLiC* often recall the spirit of the grotesque as a genre famously associated with the irreverent intermingling of human, animal and vegetable shapes, alongside a profusion of hideous demonic forms and inchoate masses rendered menacing by their very amorphousness. In *xxxHOLiC*, as in the grotesque, this representational propensity finds a direct correlative on the thematic plane, where it manifests itself in the guise of complex syntheses of ostensibly incompatible concepts and motifs. In addition, *xxxHOLiC* often deploys its grotesque elements as a means of enhancing the tragic ludicrousness of its characters' addictions. On such occasions, the freakish, bizarre and distorted shapes which punctuate the visuals serve as economical metonyms for those characters' monstrous deviation from any sense of harmony, proportion and balance.

xxxHOLiC's anatomy of these sad aberrations, which enables it to deliver a trenchant social commentary throughout, resonates with the existential messages associated with the tradition of the absurd. This is most conspicuous in its vision of life as a task which lacks any obvious purpose or destination if it is conducted exclusively in accordance with compulsive desire. Via Yuuko, CLAMP suggests that such an existence is bound to be haunted by loneliness and anguish, to be out of harmony with its surroundings, and to perceive the passage of time as an incontrovertible curse. Sad to the point of tragedy, this state of being also manages to come across, by an ironical twist of fate, as uncannily funny. The story's grotesque and absurdist elements are meticulously held together by CLAMP's unique sensitivity to the principle of texture: the concrete dimension of the work as opposed to its merely conceptual import. In CLAMP's universe, the value of texture is applied not only to the graphics — which could arguably be expected of a proficient manga artist — but also to words. This entails that the sensuous qualities of the verbal surface of the work are often accorded a privileged position in the global organization of a chapter or episode, and that the physical density of its imagery is granted no less prominent a role than either the narrative or the philosophical messages it is supposed to convey. The artists' keenness on a variety of typographical devices, including somewhat unusual ones, corroborates this contention to a tangible degree.

Watanuki's peculiar predicament and his contract with Yuuko undoubtedly provide the story with its dramatic core. However, *xxxHOLiC*'s soul is undoubtedly the magnetically unfathomable Yuuko. Her handling of language, in particular, contributes significantly to the character's overall stature and therefore deserves careful consideration. As Fumiko Yamamoto persuasively contends, "Yuuko's lines, which sometimes are profound and sometimes get right to the core of the problem, leave an impression." As the critic also suggests, CLAMP has frequently relied on a character's words "to break down preconceived notions and presenting a new perspective." Both *RG Veda* and *Tokyo Babylon*, for instance, feature comparably complex female personae with the royal musician Lady Kendappa, one of Taishakuten's most loyal retainers, and with Subaru's eccentric twin sister Hokuto, an impulsive, sharp and daring young woman who often stands out as the protagonist's polar opposite. The effectiveness of both Yuuko's and those earlier characters' lines results from CLAMP's arguably unique ability to forge "phrases that do not waste words." Undeniably, the tendency to cut lines down to the bare essentials is typical of most manga as a logical corollary of the imperative to make do with the limited amount of room at the author's disposal. However, in the case of the CLAMP artists, argues Yamamoto, "rather than simply trimming down the lines, it would seem that they extract the essence of what they want to express and work it over in order to more clearly convey what they want to say to the readers" (in CLAMP 2008d, p. 15). Sensitive to the rampant abuse to which language is quotidianly exposed, largely as a result of the lack of conviction and thought underlying its common use, CLAMP endeavors to create characters who, like the Dimensional Witch, are capable of delivering their lines with confidence and firmness because they are deeply conscious of their ethical implications and do not fear the responsibilities and duties which they necessarily entail. In this fashion, *xxxHOLiC* persistently reminds us that the meanings carried by even the most ordinary of words have the capacity to morph into life-shaping linguistic performances akin to spells.

Although Yuuko's lines may occasionally sound a bit sententious or long-winded, we are rapidly captured not only by their conceptual substance but also by their distinctively spell-binding rhythm. It could in fact be argued that there is something viscerally mesmerizing about the cadence and pace with which those lines are delivered. In an uncanny fashion, this sensation mirrors CLAMP's ubiquitous preoccupation with its key characters' mnemonic ordeals in *Tsubasa: RESERVoir CHRoNiCLE* and *xxxHOLiC* alike. Most importantly, Yuuko never comes across as a vain orator in search of lurid coups de théâtre since her words, even at their most mystifying, invariably communicate a genuine sense of conviction and commitment. There are also indications that the Dimensional Witch might not enjoy the import of her words any more than their recipients (especially in consideration of the prices likely to be demanded of them), yet feels enjoined to deliver them by her overriding sense of responsibility toward the people who seek her support and, by extension, toward the cosmic laws by which her mission abides. This sets Yuuko firmly apart from the standard image of the preacher equipped with patronizing rhetoric and fustian tropes. *xxxHOLiC*'s perspective on language, as a result, operates as a potent reminder of the sheer power of words by bringing into play several layers of signification. At all levels, the series' central message points to the power of words to allude to disparate realities — or reality zones — simultaneously, and hence to encapsulate *in nuce* the multiperspectival vision invoked by CLAMP as its pivotal worldbuilding ruse.

First and foremost, *xxxHOLiC* ventures into an exploration of the sprawling galaxy of hidden meanings attendant upon three interrelated uses of language. These comprise metaphor, which permits the poetic release of the virtually infinite array of figurative meanings lurking beneath the veneer of a word's literal interpretation; allegory, whereby words may come to incarnate abstract concepts as vibrant personifications of their latent messages; and irony, the strategy which allows words to encapsulate ideas which starkly contradict their manifest intent. Yuuko's own multiverse, the domain of magic, provides ample scope for these tropes, accommodating them at all times within its peculiar formulae, idiolects and codes. Concomitantly, in the magical realm, certain words are held to carry so great a degree of power that their casual usage by lay people is strictly forbidden. In fairy lore, for example, this trend is famously confirmed by the prohibition on the direct naming of fairies. As Susannah Marriott explains, in this respect, "there is a well-defined etiquette in discussing fairies. Never refer to the wee folk by name. To do so would be to court their wrath. Rather, use one of the many euphemisms — and make it a gracious one, such as 'The Gentry,' which cannot offend. One should never speak harshly of other folk, and that includes using harsh epithets. But just as talking of them with too much lightness can cause anger, so, too, does undue praise. It might be best simply to stay silent in places where the fay might be lurking, in woods and at crossroads, especially near nightfall."

xxxHOLiC participates in this world picture through its recurrent intimations that language should never be handled thoughtlessly or nonchalantly, and that there are times, therefore, when it may be preferable to resort to circumlocution and understatement — or even total silence. This course of action should definitely be adopted whenever there is any doubt about the relevance or propriety of the more direct words one might be instinctively inclined to employ by assessing a situation purely at face value and without taking into account the existence of latent messages beneath its empirically observable surface. Furthermore, magical thinking proposes that "the power of a secret, or sacred, name empowers those who utter it with its attributes; this is established in all the world's greatest religions. If the name of a spirit is the spirit, then in stating it one brings it into being" (Marriott, p. 104). This ancient belief resonates through many of *xxxHOLiC*'s pathos-laden moments, investing Yuuko's portentous rhetoric with an aura of almost tangible authoritativeness. Her words, on such occasions, appear pregnant with spiritual energies ready to break through their linguistic containers and spring into autonomous existence. Verbal signs, in this perspective, have the capacity to bind people more firmly than any law, and to grant wishes more commandingly than either sops or rewards.

In addition, *xxxHOLiC*'s allusions to the power of names — and attendant injunction to use them both respectfully and mindfully — serve to remind us that in the domain of esotericism, otherworldly creatures are often held to employ secret names imbued with magical or hallowed attributes, and to be capable of retaining their preternatural powers only as long as these arcane designations are left unrevealed. The creature's name and its intrinsic power — the word and its meaning, as it were — are thus radically severed. The creation of a gap between an utterance and its meaning can be regarded as a metaphor for the ultimate mystery ingrained in human language itself as a system inimical to transparent communication and more likely, in fact, to rely on ambiguity, equivocation, understatement and periphrasis than on explicit messages. According to J. C. Cooper, the taboo linked with "the Power of the Name," and used to buttress the "prohibition against using the names," emanates from "the universal belief in the creative force of sound: 'In the beginning was the Word ... and the Word was God'." The ceremonial significance of names must also be taken into consideration in evaluating the ban on referring to supernatural entities directly — and concomitant proliferation of aliases meant to provide tactful alternatives to their actual designations — to the extent that a "name is also a powerful means of exorcism and is the basis of incantation in which 'words of power' can compel elemental forces and open doors magically, as Ali Baba's 'Open sesame'." Furthermore, the employment of a person's or a spiritual entity's "true name" is seen in many traditions as a means of achieving "magic power over the soul" (Cooper, p. 64). As A. M. Hocart maintains, in this matter, "a man's name is commonly treated as part of his person. In Babylon what had no name did not exist" (Hocart; cited in Cooper, p. 64).

At the same time, CLAMP is eager to emphasize the extent to which words are always prone to saying something other than what they mean, and to meaning something other than what they say. The artists are well aware that this seemingly absurd, yet inescapable, state of affairs is a corollary of the radical displacement to which the world is subject as a result of its codification into inevitably arbitrary semiotic systems. The knowledge that disparities will always tend to obtain between the apparent and latent messages which words are designed to convey lends itself to two main uses in *xxxHOLiC*'s universe. At times, it is deliberately and maliciously deployed by characters who, out of either recklessness or spite, seek to exploit words as a means of manipulating other people and making them subservient to their own selfish schemes. At others, that same knowledge paves the way to a salutary opening up of reality by operating as an awakening agency. CLAMP's yarns repeatedly demonstrate that such a force is instrumental in the development of their protagonists — not only Watanuki, Sakura and Syaoran but also, looking back over CLAMP's prolific career, the likes of Ashura from *RG Veda*, Hikaru, Umi and Fuu from *Magic Knight Rayearth*, Kamui from *X* and Hideki from *Chobits* (among others). Indeed, it is ultimately what they need most in the legion journeys of self-discovery they undertake both across worlds and within the self.

In this perspective, CLAMP's take on language could be said to underpin its adventurous elevation of the very concept of bildungsroman to the status of a metaphysical experience. This developmental curve should not be regarded as unequivocally synonymous with growing up since it actually entails the retrieval of childhood proclivities which have been gradually suppressed by the individual's progressive socialization and subjugation to various institutions and laws. The acquisition of language plays a key role in abetting this process of incremental regimentation, insofar as it binds its users to a set of rules which inevitably delimit the spontaneous articulation of both feelings and thoughts. By unsettling the domain of language through the exposure of its inherently unstable and fractured architecture, the semiotic vision developed in *xxxHOLiC* suggests that it might be possible to rekindle the powers available to people prior to their forced enculturement, and thus rouse their innate capacities to experiment and explore, their instinctive inclination to play, and — most crucially perhaps — their preparedness to dream.

The mission dramatized in *xxxHOLiC the Movie: A Midsummer Night's Dream* brings together in a capsulated fashion many of the ethical and broadly philosophical preoccupations addressed by CLAMP in the manga. The film takes as its point of departure the day when a girl unable to enter her home seeks Yuuko's assistance and surrenders a magical-looking key as the due payment. The girl's plea happens to coincide with Yuuko's invitation to an auction to be held within a strange mansion which, it is by and by revealed, is the very place which her young client is so desperate to access. Even though the Dimensional Witch is well aware that the invitation she has received is being used as a bait by some as yet indeterminate villain, she confronts the challenge with characteristic aplomb, curious to fathom her prospective host's real identity and objectives. Seven more guests initially turn up at the auction venue, all of whom appear to be passionate collectors of bizarre objects whose accumulating mania has degenerated into a full-fledged addiction. Any pleasure these people might originally have derived from their hobbies has become engulfed in the noxious miasma of an obsession compulsion. The bidders swiftly vanish one after the other even before the auctioneer has made his appearance on the scene.

Replete with winding corridors, passageways, galleries, deformed perspectives, absurd proportions and doors which open and close of their own accord, the eerie mansion in which the drama is set oozes at every turn with sinister noises. These serve a major dramatic function insofar as they evoke at once the latent presence of buried secrets and baleful dreams, inchoate fears and submerged memories lurking everywhere just beneath the surface of the visible. The collusion of Yuuko's magical powers and the surrealistically Gothic atmosphere evoked by the mansion brings to mind James Rollins' explanation of the etymology of the term "Gothic," which, though by no means unanimously accepted by scholars in the field, is undeniably quite appropriate to the present context given its explicit association with magic. "The word 'Gothic'," argues Rollins, "comes from the Greek word 'goetic.' Which translates to 'magic.' And such architecture was considered magical. It was like nothing seen at the time: the thin ribbing, the flying buttresses, the impossible heights. It gave an impression of *weightlessness*" (Rollins, p. 406). The *xxxHOLiC* movie's representation of a setting which defies both gravity and logic with irreverent gusto communicates not only a distinctive image of space but also a vertiginous sense of instability and flux. This mood performs an ironical function within the film's overall diegesis, insofar as it feels entirely consistent with Yuuko's legerdemain, on the one hand, yet questions the rigid view of cosmic necessity inherent in the philosophy of *hitsuzen* on the other. Finally, the reason behind Yuuko's invitation to this eerie venue and the ensuing events unfolding within its unstable walls turns out to be an old promise made by its owner: a vow honored for many years and then gradually allowed to sink into oblivion. The girl seeking Yuuko's support at the beginning of the film is revealed to be the person to whom the auction's host is bound by his promise, and reappears at the end in a double incarnation: i.e., both as the elderly lady she now truly is and as the little girl she was at the time the vow was made, the latter being also the form in which the mansion's proprietor perceives her in the present. In specifically aesthetic terms, *xxxHOLiC the Movie: A Midsummer Night's Dream* owes much to the perturbing charm of its Gothic setting, the visuals' spellbinding force emanating mainly from the sheer profusion of architectural and ornamental motifs it strives to accommodate.

xxxHOLiC abounds with allusions to native mysticism and lore, compounded with frequent and meticulous references to ancient Japan and to its fascinating esoteric legacy in the design of most of its otherworldly personae—so much so that it could be seen as a perfect guide to those topics for the novice keen on studying the traditional substratum of contemporary Japanese culture. Creatures such as fox spirits (*kitsune*) and house specters (*zashiki-warashi*) make their appearance beside rain sprites (*ame-warashi*), phantoms of legion varieties, psychics, supernatural phenomena, magic lanterns and haunting photographs. Moreover, *xxxHOLiC*'s cornucopian abundance of references to the culinary arts consistently enriches the series' cultural significance. Concomitantly, in spite of its thematic and stylistic dependence on supernatural motifs embedded in time-honored legends, myths and superstitions, *xxxHOLiC* carries timeless relevance by deploying its protagonist's ordeal as the literal expression of a feeling which most ordinary people have at some point experienced in their lives. This consists of the sensation that one is being surreptitiously watched by some unspecified agent: an absent presence capable of inspiring fear against the dicta of either reason or logic. This element, combined with *xxxHOLiC*'s emphasis on pressing ethical dilemmas, yields a narrative that cannot be unproblematically dismissed as just a story about a weird kid with physic powers and an overactive imagination. In fact, the true charm of *xxxHOLiC* in all its forms lies with its multifaceted nature as an entertaining and emotional drama punctuated with philosophical messages of indisputable gravity.

While relying to superb effect on the concurrently graphic and dramatic richness of indigenous lore, *xxxHOLiC* also makes imaginative use of the symbol of the butterfly image — a motif traditionally utilized as the meeting point of varied symbolic associations in the realms of both literature and the visual arts. Butterflies have been utilized as emblems of metamorphosis and rebirth all over the world for centuries, or perhaps even millennia. At the same time, the butterfly image has often been invoked in order to communicate the evanescence of pleasure, beauty, happiness and ultimately life itself. This trope is indubitably crucial not merely to CLAMP's vision as elaborated in the context of *xxxHOLiC* but also, rather more significantly, to Japan's perception of the phenomenal world, finding paradigmatic expression in the aesthetic principle of *mono no aware* ("the sadness of things"). In Japanese poetry, in particular, the butterfly motif features consistently as an economical representation of irretrievable bliss. As Chris Eisenbraun observes in the entry of his online dictionary of symbols devoted to the butterfly, "there is a line of Japanese poetry expressing sorrow over the lost pleasures of the past, a response to the maxim, 'The fallen blossom never returns to the branch'; 'I thought that the blossom had returned to the branch — alas, it was only a butterfly'" (Eisenbraun).

It is also noteworthy, in this context, that another popular symbol of relentless metamorphosis to which Japanese literature and art have assiduously returned, the phoenix, also figures as a graphically versatile icon in CLAMP's visual repertoire. Even when the sacred firebird (commonly known as *fushichou* in Japanese) does not feature as an independent entity, its latent influence can still be sensed in myriad ornamental motifs, patterns and flourishes, as well as chromatic combinations in the case of plates and manga covers. Unlike the butterfly, whose metamorphosis exemplifies the transience of the here-and-now, the recurrent cycles of death and resurrection associated with the image of the phoenix are traditionally regarded as markers of an interminable process.

Designated in ancient Greek by means of the term also used for "soul" (*psyche*), the butterfly can also symbolize the metamorphoses experienced by the spiritual essence of both human beings and other animal as well as flowers and plants. In addition, the butterfly's ephemerality has been associated with the unfathomable domain of magic beings, as demonstrated by the fact that the likes of fairies, elves, pixies and other supernatural entities such as the figure of Hypnos, the Greek god of Sleep, are frequently equipped with iridescent butterfly wings. In Aztec mythology, moreover, the butterfly was linked both with the power of the Sun and with starlight. These ideas are mirrored by *xxxHOLiC*'s use of the butterfly motif as a means of highlighting the topoi of transformation and development, while referring at once to the spiritual, psychological and physical connotations of the transmutations experienced by its characters in the course of its multiperspectival drama. The insect's traditional association with both the supernatural realm and glowing light is concurrently invoked. No less importantly, both the manga and the anime versions of the story honor the meaning ascribed to the butterfly in the specific context of Japanese culture, where the occurrence of the creature as an individual specimen has often alluded to young womanhood, whereas the occurrence of couples of dancing butterflies has functioned as a metaphor for marital harmony. The image also plays a vital role in one of Japan's most time-honored fairy tales, "The White Butterfly." This revolves around the character of an ancient and dying man named Takahama, who has devoted the best part of his life to the memory of his former betrothed Akiko, the victim of a fatal consumptive illness said to have died shortly before the date fixed for their wedding. As Takahama approaches his final breath, Akiko returns to him in the guise of a dazzling white butterfly which vividly emblematizes her unwaveringly faithful soul.

xxxHOLiC bears several important affinities, on both the thematic and the philosophical planes, to the as yet unfinished manga series *Legal Drug* (2000–2003). The manga chronicles the adventures of two youths named Kazahaya Kudo and Rikuo Himura as they perform their daily duties as part-time employees of Green Drugstore while also undertaking side jobs which expose them to assorted supernatural phenomena. The series' utilization of protagonists employed by a store manager with unusual powers, allied to its consistent emphasis on the incidence of the mysterious and the ineffable in everyday life, foreshadows *xxxHOLiC* quite explicitly. At the same time, however, the manga's handling of the otherworldly dimension harks back to both *Tokyo Babylon* and *CLAMP School Detectives*. Finally, insofar as the entire plot originates in a chance encounter, *Legal Drug*'s narrative foundations enable CLAMP to highlight the aleatory nature of experience in a fashion which makes the incomplete manga a precursor of both *Tsubasa: RESERVoir CHRoNiCLE* and *xxxHOLiC* itself. CLAMP's latest manga, *Gate 7* (2011–), engages with a comparable mélange of elements which can be considered typical of the group's aesthetic cachet and distinctively multiperspectival vision. The story's protagonist, Chikahito Takamoto, is an apparently ordinary high school student who has just moved to Kyoto, a place to which he has always felt particularly attracted. Spatiotemporal displacement and memory erasure feature prominently in this work, just as they did in *Tsubasa: RESERVoir CHRoNiCLE* and *xxxHOLiC*. In addition, *CLAMP*'s legendary passion for the intersection of mundane and supernatural occurrences is afforded maximum leeway in this series, yielding a lavish feast of magical spells and martial exploits amid baleful monsters, illustrious historical figures, and splendidly attired people endowed with preternatural powers. As CLAMP fans the world over look forward to this series' development, the artists themselves are no doubt busy working out its forthcoming complications with characteristic ink-laced passion.

Released in manga form between 2005 and 2011, and partially adapted to anime as a TV series in 2009, *Kobato* shares some important motifs with both *Tsubasa: RESERVoir CHRoNiCLE* and *xxxHOLiC*, as characteristically borne out by its employment of the themes of spatial displacement and mnemonic impairment in conjunction with alternately daunting and melancholy intimations that the protagonist's actions are constrained within an inflexible time scale. *Kobato* also echoes the earlier productions with its aversion to conclusive resolutions, suggesting that gains and losses are as mutually interdependent in its distinctive world view as they were in Yuuko's adherence to the doctrine of *hitsuzen*. Moreover, *Tsubasa*'s key characters at one point traverse *Kobato*'s dramatic curve and are invited by the heroine to stay in her room until they are ready to world-hop once again. Yet, in spite of these conceptual similarities and dramatic points of contact with *Tsubasa* and *xxxHOLiC*, *Kobato* evinces quite an autonomous multiperspectival vision. Indeed, the plural realities portrayed by CLAMP in this story are neither exotic countries nor epic-laced alternate universes. In fact, they consist of the tormented hearts which the protagonist is enjoined to heal once she has entered the human world and confronted a series of tests in order to demonstrate her suitability as the bearer of the special jar meant to contain those hearts' afflictions. *Kobato*'s intimate scale imparts both the parent manga and its anime adaptation with an aura of artless simplicity which sets it clearly apart from CLAMP's more flamboyant forays into the exploration of multiple dimensions.

However, the impression of artlessness should not be taken as evidence of either lack of commitment or laziness on CLAMP's part, for it is actually the outcome of a studiously planned and deftly delivered narrative trajectory. In this regard, *Kobato* could be said to encapsulate one of the key lessons of traditional Japanese art and aesthetics. This pivots on the proposition that the greater the exertion fueled by artists or artisans into the creative act, the more natural and effortless their products should appear. This aspect of Japanese culture recalls the principle of *sprezzatura* fostered by Western aesthetics in the Renaissance. This denotes the studied adoption of a casually relaxed attitude to one's achievements which is intended to dissimulate any trace of toil beneath a semblance of spontaneity. At the same time, in addressing even the most mundane everyday activities as actual or potential art forms, Japanese culture dismantles the boundary between performer and spectator. In the process, it also questions radically the idea that creators undertake their practices so that others will cherish the products of their efforts in a fundamentally passive mode. In fact, creators are also spectators, and hence implied assessors, of their own performance. As Gian Carlo Calza maintains with exemplary reference to the calligraphic act, this aesthetic attitude entails that "the apogee of writing is what happens when, however profound its contents, the text flows along without visible effort, as if the brush (or the pen) were not being held back and slowed down by the effort of thought and the muscular tension demanded by writing" (Calza, p. 66). *Kobato*'s simplicity, in this perspective, can only be adequately acknowledged in the broader context of indigenous philosophy. True beauty, in this scenario, resides with the conscious avoidance of any explicit display of its qualities (be they sensuous or intellectual), let alone of the methods deployed to realize such qualities.

Relatedly, the intrinsic worth of all aspects of human endeavor should be assessed with reference to their unostentatious performance by dedicated individuals, not against their rigid societal codifications. Calza's comments on what he terms "the art of the unimportant" are especially apposite in this respect: "the apogee of elegance is to be found in what is sensed, but is indifferent to it or, at most, ahead of it. The apogee of culture is what can be recognized in a person, but is not put on display, ever. It is thus far removed from the world of the academy, which, in order to exist, has to demonstrate knowledge. The apogee of religious feeling lies in man's inner dialogue with God, and it cannot be seen, ever.... It is thus far removed from ritualism, liturgy and formal practices" (p. 66). Thus, as *Kobato* charmingly attests to, both grand and trivial aspirations, passions and yearnings are most likely to find memorable articulation in images and words stripped of the veneer of authority and pomp under which human beings so often hide the actual nature of things in a futile effort to efface their own puniness in the face of an inscrutable cosmos. It is against this comprehensive cultural background that we are implicitly invited to appreciate the unique synthesis of visual clarity, unhurried flair and grace achieved by the series one manga chapter after another, and one anime episode after another. The contingent magnitude of each consecutive task undertaken by the protagonist is relatively immaterial in comparison with the wide philosophical vision from which it emanates and to which it discreetly seeks to contribute its own embryonic lesson. This is what we are encouraged to recognize, and incrementally cherish, as the essence of Kobato's exploits — and, behind them, the core of CLAMP's own philosophy of life.

Homage to CLAMP (iii)
From "Talk About Clamp: Interview."
In *CLAMP no Kiseki Vol. 9*:

Rather than abandoning the characters and the worlds every time a work ends, CLAMP dresses them up and puts them in their next work — I think it's similar to how a movie director will use a star he likes (in various different works) ... CLAMP-san is good at recycling things like that. Also, I think that it's fantastic that they can pull out so much variation and while using the same stage even make a work comical or serious.... In a good sense ... they've always kept the fanaticism in their hearts, which is connected to the youthfulness of their works. Also, I wonder if it's that they try something new every time. They set tasks for themselves and accomplish them — watching them, you even get the sense that they enjoy leaping those high hurdles, and I think this is their greatest charm. —Shinichiro Inoue (2007)

Chapter 4
TECHNOLOGIES OF SUBJECTIVITY

> *The "bridge" in Hiroshima was built around 50 years ago. The only building in the surrounding area was the atomic dome and its steel skeleton; the rest was just a vast empty area of charred ruins. People called it the "Peace Bridge." Isamu Noguchi designed the balustrades and named them* Ikiru *(live) and* Shinu *(die), which later became* Tsukuru *(build) and* Yuku *(leave).... Some years later, a young man crossed that bridge on a bicycle: that was me. I had just started high school. "Now that's what I call design!": I remember how, whilst pedalling, I felt the power that design had for encouraging the life of mankind ... I later had the same reaction whilst looking at the* Akari *displayed in the window of Steph Simon in Paris. I have always considered Noguchi in connection with what I want to try to do. His works were a gift from beyond time and space, a message from outer space.* — Issey Miyake.

As seen in Chapter 2, CLAMP took on a major formal challenge in the execution of *Magic Knight Rayearth* in 1993–1995, thereby inaugurating a fresh perspective on the *mahou shoujo* formula, while imaginatively appropriating the aesthetic of role-playing games. Having handled that challenge with magisterial aplomb, CLAMP soon resolved to embrace another tantalizing task in 1999 by shifting to the combat genre with a work which would provide plenty of vibrant action while also taking a playful look at the world of entertainment. The result was *Angelic Layer*. Initially released in manga form between 1999 and 2001, and adapted to anime in 2001, this series offers a unique interpretation of the discourse of gaming, thereby inviting reflection on its significance as a distinctive technology capable of engendering particular configurations of subjectivity. In this respect, this title constitutes a text with unusual research resources not only for manga and anime aficionados but also for committed ludologists. The story addresses both the aesthetic and the ethical implications of the ludic discourse by means of a tournament-style plot centered on the character of Misaki Suzuhara, a girl who moves to Tokyo to attend a new junior high school while living with her aunt, her father having died when she was little and her own mother receded from her life since she was in kindergarten. The challenges which face the protagonist shortly after her arrival in the unfamiliar environment of the big city are neither of an academic nor of a familial nature, however. In fact, they proceed from her accidental introduction to a game called "Angelic Layer," in which dolls dubbed "Angels" are mentally directed by players known as "Deuses" (the plural form of "Deus"). Misaki's instant fascination with this tantalizing pursuit gains an unexpected opportunity to develop into hands-on participation in its dynamics when she meets Icchan (a.k.a. Ichiro Mihara), the creator of Angelic Layer, and acquires her own Angel, Hikaru. With Icchan's guidance and training, Misaki develops impressive skills as a Deus, showing herself able to learn from her own errors and disappointments, to incorporate her antagonists' strategies into her own gameplay, to use the subtlest of hints as sources of unique inspiration, and — most crucially — to mature and evolve as both a player and a human being.

Whereas in earlier series, CLAMP tended to accord considerable significance to the narrative side of its work, assiduously endeavoring to concoct complex storylines, in *Angelic Layer*, priority is given to the episodic orchestration of a succession of passionate confrontations, and of the martial techniques inherent in the game. In all this, CLAMP does not fail to remain faithful to its legendary fondness for crossovers, the Angel Hikaru being an adapted version of one of *Magic Knight Rayearth*'s heroines, while Shirahime from *Shirahime-Syo: Snow Goddess Tales* also features in the role of another battling doll. The group's generic reorientation does impact on its graphic vision, however, leading to the development of a fresh visual language. Thus, the prevalently baroque and ornate style characteristic of its previous creations gives way to techniques intended to maximize the evocation of lightness and speed. Commenting on the collective's stylistic priorities for this series, Ageha Ohkawa has stated that she and her colleagues "wanted the artwork to be more relaxed" because they were approaching *Angelic Layer* as "a comedy first and foremost." The comic mood is unquestionably dominant in the manga but the tone adopted in the anime adaptation, as Ohkawa herself has observed, is "a lot more serious" (interview in CLAMP 2005d, p. 25).

Angelic Layer could easily have gone no further than marking CLAMP's entry into the collectible fighting figures genre, thus joining the likes of *Pokémon* or *Digimon*. Worse still, its focus on battling skills could just as easily have imparted the series with the feel of a toy commercial for a product actually unavailable for purchase. In fact, CLAMP's refined characterization strategies make it possible for the frequent, and often protracted, sequences set in the battling arena to come across as intelligently conceived opportunities for psychological exploration. Moreover, *Angelic Layer*'s battle-centered narrative pattern enables CLAMP to develop character dynamics to as yet untested degrees. Some particularly notable moments include the very scene recording the fateful encounter bound to change the heroine's life forever. In this scene, set in the Tokyo train station, Misaki is first exposed to the sight of a combat between two dolls. As she watches this unusual spectacle unfolding on a huge screen, utterly captivated by its message, Misaki meets Icchan. From this point onward, her entire existence will become increasingly inextricable from the world of Angelic Layer. Even though it is not immediately disclosed that this encounter is not quite as accidental as one might at first believe it to be, the somewhat solemn atmosphere pervading the scene hints at its momentous significance in the context of the story as a whole. Another memorable sequence consists of the one in which Misaki loses an important battle to Hatoko, a prodigiously accomplished Deus even though she is merely a five-year-old kindergartner. Though initially devastated by the defeat, the heroine bravely turns her loss into an inspiring lesson which propels her evolution as a Deus. As the series progresses, it becomes clearer and clearer that Misaki's uncanny flair as a Deus — an ability seemingly unimpaired by her general lack of athletic prowess and gaming experience — stems precisely from her resilience, perseverance and determination. While quick reactions and fine-honed instincts indubitably abet Misaki's performance, her greatest power lies with those fundamental ethical principles. The girl's moral stamina is confirmed by her mature approach to personal relationships both beyond and within the boundaries of Angelic Layer. This is demonstrated in the course of several interrelated scenes, and most vividly conveyed by Misaki's attitude toward Koutarou as his kindness and supportiveness gradually morph into romantic affection, which prompts her to reassess the nature of her own true feelings toward the boy.

Within the ludic domain, Misaki's ethical integrity is borne out by her incremental realization that an Angel's safety lies entirely in its Deus' decisions. Therefore, as her talent grows with each successive confrontation, so does her sense of responsibility toward Hikaru. By and by, this realization leads Misaki to an even more vital discovery: the fact that the bond which develops between a Deus and an Angel over time is not just an outcome of the refinement of combat tactics but actually constitutes the basis of a unique partnership with profound psychological and physical implications. Relatedly, Misaki gradually learns that a battle is genuinely enjoyed only when a Deus is in a position to trust his or her Angel unequivocally. It is indeed her unwavering faith in Hikaru that enables the protagonist to overcome an apparently unbeatable maneuver, the "Wizard's Move," and snatch a glorious victory out of the jaws of defeat in one of the most memorable battles ever. Coupled with this moral lesson is Misaki's firm belief in the importance of mutual respect: no triumph, in this perspective, can ever be fully savored unless one is able to admire the opponent's skills, tenaciousness and martial honesty. It is a frank recognition of these qualities that enables Misaki to experience real elation in the aftermath of a hard-won victory over a valiant adversary. One of the most deeply affecting scenes in the entire series is the one in which its is finally revealed that the shy and mysterious female figure who appears to have been watching over Misaki from an early stage in the action is her beloved mother Shuuko, the Deus controlling the strongest of all Angels, Athena, and the final antagonist facing Misaki once the girl has received the title of National Champion. It transpires that Shuuko has been forced by her pathological timidity to live apart from her daughter and that in the years of their separation, she has contributed to the creation of Angelic Layer. Much as Misaki may be brimming with happiness at the prospect of an especially tantalizing battle, it is the revelation of her opponent's true identity that provides the greatest source of bliss in her life.

The character of Shuuko comes across as eminently credible within the fabric of the original manga in both narrative and graphic terms, largely because the manga's predominantly humorous tenor makes it quite possible for its readers to accept situations and behaviors which in more serious or more realistic circumstances would smack of sheer absurdity. Yet, it posed a major challenge for the producer of the anime adaptation, Masahiko Minami, insofar as the series' tonal shift toward gravity required him to provide more solid emotional causes for Shuuko's anomalous conduct. "I had a problem with the reason Misaki's mother didn't see her own daughter even though she lived in Japan," Minami has stated. "In the manga, it's kind of funny, with the mother being so incredibly shy that she can't even face her own daughter.... However, I didn't want to take that relationship in the anime in a comedic direction. Instead, I wanted to explore the psychology of a mother who couldn't even face her child; I wanted to focus on the mother/daughter relationship." Since the manga and its anime adaptation came into being almost concurrently, Minami and his colleagues were not always in a position to rely on the parent text for guidance or reference. As a result, they had "to fill in the gaps" themselves, and this inevitably caused the TV series to "drift" from its parent text. "However," Minami is eager to stress, "CLAMP accepted that fact, so it wasn't a problem." CLAMP's preparedness to go along with Minami's revisions without presuming to impose its veto on the basis of authorial omniscience offers eloquent confirmation of its artists' flexibility. The team's commodious take on art as a multifaceted and multiskilling phenomenon finds an apt ethical correlative in its resolutely anti-dogmatic approach to their chosen medium at large and to its adaptive potentialities in particular. It is with its rendition of the ludic fights that the anime adaptation proves most faithful to the source text on the visual plane — even though, ironically, this is the very area in which it also asserts its innovativeness most vigorously by capitalizing not solely on the resources inherent in the moving image but also on the expressive capacities of the animators' own drawings. "I focused on trying to make the angels' battle scenes look good," Minami explains, "especially on how to draw them. We also paid a lot of attention to the virtual arenas where the battles took place." Minami was also fascinated with CLAMP's costume designs for this series, and particularly intrigued with their knack of appearing "simple, yet unique; familiar, yet original." As Minami commends CLAMP's "fantastic fashion sense," we are again reminded of its members' outstanding versatility as not merely multiskilled but also multivisionary creators (in CLAMP 2006, p. 31).

As argued in Chapter 1, Japanese culture has evinced a deep-rooted fascination with dolls for many centuries, enthroning these creatures as major actors in a wide range of artistic activities and forms of popular entertainment, as well as in ceremonies and festivals. As virtually ubiquitous presences, dolls have time and again proclaimed their privileged cultural status both in the guise of stylized ritual icons and in that of everyday playthings. CLAMP has explicitly commented on the influential role played by specific doll designs, popular in their childhood and early youth, in the shaping of the seminal idea at the heart of *Angelic Layer*. "The Rika-chan [similar to Barbie] doll boom started when we were little kids," Ohkawa has explained. "While I don't really play with dolls (laughs), the other three had a lot of experience playing with them. We were talking about how it would be cool to have dolls that could move on their own." According to Mokona, this initial idea gained both substance and originality with the advent of a more sophisticated doll type, from which CLAMP derived further inspiration: "eventually, you had dolls with joints, like Jenny-chan. We thought it would be cool to have dolls that could be controlled by a person's thoughts, not just move on [their] own" (interview in CLAMP 2005d, p. 25). Not many people would automatically think of a Barbie-style doll as the inspirational basis for a story about autonomously mobile dolls, let alone transition quite effortlessly from the model of a jointed doll to the ideation of a doll activated by psychokinetic means — but then, not many people either within or outside the realm of popular entertainment share CLAMP's flair for translating even the most prosaic of cultural realities into a trigger for the articulation of an utterly original poetry of images. By emplacing the doll figure as a pivotal aspect of the new story, CLAMP was also able to challenge several of the conventions typically associated with combat-based yarns. First of all, the common assumption that girls are more likely than boys to play with dolls enabled the artists to make their chief character female even though a plot of that kind would normally feature a male protagonist.

This basic casting shift paved the way to no less significant formal reorientations. Even though *Angelic Layer*'s affiliation with the action/combat genre makes it eminently attractive to boy readers and viewers, it is immediately clear that it does not quite conform to the classic tenets of the *shounen* category. According to Hidekazu Katoh, the author of a helpful essay on "Understanding *Angelic Layer*," this series' departure from the mainstream approach is evident right from the start, being succinctly communicated by CLAMP's atypical handling of the motif of physical inadequacy. "Misaki's inferiority complex about being short reflects the worship of physical strength," Katoh observes. "This type of complex is more common in boys than girls. If the story was done by a typical *shounen* manga creator, he may have just given the boy a power to compensate for his height. However, CLAMP doesn't give Misaki power. They give her inner strength." No less striking, according to the critic, is the story's unconventional climax, and particularly its assertion of the importance of emotional strength as more valuable and durable an achievement than any sensational victory or canonical rite of passage. "The struggle that children have with their parents is a human ritual that signifies the child's building independence. While it's an important part of growing up, it's more important to build one's independence than just to 'win.' That is why Misaki can smile through her defeat, and enjoy living with her mother" (in CLAMP 2005d, p. 25). As shown later in this chapter, CLAMP would make its first decisive intervention in the realm of manga geared toward young men with *Chobits* by subjecting a familiar plot motif to radical reconceptualization. *Angelic Layer* could be regarded as *Chobits*' worthy predecessor in its own effort to both appropriate and rework an established formula with unique experimentative vigor.

While it lays emphasis on the importance of games as both leisure-oriented events and social agencies, *Angel Layer* also proposes that games are not only a source of fun. Nor can they be reduced to the status of tools for facilitating human interaction. It would, of course, be foolish to deny that games are designed to generate pleasure in the forms of both fleeting entertainment and a more lasting sense of emotional well-being. Angelic Layer's inventor, Icchan, underscores this point, adamantly maintaining that Angels are dolls, and that the most crucial thing for a competitor to learn is to enjoy how to play with them. Concurrently, the series emphasizes that games hold social significance as both vehicles and arenas for the stimulation of intersubjective dynamics — an especially valuable function in an era of rampant atomization and anomie. The danger, as *Angel Layer* frankly reminds us, resides with the power of games to erode any extant vestiges of authenticity from cultures in which simulacra already occupy virtually all of the social space by attenuating further their users' tenuous connection with the real, and by luring them into an escapist mirage of self-perpetuating illusions. In this respect, games stand out as technologies of subjectivity of incomparable force in their knack of constructing individual and collective identities alike in accordance with distinctive pleasure-oriented and cohesive priorities, with both constructive and debilitating consequences.

In its distinctive construal of the graphic and dramatic language of an imaginary ludic system, the anime version of *Angel Layer* could be said to carry not only entertainment value but also documentary weight. This lies with its allusions to the synergetic dialogue between anime and games: a phenomenon which has played a vital part in the gradual familiarization of Western audiences with the visual rhetoric of Japanese animation. An especially notable aspect of this process is the gaming sector's consistent infiltration by particular anime styles. This phenomenon has been exhaustively documented by Chris Kohler in *Power-Up: How Japanese Video Games Gave the World an Extra Life*, the first among the growing number of critical volumes devoted to the analysis of gaming to have drawn attention to the East as the cradle of this art form. Kohler's pivotal contention is that Japanese game designers have progressively been developing a visual repertoire capable of worldwide appeal precisely on the basis of a culturally defined design ethos which originates both in traditional Japanese art at large and in the specific media of manga and anime in particular. According to Kohler, many of Japan's most proficient game developers benefit from their education in the creative context of art and design colleges rather than in the pointedly technical areas of coding and programming as was often the case with their early Western counterparts. Furthermore, many of those artists started out as manga illustrators and anime artists, and therefore accrued at an early stage in their career graphic skills which would enable them to enrich their games with intriguing storylines and sensitive characterization by recourse to techniques acquired in those initial positions.

On the historical plane, the collusion of anime and games has been profoundly influenced by commercial priorities. Even though the earliest games in Japan had tended to look at anime as a superior source of visual inspiration, there came a point when their status altered from that of Cinderella-like derivatives to that of independent market forces. As Jonathan Clements and Helen McCarthy have commented, on this point, "the large unit costs of games means that a successful gaming company has much higher budgets [than anime] to play with. By the late 1990s, with anime budgets squeezed ever tighter, many of the talents who might have previously worked in TV animation instead migrated to the higher returns of computing.... Those anime that flourished on television often did so with the heavy backing of gaming concerns.... Their emphasis is often based on the collecting of cards, toys, or other cheaply mass-produced items that can be marketed to young consumers during the commercial breaks" (Clements and McCarthy, p. 218). An especially vivid evaluation of anime's bearing on the gaming industry has been offered by Jodi Heard in her portrayal of the distinctive aesthetics of E3 Expo (i.e., Electronic Entertainment Expo), an event held in 2003. (E3 is an annual trade fair for the computer and video game industries regularly hosted by the LA Convention Center.) "For someone who has never been to the mother of all gaming conventions," Heard avows, "it can stun you into silence when you first walk in.... Wandering around the thunder and light show of E3, images from millions of games, released or yet to be released, are everywhere.... Then after a moment, after you have visited all the booths you can and the urge to see everything dies down, you start to notice something; a familiar bat of eyelash here, a wave of a hand there, a character design that resembles someone you know.... Everywhere you go there are the haunting wisps of anime.... That familiar cadre of colour palette, animation cues, and character designs called anime art for lack of a better description, makes its appearances in a variety of levels and forms in the video game world." What is ultimately most tantalizing about the dialectical interplay of anime and games is its knack of stretching well beyond the compass of Japan and its unique visual codes to impact on the gaming sector in its entirety: "it seems the anime influence is visibly everywhere," argues Heard, "but it is no surprise that this happens. Most of the best and most popular companies that put out titles are from Japan where such design trends are almost inherent. But what is surprising is [that] the impact of the anime genre is now intruding on the designs in non–Japanese companies" (Heard).

The market for games overtly influenced by popular anime releases and by the manga on which these are in turn often based has been rapidly expanding over the past couple of decades. As Kevin Gifford has stated, this process initially issued form "a simple formula over in Japan — if a manga published in *Shounen Jump* hits it big and gets its own long-running TV show, then Bandai or Sony or someone will — repeat, *will*— make it into a 3D one-on-one fighter game" (Gifford, p. 137). The privileged position granted to *Shounen Jump* is hardly surprising given its status as one of the longest-running manga anthologies published on a weekly basis in Japan with monthly editions released by Viz Media in North America and Europe. At times, the game in question merely provides a group of characters from the source text and appropriate settings in which their fights can be staged. However, the established formula has been gradually receiving imaginative reassessment as game designers have sought to create ludic packages capable of communicating both narrative and aesthetic values of their own, instead of blandly emulating the ambitions fostered by their manga or anime predecessors. In such cases, the game shows itself capable of transcending the aesthetics of the arcade-style fighter typology, and of imbuing each scenario with an engaging atmosphere through the simulation by electronic means of some of the principal graphic conventions associated with manga and most passionately cherished by their readers. An especially effective strategy, in this regard, consists of the rendition of visuals which seem to have been executed in pencil by recourse to special shading equipment.

The coalescence of anime and games would appear to consist of a fundamentally two-way process. On the one hand, Western audiences have grown more responsive to games created by Japanese companies thanks to their previous exposure to anime and their attendant recognition of certain visual conventions. On the other hand, game players already familiar with Japan's pictorial proclivities thanks to their involvement in the ludic experience have become more open to the medium of anime. Jack Niida, marketing coordinator for the Japanese videogame production company Nippon Ichi has helpfully elucidated this double-edged phenomenon. Focusing specifically on the reasons behind Nippon Ichi's decision to move to the United States in 2005, he has stated: "we thought it was the right timing, because the American market seemed to be getting more accustomed to Japanese anime-style artwork ... and our titles are all pretty much anime-influenced.... The anime crowd is pretty hardcore, so we thought it was a good match, and it turned out to be." In response to the invitation to explain to what he would attribute the increasing responsiveness to Japanese styles among Western consumers, Niida has also noted: "I think it's because of the growing anime influence, Americans are becoming more accustomed to it ... back in the old days you had Japanese titles with anime-related characters but they changed the art style to suit the Western taste, but ... nowadays they can just bring the original artwork over, which is great for people like us" (Niida).

With both its narrative format and its visual style, *Angel Layer* offers fictional confirmation of the arguments delineated above regarding the mutual influence of anime and games, and the impact of this cross-media dialogue on contemporary audiences. As an anime adaptation revolving around an imaginative interpretation of the codes and conventions of games, the series actively partakes of both forms. In so doing, it draws attention to the influence exerted by anime on games, on the one hand, and by games on anime on the other. *Angel Layer* is in a position to attract regular anime viewers as yet unacquainted with game-specific criteria to the world of gaming through its engaging take on the ludic event, and on its social and emotional repercussions. At the same time, it is able to appeal to viewers who are relatively new to anime but cognizant of gaming formulae insofar as it can help them relate more intimately to its own yarn than would be the case with an anime which bears no obvious thematic connection with the ludic domain. This process brings into play particular technologies of subjectivity centered on the mechanisms through which specific media are able to fashion specific audiences on the basis of the rules, expectations and goals associated with their reception. It is worth stressing that *Angel Layer* also underscores the role played by stylistic considerations in the establishment of an ongoing anime-game dialectic by applying the same essential set of graphic ingredients to the representation of the anime's human actors and to the ideation of the artificial beings they deploy in the game.

It is also worth noting, in this context, that parallel developments in the anime and gaming industries offer convincing evidence for the steady ascent of both forms to the status of fine art, and that this development serves to advance one more form of cultural synergy: namely, the creative dialogue between so-called mass culture and so-called high art. Indeed, both anime creators and game designers have been increasingly hailed virtually the world over not merely as entertainers but also as artists capable of creating impressive visual artifacts, endowed with highly sophisticated technical and aesthetic qualities. Anime production and game design, therefore, have incrementally achieved recognition by disparate cultures as valid art forms in the traditional and academic sense of the term. Janet Hetherington's comments on the evolution of game-related art, specifically, provide a thought-provoking critical intervention in the synergetic field here outlined. "Art can be defined as the production, expression or realm of what is beautiful" Hetherington maintains. "It can also be described as objects subject to aesthetic criteria. Today, some of the most recent additions to the world of art are coming from an unexpected source—videogames. Artist Andy Warhol (1930–1987) first took everyday things and raised them to a new level of artistic awareness in the 1960s.... Today's artists are again looking to pop culture for inspiration, and videogames are providing that inspiration." The tendency outlined by Hetherington could also be traced back to the work of Marcel Duchamp (1887–1968), and especially to the Dadaist artist's transposition of a "readymade," or "found object" (*objet trouvé*), from the domain of the quotidian to that of putative high culture. The electronic game is indeed a product that is habitually valued in strictly utilitarian terms for its entertainment value, yet can accrue a new status and an alternate significance by being reimagined and recontextualized within the art world. Relatedly, games are beginning to infiltrate the erstwhile highbrow (and, by and large, rather prejudiced) citadel of the museological kingdom by means of exhibitions and conventions which provide the public with occasions "to see the work and talent that goes into creating the videogames they enjoy" (Hetherington). To reinforce her central hypothesis, Hetherington cites Lorne Lanning, president and creative director at Oddworld Inhabitants: "each year the game industry continues to attract incredible artistic talent from around the globe," Lanning contends. "Yet much of the work created by these artists goes into the preproduction process and is rarely seen in its original form by the art-loving public." Events like the annual exhibition "Into the Pixel" offer tantalizing opportunities to gain precious insights into this normally invisible process. Lanning describes "Into the Pixel," inaugurated in 2003, as "an exciting opportunity. It allows the artistic works to be seen and judged by the artistic merits of the creators and not by the commercial success that is all too often mistaken for quality in our mass-market medium" (cited in Hetherington).

Manifold and interlocking levels of synergy can be identified within the bundle of processes described above. At one level, anime nourishes games and is in turn sustained by them, as both forms acquire popularity by mutually abetting each other and by imprinting their stylistic features onto each other. Simultaneously, anime's increasing recognition as an art reflects, and is reflected by, the promotion of games themselves to artistic standing. Vladimir Cole's observations on the subject deserve particular attention in this context: "The Associated Press writes, 'The popularity of anime, that uniquely Japanese form of animation, can be traced directly to the growth of video games, especially the *Final Fantasy* series and other role-playing epics like *Dragon Warrior*.' The relationship between the two media is more complicated than that. First of all, anime has been around for nearly 100 years, so it's far more likely that anime has had greater influence on games than the other way around. Second, the relationship is more symbiotic than the article implies. Fans of the two entertainment forms tend to appreciate many of the same techniques, plot devices, and tropes. It's difficult to imagine either form of entertainment evolving to the state that each is in today without the other. Anime is constantly referencing video games and games anime" (Cole).

Angelic Layer can be seen to carry documentary value not only insofar as it attests to the popularity of a certain type of ludic venture and attendant rise in the number of both actual and virtual communities held together by such an enterprise but also to the extent that it bears witness to the ascendancy of the visual image in contemporary cultures at large and in Japanese society specifically. The anime's cinematic nature allows it to convey this idea more forcefully than the source text, insofar as the intense dynamism which characterizes its action from beginning to end imparts its images with a sense of urgency and momentum which figuratively reinforce their centrality. The visuals' chromatic vibrance abets this impression with frequently exhilarating effects. Thus, while both the manga and anime versions of *Angelic Layer* lay emphasis on the ascendancy of visuality, the anime is in a position to bring that message to fruition in a more impactful fashion by virtue of its kinetic energy and colorfulness. The ubiquity of visual images in contemporary culture is thrown into relief practically from the start, and specifically through the sequence in which the protagonist first discovers the existence of Angels. Japanese culture is markedly visual at all levels, and its social, economic and semiotic structures, therefore, are veritably saturated with images. The ubiquitous presence of visual images is corroborated by the privileged place granted by Japanese art to a wide variety of both time-honored and innovative patterns, emblems, symbols and stylized figures. Even the most casual audiences will be quick to recognize that the art of anime itself relies on specific visual codes and conventions which make its products recognizable qua anime in spite of the impressive diversity of styles exhibited by that form over its kaleidoscopic history. Anime, in this regard, constitutes a relatively modern articulation of what is actually an inveterate proclivity, as epitomized by the ideographic (and, by implication, pictographic) character of Japan's writing systems, and particularly *kanji*, as both an abstract system of signs and an intensely physical reality unto itself. In contemporary Japan, the enduring vigor of the country's visual sensibility at both the Westernized and the indigenous ends of the graphic spectrum is embodied by the overwhelming quantity of visual data which assail the senses in Tokyo's shopping district, on the one hand, and the more mellow but comparably awe-inspiring flow of traditional imagery which permeates the Kyoto area, on the other.

As Mark W. MacWilliams persuasively argues with reference to two of the most eminent thinkers of our time, "modern Japan is what Michel de Certeau describes as a 'recited society' where people walk 'all day long through a forest of narratives from journalism, advertising, and television, narratives that still find time as people are getting ready for bed to slip a few final messages under the portals of sleep...' Japan is also what Susan Sontag refers to as an "image world," since much of Japanese mass media is involved in producing and consuming images, at a time when they have 'extraordinary powers to determine [people's] demands on reality and are themselves coveted substitutes for firsthand experience...' ... The animated images that flicker across the screen and all the pages of comic magazines and books are a major source of the stories that not only Japanese, but also an increasingly global audience, consume today" (MacWilliams, p. 3). The cultural propensity to ideate human life as a series of image-laden stories — which is effectively tantamount to a propensity to live through images — is a contemporary trend of global significance which finds paradigmatic expression in the culture of Japan. Nonetheless, in observing the part played by the visual dimension in Japanese society, it is vital to acknowledge the ongoing pre-eminence of that reality over the centuries instead of deeming it automatically synonymous with contemporaneity. Concurrently, it is necessary to appreciate the bearing of visuality as a twofold phenomenon which alludes at once to the condition of being visual (i.e., visualness) and to the kinetic event whereby people and things are experienced as specifically visual entities (i.e., vision). These structures of vision and visuality, or scopic regimes, define what and how people are *invited, made* or *allowed* to see within the boundaries of their society minute by minute, in the contingent present (as well as the extent to which they may be able to perceive the invisible therein). (Invited, Made, Allowed: these words' initials, incidentally, form the acronym IMA, the Japanese word for "now.") In elaborating these themes, *Angelic Layer* intimates that what human beings see within the bounds of a particular society — real or virtual as the case might be — is always a function of technologies of subjectivity designed to shape their sensory and mental responses, and hence induce them to embrace specific ideologies and patterns of behavior held consonant with the data delivered by visual experience. Norman Bryson tersely defends this proposition in his insightful discussion of "The gaze in the expanded field," where he argues that whenever we use our eyes, we do not merely perceive "light" but also "intelligible form." The abstraction of form from the raw materials of optical experience, Bryson maintains, is a direct consequence of the socialization of vision: "for human beings collectively to orchestrate their visual experience together it is required that each submit his or her retinal experience to the socially agreed description(s) of an intelligible world. Vision is socialized, and visual reality can be measured and named, as hallucination, misrecognition, or 'visual disturbance.' Between the subject and the world is inserted the entire sum of discourses which make up visuality" (Bryson, p. 91).

Published in manga format in 1992 and 1993, and adapted to anime in 1997, *CLAMP School Detectives* represents the culmination of a trilogy in both thematic and structural terms. This was inaugurated by the manga *Man of Many Faces*, released in 1990 and 1991, and continued with the manga *Duklyon: CLAMP School Defenders*, released in 1992 and 1993. Set in the prismatic microcosm of CLAMP School, *Man of Many Faces* focuses on the character of Akira, a student whose lack of a father is more than abundantly compensated for by the presence in his life of two blaringly nutty mothers. Keen on exploiting the boy's culinary flair by employing him as a chef, the two women also love to have him steal for them so as to satisfy an insane passion for fanciful objects of all sorts. An obedient son, Akira regularly adopts the alternate identity of the thief "20 Faces" as a notoriously skilled and elusive thief garbed in a fetching mask and tuxedo. *Man of Many Faces* shows that even though CLAMP had made a sensational debut onto the mainstream with the groundbreaking epic fantasy *RG Veda*, its members were already eager to experiment with disparate forms instead of seeking to carve a clear-cut niche for themselves within a single sector of the manga market. Indeed, whereas *RG Veda* is predominantly serious in its treatment of heroic exploits of earth-shattering proportions, *Man of Many Faces* is essentially a lighthearted romantic comedy grounded in contemporary society and capable of appealing to both kids and adults on the basis of precisely such unassuming qualities. Young readers are given an opportunity to immerse themselves in a lively yarn sustained by personae with whom they can readily identify as both manga equivalents of their own daily selves and fantasy role models to be emulated or aspired to in imagination and dream. Grownups, in turn, are most likely to feel drawn to CLAMP's flair for clever dialogue and quick repartee: traits of the team's distinctive cachet which *Man of Many Faces* could be said to have launched. At the same time, older audiences are likely to enjoy CLAMP's deft reconceptualization of the mystery genre through the lenses of a boldly handled romance.

In addition, even though the series' prevalent tone is light, when its characters engage in debates about the nature of love, which they often do, their words carry philosophical connotations which cannot be dismissed as mere pretexts for witty banter. In fact, they invite recognition as poignant reflections on emotional challenges which most people at some point have to confront in their ordinary existence. They might not take us into the far reaches of metaphysical speculation but this does not render them either peripheral or superficial elements in CLAMP's overall vision insofar as they have the power to fathom the vicissitudes of the human heart no less sensitively, though less spectacularly, than many of the later works. As argued in the foregoing chapter with reference to *Cardcaptor Sakura*, CLAMP's take on love is exceptionally commodious. The analysis of *Chobits* presented later in this chapter will further consolidate this contention. *Man of Many Faces* makes its own seemingly modest, yet memorable, contribution to this important aspect of the group's philosophy, in many ways foreshadowing later articulations of its main concerns of the kind one encounters in mature series such as *Tsubasa: RESERVoir CHRoNiCLE* and *xxxHOLiC*.

The views expounded by the female lead, Utako, and her younger sister Mako vividly encapsulate CLAMP's perspective on love as promulgated in *Man of Many Faces*. Its core consists of the disarmingly simple proposition that romance has far less to do with chivalric ideals of the kind one sees celebrated in the ethos of courtly love than with a mature understanding of its value as a form of cooperative responsibility. This understanding is founded on the cultivation of one's moral probity, insofar as caring for a person of one's choice means facing the possibility of placing that person's well-being ahead of one's own gratification, yet should not entail utter self-denial — i.e., a draconian suppression of selfhood. Indeed, for love to keep growing and transcending the boundaries of vapid infatuation, one must be able to foster both the loved one's and one's own integrity. This idea is pithily summed up by Utako's assertion that romance is bound to be a one-way street. This is not tantamount to saying that people in love should feel at liberty to pursue their private fantasies regardless of their partners' feelings and values. What Utako seeks to suggest, rather, is the idea that each person is likely to experience love in a subjective way, and that we should never expect or presume the person we love to share our own emotions down to the last detail. Reciprocal trust and respect depend to a vital extent on the ability to acknowledge, honor and foster difference — and the right to difference. In this matter, *Man of Many Faces* evinces underlying affinities with the moral perspective elaborated by CLAMP in *Tokyo Babylon*, here examined in Chapter 2, by intimating that the development of the capacity to care for others genuinely and disinterestedly is dependent on one's ability to understand oneself and one's own natural proclivities. Utako's position also entails that the impact which one's emotions are bound to have on disparate aspects of everyday life is not something which can be unequivocally quantified or predicted. Thus, even ostensibly trivial situations are liable to assume unexpected significance if they come to be associated, either empirically or symbolically, with a loved one and his or her personal inclinations, tastes or even idiosyncrasies. Chef prodigy Akira conveys an analogous message in the context of the later campus-based series *CLAMP School Detectives* as he announces that love is the most crucial gastronomic ingredient of them all. The sheer desire to cook a scrumptious dish for a person one deeply cares for has the power to make even the most ordinary recipe taste incomparably delectable.

The second segment of the trilogy peaking with *CLAMP School Detectives*, the manga *Duklyon: CLAMP School Defenders*, is also set in the pentagram-shaped compound of CLAMP School. This series chronicles the exploits of two teenagers, track-and-field specialist Kentarou Higashikunimaru and kendo expert Takeshi Shukaido, in a predominantly comedic fashion. The series playfully attests to CLAMP's appetite for adventurous experimental gestures by delivering a sustained parody of numerous codes and conventions associated with *shounen* manga — and, most pointedly, with the subgenre known as *tokusatsu*, a type of story which usually pivots on the figure of the monster-fighting superhero clad in a showy armored suit. However, in the execution of this manga, CLAMP has clearly not confined itself to the delivery of a mere spoof or pastiche, which presumably would have been insufficient to satisfy its artists' experimentative leanings. In fact, as the commentary accompanying *Duklyon: CLAMP School Defenders* in the fifth volume of the *CLAMP no Kiseki* collection explains, "this series is filled with parodies of *tokusatsu*, but of course, the readers who don't know the original *tokusatsu* can enjoy it without a problem. That's because *Duklyon* is not just a parody. It's a standalone entertainment inspired by *tokusatsu*'s simple story structure ... done with a little poetic license." The manga's cumulative effectiveness, accordingly, does not stem from its imitative flourishes but rather form its creators' affectionate grasp of "the genre's essence" (in CLAMP 2005e, p. 20).

While Kentarou and Takeshi take it upon themselves to embody the classic *shounen* role with something of a vengeance, the supporting characters and the setting consistently fuel the series' parodic thrust. The main character, beside Kentarou and Takeshi, is Eri Chusonji, the formidable lady who dispenses information and instructions, as well as an overgenerous helping of mallet bashing meant to discipline incompetent subordinates. As for the manga's key setting, this is the quintessential two-level world one frequently encounters in superhero yarns of the supposedly serious variety. Thus, "Duklyon" is a bakery on the surface but secretly accommodates the headquarters of the organization of the same name, which is responsible for thwarting the aspirations to world domination harbored by the Imonoyama Shopping District and its leader, the seemingly meek Kotobuki Sukiyabashi, who also happens to be one of the protagonists' classmates. An especially charged stage in the heroes' mock-epic adventures is marked by the abduction by the infamous denizens of the Imonoyama Shopping District of the president of the Elementary School's student council, Utako Ohkawa — a character which this series shares with both *CLAMP School Detectives* and *Man of Many Faces*. The manga's tenor has been perfectly captured by jennaria [*sic*] in the *XamJapan* review of the manga. In this context, its parodic status is assessed as a concomitant of the series' juggling with diverse forms, and hence acquires additional layers of meaning. *Duklyon: CLAMP School Defenders*, the reviewer proposes, immediately declares its irreverent approach to generic conventions by combining elements of at least four manga categories. Thus, it "is sort of *shoujo*, and a little bit BL [Boys' Love], and kind of *shounen*. Mostly, though, it's a parody. It sets itself up with an absolutely straight face: the bickering partners, the secret identities (which aren't very well kept), the nonsensical excuses when they have to go take care of Duklyon business. There's a secret headquarters, and an opponent who's Trying To Take Over The World.... And finally there's a big epic romance between the opponent and the girl who seems to sort of command Duklyon. (Or aids them? It's not really clear. She seems to be in a vaguely Moneypenny position to their James Bond)" (jennaria).

With the transition to *CLAMP School Detectives*, CLAMP's passion for character crossovers asserts itself for the first time as a major aspect of the team's creative signature. In a sense, this facet of *CLAMP School Detectives* could be considered sufficient unto itself to establish the series' standing as a milestone in CLAMP's career. Upon embarking on this series in either its manga or its anime incarnations, it is also vital to appreciate its distinctive use of its location in comparison with the first and second parts of the trilogy. While both *Man of Many Faces* and *Duklyon: CLAMP School Defenders* tend to concentrate primarily on their personae and relationships, *CLAMP School Detectives* posits CLAMP School as an axial dramatic agency. One of the reasons for which this setting suddenly ascended to unprecedented eminence is that CLAMP's members were eager to devise a narrative mechanism which would allow them to synthesize their separate creative efforts into a unitary vision. As Ohkawa explains, "the way CLAMP works now, we all work together on a common story, but when we were making *doujinshi*, we each had our own stories and characters. At one point we decided to play around with making a common world for all our characters to live in.... The common world we created at that time was the CLAMP School" (interview in CLAMP 2005e, p. 9). This early development in the team's evolution indicates that the highly collaborative spirit for which its artists are justly renowned was already operational in embryonic form within their interpersonal alchemy from a very early stage.

Like several other series which have contributed substantially to the establishment of CLAMP's global fan base across disparate generations, *CLAMP School Detectives* owes much of its charm to subtly nuanced characterization. As anticipated in Chapter 1, the depiction of the story's three protagonists clearly indicates the tone adopted by CLAMP in the conception of this specific character gallery. Nokoru Imonoyama is portrayed as the youngest member of the illustrious Imonoyama *zaibatsu* (or financial corporation), the founders of CLAMP School. Endowed with so prodigious an IQ that NASA are eager to enlist the kid in their ranks despite his tender age, Nokoru has a tendency, supposedly inherited from his elders, to embark on the most bizarre of tasks just for the fun of it. His decision to establish the CLAMP School Detective Agency stems from another unusual proclivity: Nokoru's knack of sensing the presence of a lady in distress at a considerable distance. While Nokoru is primarily distinguished by his intellectual capacities, as well as his classic good looks, Suoh Takamura excels at virtually all major martial arts, having achieved a third-dan black belt in karate, aikido, kendo and judo while also being proficient in kyuudou (Japanese archery). As a descendant of a ninja clan, Suoh certainly appears to be honoring his ancestors' legacy. Finally, Akira Ijyuin is depicted as a world-class cook and as the son of the notorious "20 Faces," the putatively uncatchable thief of legendary repute and the protagonist of the yarn developed independently in the manga *Man of Many Faces*, as outlined earlier. The balance of mental and practical abilities exhibited by the engaging character triad on which *CLAMP School Detectives* relies is especially remarkable when one takes into consideration the predominantly blithe, at times even downright farcical, mood which pervades the work in both its manga and anime incarnations. A number of supporting and ancillary personae are brought into play to complement the personalities and behaviors evinced by the series' axial triumvirate. The president of the Kindergarten Student Division Council, the aforementioned Utako Ohkawa, and the flutist Nagisa Azuya play especially notable parts, in this respect. The overall character dynamics are further abetted by the incorporation of a romantic strand based on Akira and Utako's mutual attraction and on Suoh's reciprocated crush on Nagisa. In fact, Suoh even goes as far as give his romantic ideals free rein by fantasizing about Nagisa as a wisteria fairy or an illusion before eventually convincing himself that she is a normal girl in flesh and bone.

As they unflinchingly endeavor to stay true to their ideals against all odds, the detectives never seem to regard the tasks laid before them by fate as paltry, uninteresting or otherwise unworthy of their wholehearted efforts as latter-day embodiments of the knight in shining armor. Therefore, while one adventure might require them to succor an elderly lady harassed by an unscrupulous brother-in-law, the next exploit might entail the deployment of their multifarious talents in unraveling the mysteries surrounding a supposedly haunted art room, identifying the sender of a missive threatening to cancel the school dance, or simply finding the owner of a silk stocking. Some of the series' older readers and viewers have occasionally expressed marginal dissatisfaction with its overall lack of conflict, lamenting its proclivity to solve problems and overcome obstacles just a little bit too smoothly. Whether or not one subscribes to this critical evaluation of *CLAMP School Detectives*' modus operandi, it can hardly be disputed that in its climactic manga chapters and corresponding anime episodes, the series reverses any such tendency to foreground conflict as a major narrative and dramatic factor. In these segments, the series foreshadows *Cardcaptor Sakura* by assigning a special dramatic function to the character of a new transfer student. Every bit as clever and ingenious as the wonder boy Nokoru, this freshly introduced persona appears to have a score to settle with the formidable detectives, and particularly with Nokoru himself, and to be determined to go to considerable lengths to achieve his goal. One of his first nefarious moves consists of an attempt on the lives of Akira, Suoh, Utako and Nagisa, which forces Nokoru to put all of his legendary resourcefulness into action. He then proceeds to go after the school blimp, the protagonists' den, and then to kidnap all the apes in Banana Park. However, it is when the new student decides to devote his strategic cunning to eroding Nokoru's self-confidence seemingly beyond repair that *CLAMP School Detectives* strikes its most somber chords. In other words, the opponent's psychological warfare is far more disturbing that his physical tactics. In showing what it is like for a person who has never had any reason to doubt his abilities and popularity suddenly to be confronted with the agony of defeat, loneliness and loss, the series supplies us with a psychological portrait which feels eminently realistic in spite of the action's ongoing commitment to the delivery of a fundamentally comic experience.

Even when its conflict levels remain relatively low, *CLAMP School Detectives* is able to make proficient use of its character dynamics and hence convey an unmistakable sense of vibrant human interaction. Thus, while it would be absurd to deny that virtually all of the series' personae (peripheral figures included), are thoroughly individualized down to their minutest quirks, it is no less important to recognize that CLAMP's sensitive grasp of intersubjective chemistry has the power to bring those singular presences together into a harmonious constellation. This ultimately stands out as a composite personality construct, capable of asserting its distinction as a character in its own right, as well as acting as a potent reminder that the whole can never quite be reduced to the sum of its constituent parts. As noted, the basic plotting mechanism through which this integration is sustained consists of the sequential arrangement of adventures enlisting the three protagonists' impressive abilities as they strive to protect the female population of their prestigious school. It is through its assiduous reliance on this simple device that *CLAMP School Detectives* prompts us to observe from a fresh perspective the technologies of subjectivity by means of which human beings come continually into existence as social entities from one moment to the next. Indeed, the series proposes a thought-provoking interpretation of those processes, whereby the individual is neither nostalgically glorified as an ideal point of reference, supposedly suppressed by the collective demands of his or her society, nor dwarfed as a marginal category in the service of some grand (and equally vacuous) collectivist ideology.

In fact, individuals are allowed to stand out as carefully defined agencies, and situated in narrative scenarios which grant them plenty of leeway for autonomous (if not always well-advised) action, opportunities for the exercise of free will, and chances to learn from their own mistakes no less than from the models proffered by others. At the same time, however, their integration in a communal ensemble requires them to grow up by acknowledging the fundamentally relational nature of their identities. This, in turn, urges them to assess the extent to which their own personal aspirations should or could be pursued without either endangering the self's relative freedom or eroding the advancement of the general good. The ethical issues addressed by CLAMP in *Tokyo Babylon* come into prominence again in the context of *CLAMP School Detectives* insofar as this series' characters, like Subaru Sumeragi and his associates and patients, are finally enjoined to ponder the difference between individualism and selfishness, and hence between altruism and empathy. This entails their preparedness to recognize that even though it may well be impossible to experience another person's suffering as though it were one's own pain, this incapacity is not automatically bound to make us callous. In fact, it may pave the way to the achievement of a refined sense of self-understanding whence genuine compassion may then arise.

It would be absurd to deny that the comic side of *Man of Many Faces* and *Duklyon: CLAMP School Defenders* comes to full fruition in *CLAMP School Detectives* through CLAMP's intermeshing of a colorful setting and a rollercoaster ride of sprightly antics. Nevertheless, it would be equally inapposite to ignore that the series' treatment of intersubjective relations also hosts some serious subtexts which no committed fan can afford to neglect. The relative gravity which *CLAMP School Detectives* interstitially accommodates is most palpable in its treatment of the romance strand — and especially its intimations that whereas Akira and Suoh are entitled to have sweethearts in the persons of Utako and Nagisa respectively, it is Nokoru's fate to remain single. The golden boy's retention of this status, it is suggested, is in fact instrumental in the realization of his utopian vision of a world in which no woman in need of support will ever be left unassisted — and, by extension, in the healthy functioning of CLAMP School as a whole. As to what might happen when a character entrusted by the order of things to operate as his community's scion and fulcrum — and hence expected to sacrifice personal desires to the fulfillment of these noble functions — yields to self-interest in the name of love, *Magic Knight Rayearth* exposes the gravity of such a choice through Princess Emeraude's dismal fate. Katoh elaborates this idea to notable effect in the essay "Understanding *CLAMP School Detectives*": "in *Magic Knight Rayearth*, Princess Emeraude must choose between supporting her world as Pillar and loving her special someone, Zagato. As much as it pains her, she can't help but love Zagato. As a result, Cephiro becomes a wasteland filled with monsters until Emeraude reaches her tragic end. If I apply this model to [*CLAMP School*] *Detectives*, the women's utopia would be destroyed like Cephiro should Nokoru find his special someone" (in CLAMP 2005e, p. 8).

An even more serious subtext consists of the series' engagement with the role played by disparate technologies of subjectivity in CLAMP's overall philosophy. It is in relation to this topos that the full import of its location as not only a versatile setting but also a dramatic force in its own right should ultimately be grasped. Like *Angelic Layer*, *CLAMP School Detectives* offers a relatively jovial take on the topos of the construction of subjectivity by recourse to various technologies. The chief technology in question, in this instance, does not consist of either industrial machinery or a cybernetic apparatus but of the structures of power sustaining the massive campus wherein the protagonists carry out their mock-chivalric exploits. This interpretation of the word technology is inspired by the writings of Michel Foucault and specifically by the contention, promulgated by the philosopher virtually throughout his whole career, that structures such as the academic, penal, juridical and medical systems (among others) constitute the key institutions by means of which individuals are disciplined, regimented, restrained, and gradually turned into compliant subjects. Social formations of this kind shape subjectivity by acting directly upon the human body.

In this scenario, the body comes to constitute both the primary channel through which societies can control their subjects—and hence a technology in its own right—and the product of the disciplining strategies designed to maximize the organism's utility and to exploit its energy. The management of the individual body (anatomo-politics) is thereafter extended to the control of entire communities and populations as functional machines. *CLAMP School Detectives*, despite its superficial breeziness and relatively undemanding storytelling style, implicitly expounds the proposition that "ideology's disciplinary strategies impact directly on the human body as the primary object of both the social sciences (psychology, medicine, sociology, criminology) and of the institutions through which such sciences articulate their ideologies (hospitals, schools, prisons, law courts). The body's drives are thoroughly manipulated for the purpose of producing efficient and docile subjects, and subjugated to abstract notions of propriety and usefulness that make the soul the prison of the body" (Cavallaro 2001, p. 82).

While robot-girl series are by no means rare, CLAMP's treatment of this somewhat overused concept in the manga series *Chobits* (2000–2002) is so fresh as to enable the story to stand out as a veritable gem in a crowd of lookalikes. Taking as its narrative premise the standard plot motif about an enchanting girl who accidentally ends up in the home of a socially maladjusted young man, CLAMP soon subverts the established narrative mould. Non only is the girl in question a computer, which could be deemed sufficient unto itself to disrupt established conventions: she is also revealed to harbor unique affective potentialities. This message is deftly conveyed by recourse to ever-increasing intimations that she has been created out of love, and that it is somehow her destiny to experience this emotion herself in ways which transcend a machine's systemic limitations. As argued in the preceding chapter, CLAMP's work seeks to question romantic conventions, proposing that love is capable of taking many unexpected guises and that it is therefore spurious to attempt to delimit its scope by categorizing its expressions in terms of specific relationships. *Chobits* develops this theme in utterly unprecedented directions, treading the tortuous path between biology and technology under the banner of one fundamental principle: the idea that love is love regardless of how it manifests itself. This renders *Chobits* a vibrant affirmation of the human capacity to love anything in existence. Relatedly, *Chobits* never demurs from taking an earnest look at romance in order to expose the nebulousness of the boundaries meant to distinguish the real from the fake, the sentient from the inert. By applying the proposition that love never loses its essential meaning to the relationship between a human being and a computer, CLAMP is also able to put forward its particular vision of a future in which natural and artificial entities are not as sharply differentiated as might have been the case in earlier periods. This vision, as shown, reaches its apotheosis with *Tsubasa: RESERVoir CHRoNiCLE*'s outstanding approach to the topos of cloning.

As a romantic comedy, therefore, *Chobits* boldly challenges common expectations, delving into the philosophy and psychology of emotions in a fashion unknown to the genre. Unsurprisingly, *Chobits* rapidly came to be regarded as the opening of a fresh chapter in CLAMP's career. It is also worth noting, on this point, that this was CLAMP's first deliberate attempt to reach an audience consisting primarily of male readers in their late teens. Up until this point, the team's works had been geared toward a fundamentally female readership with *shoujo* preferences. The publication of *Angelic Layer* in the magazine *Shounen Ace* had begun to alter that basic trend and demonstrated CLAMP's ability to create stories geared toward boys in spite of its markedly unconventional take on the *shounen* formula. However, for many regular readers of *Young Magazine*, it was *Chobits*' publication that signaled their first exposure to CLAMP's talent. Asked to comment on the circumstances surrounding CLAMP's decision to target a different demographic, Ohkawa has stated: "we wanted to do this story, so we decided to present it to a guys' magazine.... We had a lot of letters with comments saying Chi was really cute. However, once the story got more complex ... (laughs). I think it was quite a stretch for fans that wanted a simple happy story" (interview in CLAMP 2007d, p. 11). Ohkawa does not need to spell out what happened "once the story got more complex": as intimated in the preceding chapters, CLAMP has been heartily challenging rules practically from its inception, taking quite a few readers by surprise yet invariably retaining — or indeed enhancing — its fan base through its uniquely absorbing narrative and pictorial skills. Accordingly, even though *Chobits*' unfolding might have shocked readers accustomed to more conventional *shounen* yarns, there is no doubt that it rapidly gained a substantial following. Indeed, it was the manga's huge success that led to its anime adaptation, and hence to further growth in the cohorts of CLAMP's devotees on cross-media terrain. The anime adaptation comprises a TV series, aired in 2002, as well as the ancillary six-minute special *Chibits* released in 2004.

It is through its sensitive character portraits that CLAMP's philosophical position on the capaciousness of love, delineated earlier in this analysis, fully manifests itself. Central to this aspect of the story is the male lead's gradual realization that love means acceptance no less than attraction, and patience no less than excitement. The human appearance exhibited by a "Persocom" on the purely physical side may be the contingent reason for which a human being is able to fall in love with it. However, a recognition of the empirical trigger of one's infatuation is not enough to explain one's ability to move from instinctive and momentary attraction to a long-standing commitment likely to entail the reality of sorrow and loss as well as the promise of happiness. Furthermore, Hideki must learn to negotiate the unpalatable inevitability of difference, and hence come to terms with the fact that much as Persocoms appear to behave and talk just like humans, they are incapable of sensing either grief of physical pain unless they have been deliberately programmed to do so. In fact, even if their programming equips them with the potential to experience those affects, it is always possible to erase the data in which unpleasant occurrences are embedded and thus return the Persocom to its pre-traumatic condition. Hideki's exposure to this discovery throws the fundamental difference between humans and Persocoms sharply into relief. At the same time, however, it is repeatedly suggested that even though Persocoms will not remember anything they have learned or experienced once the relevant data have been deleted, as long as the humans who have cared for them remain able to remember, the memories themselves will survive. This is the key lesson Hideki acquires from Hiroyasu Ueda, a character who has experienced first hand the tragedy of difference, having married a Persocom and had to endure the creature's death. Ridiculous as Ueda's proposition might sound if assessed from a purely logical point of view, it is perfectly consonant with CLAMP's philosophy of feeling. Once again, *Tsubasa: RESERVoir CHRoNiCLE* stands out as the title in which this vision comes to stunning fruition. There can be little doubt that Hideki draws comfort from Ueda's lesson, as this enables him to view his whole connection with Chi in a new light — to the point that when her abductor ungallantly describes her as a Persocom endowed with some "brilliant engineering," Hideki angrily declares that Chi is Chi and nobody should be so brash as to dismiss her as no more than a robotic apparatus. It is by honoring this moral stance against the odds that Hideki's actions are capable of imparting *Chobits* with a fairy tale ending despite the plot's progressive darkening in the latter part of the series.

Even though *Chobits* is by no means a mystery yarn in the classic sense of the term, it does accommodate a stirring mystery element in its handling of the riddles surrounding the heroine's identity. This intriguing facet of the story progressively asserts its dramatic weight, gaining intensity as it evolves over three main stages of the narrative. Some tantalizing questions are first raised not long after the heroine's discovery by Hideki in the trash and "adoption" as a member of his household. Although at this juncture the Persocom is incapable of uttering any word other than "chi," and knows nothing about either herself (name included) or her provenance, the possibility arises at any early stage in the drama that she might be the legendary "Chobit": a Persocom which does not only combine the technological properties of a computer with the appearance of a human, as all Persocoms do, but is also endowed with an autonomous consciousness. While twelve-year-old genius Minoru seems to think that the Chobit is no more than a myth, it becomes obvious that Chi is not an average Persocom once she has crashed all of Minoru's own Persocoms, including the technologically advanced Yuzuki, who has been programmed with the personality of Minoru's sister. The next major challenge, for both Hideki and the audience, coincides with the intimation that Chi has an alter ego in the form of another Persocom that looks exactly like her. A strong creature enveloped in an aura of ineffable sadness, this enigmatic Other seems to remember Chi's past and to have the ability to learn everything which Chi herself is taught. We will later learn that this double is Freya, a Persocom created as Chi's twin sister and the victim of an irreconcilable conflict between her love for her mother and her love for her father, which has caused her internal processors to malfunction and eventually crash beyond repair. Since Freya's memories have been transferred into Chi, they sporadically surface in the guise of the phantasmatic Other. The final and most drastic disclosure concerns Chi's origins. Created to fulfill the role of a little daughter for the wife of the very inventor of Persocoms, Ichiro Mihara, and named Elda, she was indeed conceived as the quasi-mythical Chobit and equipped with a program bound to make her presence hazardous for other entities of her ilk. Ichiro, incidentally, shares his designation not only with the inventor of Angels from *Angelic Layer* but also with a real-life person: the creator of the *Streetfighter X* series, a popular fighting game, as well as a software expert who has worked for a number of major companies including Square, Capcom and Arika. In the "Greeting to CLAMP" published in the fourth volume of *CLAMP no Kiseki*, Mihara describes himself as "just an old classmate of CLAMP's, and a regular guy, although people seem to forget that" (in CLAMP 2005d, p. 26).

Chobits does not confine itself to exploring the interaction between humans and machines. Nor is it satisfied with simply lending erotic connotations to its dynamics by focusing on the relationship between a young man and an uncommonly cute interpretation of the computer. In fact, the story also endeavors to deliver some intriguing social commentary through its portrayal of the male lead's precarious social standing and uncertain future in the supposedly productive world of motivated adults. Thus, while watching the Persocom Chi as she sweetly stumbles through basic social situations with mirthful results will leave many viewers with a sense of warmth in their hearts, it is impossible to dismiss the drama's more serious motifs as mere padding. In fact, *Chobits*' broadly cultural import gradually asserts itself as no less defining a marker of its dramatic identity than the playful or sexy dimensions. As it advances toward its bittersweet climax, in particular, *Chobits* gains incremental gravity insofar as the technologies of subjectivity underpinning its drama reveal their darker connotations. This aspect of the story is most frankly exposed by the installments in which the heroine's true identity and her imbrication in a tragic family history are disclosed. It is at this point that *Chobits* engages most dispassionately — and most memorably — with the multifarious processes through which the identities of humans and machines are simultaneously constructed, and technologies thereby assert their authority as the guarantors of both natural and synthetic identities. The very notion of a natural identity is implicitly called into question by these speculations, to the point that it is feasible to deduce that all identities — human and robotic, organic and artificial, innate and imposed — may ultimately amount to constructs.

As argued in Chapter 1, synthetic beings such as Angels and Persocoms are heir to a venerable tradition as recent expressions of an atavistic human urge to replicate the human form by mechanical means. In Japan, this proclivity has manifested itself as an inveterate fascination with dolls which has persistently punctuated the evolution of both the traditional visual and performance arts and the realm of contemporary popular entertainment. Alongside games, manga and anime have constituted, needless to say, the two primary areas in which those creatures have found ideal grounds for dramatic growth. In explaining how CLAMP first came up with *Chobits*' basic plot, Satsuki Igarashi has emphasized the primarily humorous side of the experience: "back then, when our computer had problems, all we would get were these inscrutable error messages. However, we had no idea what was wrong because it wouldn't tell us anything more" (interview in CLAMP 2007d, p. 11). The idea of a talking Persocom, in the light of these remarks, would seem to have issued from an instinctive desire to communicate with an non-human inorganic entity. However, CLAMP's interest in the controversial image of the humanized automaton extended far beyond the scope of contingent technological mishaps. Indeed, its members were well-aware of their culture's long-standing fascination with such a creature when they started developing *Chobits*' characters and fundamental narrative premises. Especially important, in this regard, was the decision to make Chi into a personal computer rather than a robot. As Ohkawa has explained, this choice was intended to amplify the intensity of the affective obstacles confronted by the story's protagonists, insofar as "it's easier to get emotionally attached to robots" than to "a personal computer" since "the latter is still thought of as a machine, completely devoid of any life" (interview in CLAMP 2007d, p. 11). The hurdles faced by Hideki and Chi in the course of their tortuous romance obviously posed as many difficulties for the artists themselves, prompting them to raise the bar of what could be expected of a story about personalized machines without sinking into sheer absurdity.

As Shinta Tanbe argues, when it comes specifically to "tales of love between humans and dolls," the relationship appears to be "doomed from the start." The critic cites E. T. A. Hoffmann's "The Sandman" as a paradigmatic illustration of this trend. Ohkawa corroborates this contention with reference to her own personal experiences as a reader and spectator: having "been heavily influenced by *Astroboy*," she has personally tended to conceive of robots as fundamentally "tragic figures." Furthermore, the fact that love relationships between human and non-human entities have "always ended in tragedy" in the domain of "Japanese folklore" has "always bothered her" (interview in CLAMP 2007d, p. 11). Tanbe also notes that in the few instances where a happy ending is granted, as in the case of the tale of Pygmalion, this is often the outcome of divine intervention. The core of the problem seems to be a pervasive uneasiness about the status of artificial beings — such as dolls, robots, androids and computers — as entities devoid of feelings. This assumption, the critic explains, has even led some religious creeds to "ban the creation of dolls. It is well known that when Honda created the robot ASIMO, they asked the Pope for his moral opinion on creating a machine that resembles humans." In the manga version of *Chobits*, the contention that synthetic entities lack emotions is incontrovertibly asserted by the Persocom Freya. This is radically opposed by Hideki's claim that Chi's heart is real — so real, in fact, that he can feel it pulsating inside his own being. This response cannot be taken simply as corroboration of "the Freudian idea that love for dolls equals narcissism," which is based on the assumption that "when a man loves a doll, it is only infatuation and the glorification of the doll's existence on the part of the man." In fact, as long as feelings can be consciously perceived and acknowledged as such, they truly exist.

In this regard, CLAMP's perspective on the possibility of love between humans and nonhumans echoes Descartes' famous dictum "*cogito, ergo sum*": the conscious apprehension of feeling, like the awareness of thought, can be taken as evidence for existence. "There is a story," Tanbe concludes, "that claims that Descartes loved a doll that resembled his deceased daughter, Francine. Could this be only a coincidence? CLAMP's philosophy states that 'the love and feelings that one holds are true and real.' They are saying that despite the fact that machines may not have feelings, the actual emotion of love is still very real and cannot be denied" (in CLAMP 2007d, p. 10). *Chobits*' treatment of the romantic component does not pander to the customary penchant for tragic endings described by both Tanbe and Ohkawa. Yet, this aspect of the story should not be taken as symptomatic of a pervasively optimistic outlook. In fact, *Chobits* addresses quite uncompromisingly the doll figure's darker connotations by showing that its latter-day dolls are by no means the innocent toys which stereotypical Western perceptions of those creatures make them out to be. While the heroine herself is shown to be potentially dangerous, it is through the dramatization of Freya's experiences that *Chobits* brings the darker connotations of the doll figure into sharp focus. As anticipated, Chi's twin sister is indeed depicted as a receptacle of destructive emotions eventually conducive to heartbreak, insofar as the incompatibility of her erotic attraction toward her father and sense of filial duty toward her mother precipitates the hapless Persocom's descent into a state of cybernetic catatonia, and to a "death" tinged with figuratively suicidal drives.

Chobits' integration of poignant drama and intelligent humor, allied throughout to genuinely endearing character portraits, consistently ensures the story's unflagging appeal. In fact, the series' comedic dimension and its approach to characterization are intimately bound up insofar as the humor owes much to the characters' ability to carry the story as the often startling emergence of disparate facets of their personalities abet impeccable comedic timing. With the brief special *Chibits*, the franchise allows the main series' comic strand to gain full sway in an eruption of farcical humor centered on an underwear-related incident. A portmanteau combining the word *chibi* (small) and the main title *Chobits*, *Chibits* is a fitting designation for this zesty morsel of anime cuteness. Several viewers who feel drawn to the main anime primarily on account of its more serious subtexts might find *Chibits* downright unappealing or even accuse it of dwarfing the parent series' philosophical potential. However, its vivacious animation and utter unpretentiousness will feasibly strike many spectators as assets which appropriately complement the franchise's overall import.

In its treatment of the romantic dimension, *Chobits* echoes a variety of CLAMP productions in which love plays a conspicuous part. The wistful aura surrounding the protagonists' relationship often brings to mind the atmosphere immortalized by CLAMP with *Tsubasa: RESERVoir CHRoN-iCLE*, while the story's emphasis on the heroine's irreducible alterity occasionally recalls CLAMP's handling of the relationship between Shuichiro and Kohaku in *Wish*, a title addressed in the previous chapter. In situations which draw attention to Chi's role as something of a pupil, *Chobits* bears affinities to the manga *Suki*, released in 1999–2000, where CLAMP focuses on the romantic liaison developing between a school girl, Hinata Asahi, and her school teacher and neighbor, Shiro Asou, amid myriad twists and surprises. A predominantly warm tale characterized by soft lines atypical for CLAMP, *Suki* anticipates *Chobits* most explicitly in its deployment of narrative multilayering. In this instance, this technique revolves around the use of a storybook about teddy bears which serves both as an allegorical commentary on the relationship between Hinata and Shiro and as a means of elucidating particular plot developments. Finally, the variety of often conflicting emotions evoked by *Chobits* as the drama progresses, tangentially reaffirms the central message conveyed by CLAMP in the manga *The One I Love* (1993–1995). This consists of a series of twelve short love stories focusing on simple situations which virtually any woman could plausibly experience. Endowed with a slice-of-life feel which many readers would not automatically associate with CLAMP, this engaging collection is nonetheless permeated with a psychological acuity typical of its creators.

In its artistic engagement with various technologies of subjectivity, CLAMP is most concerned with those which are specifically geared toward the compartmentalization of individuals on the basis of particular abilities and functions. A pointedly thought-provoking interpretation of this ideological phenomenon is offered by the manga *Clover* (1997–2001), one of CLAMP's most ambitious and frankly experimental projects. What prevents this production from plummeting to the very depths of unrelieved tragedy is its ubiquitously lyrical tone. This is a quality which the animated adaptation released in 1999, though consisting merely of a seven-minute special, endeavors to accommodate with spellbinding grace. The original manga, of which the adaptation captures the most salient aspects in an allusively condensed fashion, focuses on the dark destiny befalling children endowed with psychic powers in a world set in an unspecified future. Rigorously trained at the behest of a council of mighty psychics known simply as "Wizards," the children are ranked as "One-Leaf," "Two-Leaf," "Three-Leaf" and "Four-Leaf Clover" according to the intensity of their capacities. The most competent Clovers are cut off from the rest of the world and categorically forbidden to enter any relationships with its inhabitants, which effectively condemns them to a fate of tragic loneliness. The manga focuses on the character of Su, the world's only full-fledged Clover, and the experiences she undergoes when a Wizard allows her to explore the outside world, sensitively highlighting the inextricability of the joys and sorrows to which Su's flight from her isolated existence inevitably exposes her. Indeed, even as she discovers the pleasures of companionship, language and song, thereby gradually coming to grasp the meaning of happiness, the Four-Leaf Clover must also continually negotiate the lethal dangers posed by those who unscrupulously seek to exploit her powers.

While the manga's speculative content is in itself engaging, what firmly abides in memory is *Clover*'s unique approach to storytelling, where conventional chronological strictures are defiantly eschewed in favor of narrative loops and chains of association. These formal elements, moreover, are consistently allied to a preference for graphic minimalism which manifests itself most strikingly in the reduction of text to the bare essentials, and in a subtly diversified juxtaposition of black and white portions of space as correlatives for the characters' feelings. As Tanbe points out, *Clover* captures the spirit of poetry at its most trenchant. Citing the distinguished poet Sakutarou Hagiwara, credited with creating the colloquial free verse, the critic reminds us that poetry has the "power to express ideas that cannot be expressed in the human language. Poetry is created with words that are more than just words." This proposition, argues Tanbe, is applicable to *Clover* to the extent that in this work, "emotions are expressed in their most raw form ... without simply relying on words." The manga's poetic qualities are not confined to its handling of verbal language, however, for they actually encompass the graphic dimension with no less palpable intensity. Thus, "the poetry of this work is apparent in a way that a piece of paper has become drenched in a character's feelings" (in CLAMP 2005b, p. 18).

Comprising the TV series *Mouryou no Hako* (2008) and the OVA *Mouryou no Hako: Hako no Yuurei no Koto*, the title addressed in this segment is one of the two major anime included in this study which have not issued from a CLAMP manga, the other production being *Code Geass*. Based on a novel by Natsuhiko Kyogoku, the animation nonetheless derives much of its distinctive flavor from CLAMP's original character designs. Moreover, given *Mouryou no Hako*'s generic affiliation with the traditions of the supernatural thriller and the suspense-driven psychodrama, it is hardly surprising that CLAMP should have felt drawn to its story. Indeed, the collective's members have explicitly professed their liking for those forms in the course of an interview addressing the genesis and development of the *xxxHOLic* franchise. Thus, in response to the question "do you all like occult things?" Ohkawa has stated: "I love them (laughs). To express that in movie titles, I like *Angel Heart, The Dead Zone, Omen*," while Tsubaki Nekoi has expressed a particular fondness for "Baku Yumemakura-sensei's *Yamigarishi* [*Darkness Hunter*] novel series," and Mokona has admitted to finding "Kamon-sensei's *Kaidan Tsure-zure Gusa* [*Idle Ghost Story* Essays] ... really scary" (interview in CLAMP 2008d, p. 5).

Mouryou no Hako stands out as a memorable instance of what the art of anime is capable of accomplishing when it turns its attention to the mature treatment of a complex textual construct by interweaving multi-faceted visual symbolism with an impactful storyline, subtle narrative and cinematographical layering, and an imaginative script. The technical genius for which its animation studio, Madhouse, is justly renowned all over the globe abets *Mouryou no Hako*'s dramatic vigor to great effect. It could hardly be denied that CLAMP's character designs contribute vitally to this achievement. On the whole, none of the characters is either accorded a substantial amount of screentime or accompanied by a detailed background. Yet, all of the actors — protagonists and supporting figures alike — exhibit such a wealth of subtle expressive details as to imprint themselves on the spectator's memory with almost tangible force. Concurrently, each persona bears a distinctive stage presence, and this renders the entire cast a pleasure to watch while yielding an ironical display of colorful somberness. The result of this felicitous combination of choice ingredients is a series which unfailingly challenges many of the generic conventions commonly associated with the interrelated traditions of mystery, detective and crime fiction. Nor is *Mouryou no Hako* reluctant to challenge the formal expectations harbored by the average anime audience, as demonstrated by its incorporation of exceptionally protracted dialogical sequences the likes of which one only encounters in Mamoru Oshii's anime at its most cerebral.

This aspect of the anime's formal constitution is best understood in the context of its handling (and eventual disruption) of the conventions inherent in the mystery narrative. As George Grella maintains, this type of story is sustained by a belief in a "benevolent and knowable universe" (Grella, p. 101). *Mouryou no Hako* destabilizes the mystery plot's mood of permanence and harmony by amalgamating it with an investigative adventure which, conversely, stands out as stubbornly unstable, jumbled, often unsystematic and at all times prey to the erratic rhythms of chance and contingency. In such a world, no degree of philosophizing — no matter how punctilious and methodical — is likely to be able to either foreclose or contain the onslaughts of violence and chaos. In this respect, the anime's penchant for indulging in extensive intellectual disquisitions could be interpreted as an ironical comment on the ultimate futility of rational calculation in the face of humanity's most brutal drives. At this level of its multilayered narrative, *Mouryou no Hako* echoes CLAMP's own *xxxHOLic* as described in the preceding chapter. Thus, in chronicling a series of cases triggered by multiple murders and related dismemberments, the anime insistently invites us to reexamine any preconceptions and received assumptions we may harbor regarding the proper treatment of the whodunit. On numerous occasions, we are encouraged to feel that even the private investigator hired by the mother of one of the victims, alongside the antique book seller and the other supporting characters who assist his efforts to unravel the murder spree, have to discover the rules of the game as they play along. In other words, these personae cannot rely on established criteria in pursuing their mission any more than the viewer can depend on existing generic conventions to make sense of the story. Moreover, *Mouryou no Hako* does not confine itself to unsettling accepted generic rules. Time and again, it actually endeavors to erect an alternate dramatic discourse of its own conception on the detritus left behind by its bold dismantling move, caring to process that material so as to transform it into something crisp and fresh instead of irreverently discarding it or presuming to consign it to oblivion out of sheer arrogance. In the process, the anime shows itself capable of breaking one taboo after another with methodical resolve, thus evoking the cumulative impression of a relentlessly advancing wave.

In order to negotiate the complexity of *Mouryou no Hako*'s multilayered narrative, with its multitude of puzzling flashbacks and cryptic allusions, scarce gratification is likely to be obtained from a clinical dissection of its enigmas. In fact, it is considerably more helpful to evaluate its connections, both explicit and covert, with the broader traditions of mystery, detective and crime fiction. G. J. Demko's observations are especially useful in offering a point of entry to this dauntingly extensive area of critical inquiry. "The mystery genre," argues Demko, "has been, and is, enormously popular in Japan.... Crime stories had a rather early start in Japan as evidenced by the publication of a collection of criminal cases by Saikaku Ihara in 1689." However, *Mouryou no Hako* does not merely attest to the popularity of the genre on home turf but is actually eager to emphasize the specifically Japanese components of its take on the mystery genre in both thematic and aesthetic terms. Hence, it bears witness to a long-standing indigenous preference for a specific type of yarn. This, as Demko explains, pivots on the relatively "old fashioned tendency to emphasize the puzzle-solving dimension of the genre. Given the absence of guns, murders are often rather messy and/or very imaginatively performed — methods may vary from axes to sound." The anime could be said to pander to the local appetite for puzzle-solving techniques in its deft juggling of riddles and explanations. For example, it is not unusual for the series to dwell on scenes which initially appear to bear no direct impact on the main action — and to have been introduced just for the sake of fleshing out the setting or steering the audience onto a side-track — and then unexpectedly disclose their actual relevance to the main plot. *Mouryou no Hako*'s preparedness to maximize the puzzle-solving dimension is further attested to by its carefully conceived bipartite structure. The first segment encompasses the initial six installments and is primarily devoted to the introduction of all of the key characters, as well as its main narrative devices. In this segment, the series' symbol-laden iconographic infrastructure is also thrown into relief, though its meaning remains as yet largely unclear. In the remaining eight episodes, the sinister tangles produced by the events dramatized in the preceding installments are gradually unraveled. This structural division impacts directly on the show's generic identity, insofar as the mystery-setting component often comes across as a peculiar synthesis of old-school investigative work (combined with a beginners' guide to Japan's folkloric mysticism), while the second serves a fundamentally explanatory role and dispenses almost totally with the spiritualist subtexts woven in the preceding episodes.

These revelatory strategies enable *Mouryou no Hako* to convey the impression that it is in full control of events at every turn, that it is never likely to lose sight of its aims, and that we may therefore rest assured that regardless of how many befuddling events we may have to witness, everything will come together in the end — the taste for meticulous puzzle-solving procedures will not, in other words, be left unsatisfied. Nonetheless, even as it fulfills one major expectation typical of indigenous aesthetics, *Mouryou no Hako* adventurously defies another — no less significant — cultural dominant: the proclivity to couch most mystery plots as "police procedurals," with an attendant "dearth of flashy and flamboyant private eyes" (Demko). Even though the anime does feature what could be loosely regarded as an investigation, it is far more interested in exploring the kaleidoscopic possibilities brought into prominence by the interplay of a metaphysical belief in the ultimate authority of the otherworldly and an empirical faith in the primacy of the mundane as these incessantly clash and collude by turns. Concomitantly, as adumbrated in this study's opening chapter, the series exhibits a sustained penchant for intermeshing classic elements characteristic of the mystery, detective and crime genres with motifs drawn from traditions which veer instead toward the supernatural and the occult.

According to Maurizio Ascari, in the early stages of its development, detective fiction aimed to supplant existing forms which capitalized on supernatural and irrational occurrences by recourse to "riddles and enigmas which respectably set the mind to work with crystal-clear lucidity. Death and crime ... were exorcised by the focus on the enquiry, an incontrovertible proof of the enlightened human potential for good" (Ascari, p. 1). *Mouryou no Hako* evinces a tongue-in-cheek attitude toward this critical position, deploying its intradiegetic detective as a reasonably clear-headed observer of events, and physically distancing him from the crime scene itself for a considerable part of the drama, as though to underline his transcendental omniscience. At the same time, however, the anime's dialectical structure insistently highlights the nature of its private eye's task as a strenuous battle bringing into play incompatible intentions and goals, and thus appearing to preempt the very possibility of a smooth resolution issuing from logical and even-tempered objectivity — in other words, the very qualities supposed to accompany the detective typology depicted by Ascari. None of *Mouryou no Hako*'s personae is portrayed as so impartial as to be capable of undertaking truly dispassionate detection.

At the same time, the anime's in-text detective can be said to orientate the audience's own experiences and interpretative efforts in much the same way as fiction authors can be expected to do, lending credence to Paul Auster's contention that detectives and authors carry out analogous tasks: "the detective is the one who looks, who listens, who moves through this morass of objects and events in search of the thought, the idea that will pull all of these things together and make sense of them. In effect, the writer and the detective are interchangeable. The reader sees the world through the detective's eyes, experiencing the proliferation of its details as if for the first time" (Auster, p. 15). Likewise pertinent, however, is the comparison of readers themselves to detectives — a hypothesis foreshadowed by Sherlock Holmes when he elliptically compares his task to that of Watson's audience by declaring: "for I hold in this hand several threads of one of the strangest cases which ever perplexed a man's brain, and yet lack the one or two which are needful to complete my theory" (Doyle, pp. 139–140).

The numerous cryptic messages sprinkled throughout *Mouryou no Hako*, with the image of the titular box in pride of place, form an intricate network of texts which provide the anime's structural mainstays. As Patricia Merivale and Susan Elizabeth Sweeney argue, "in many metaphysical detective stories, letters, words, and documents no longer reliably denote the objects that they are meant to represent; instead, these texts become impenetrable objects in their own right. Such a world, made up of such nameless, interchangeable 'things,' cries out for the ordered interpretation that it simultaneously declares to be impossible" (Merivale and Sweeney, pp. 9–10). It could indeed be suggested that in *Mouryou no Hako*, the web of hermetic texts constitutes a character of independent caliber. Invested with tangible presence, this dense ensemble of signs is tenaciously reluctant to yield to the conventional assumption that a text should operate as a visible path to an objective meaning. In the process, the anime prompts both its characters and its spectators to yearn all the more keenly for reparative answers in life no less than in fiction — even as it consistently intimates that such an outcome, though perhaps achievable within the margins of a fictional package, is starkly irreconcilable with the real world and its unpredictable rhythms. This state of affairs echoes the semiotic spectacle staged by Edgar Allan Poe in "The Purloined Letter," where the titular missive is seen to carry incomparable weight for all of the key characters without its subject matter ever being revealed — or unequivocally shown to exist at all for that matter. In wrenching meaning from content, both *Mouryou no Hako*'s esoteric references and Poe's letter invite us to reflect on the nature of the linguistic sign as an arbitrary entity which may acquire meaning without actually communicating anything or, alternately, may appear to convey momentous messages without actually hosting any authentic meaning. *Mouryou no Hako*, incidentally, also partakes of Poe's philosophy by suggesting that the best way to solve riddles may be to identify with the criminal's mentality and hence deduce his or her distinctive style, protocol and methods. The investigative technique advocated by Poe, and consistently reflected in his tales' structural attributes, pivots on the replication of one's adversaries' thought processes to turn their reasoning against them and hence trap them in nets of their own making.

No less importantly, *Mouryou no Hako* makes it patently evident that the excitement unleashed by the playful amalgamation of disparate narrative elements far exceeds in value the reward of orderly solutions. In this respect, the series bears affinities with CLAMP's consummately eclectic modus operandi. At the same time, the anime's syncretic tendencies would appear to substantiate Julian Symons' proposition concerning the essence of detective fiction: "the detective story pure and complex, the book that has no interest whatever except the solution of a puzzle, does not exist, and if it did exist would be unreadable" Symons provocatively maintains. "The truth is that the detective story, along with the police story, the spy story and the thriller ... makes up part of the hybrid creature we call sensational literature" (Symons, p. 15). *Mouryou no Hako* recalls sensational literature most blatantly in the scenes where the pervasively uncanny atmosphere surrounding its events verges on the melodramatic, while also incorporating elements of unmistakably Gothic provenance. In such scenes, the anime puts to maximum advantage the theatrical potentialities inherent in its supernatural substratum at the same time as it endeavors to expose the social roots of its grisly crimes, and thus highlight the omnipresence of perverse passions throughout its cultural fabric. As the investigation unfolds, the synthesis of discreet social commentary and sensational drama is incrementally enthroned as one of *Mouryou no Hako*'s governing aesthetic principles.

While the generic features outlined above indubitably play a key role in the shaping of the anime's individual identity as an adaptive, yet adventurous, work, more crucial still is its informing dramatic tenet. This ultimately coincides with the fundamental quest spirit: an ancestral narrative mechanism enshrined in human history for millennia on which mystery, detective and crime fiction capitalize even as they share it most liberally with other (both germane and quite separate) genres and media. In *Mouryou no Hako*, the quest drive also operates as a catalyst enabling the mutual interpenetration of the worlds of mystery and detective narrative as defined by Carl D. Malmgren. "Mystery fiction," the critic maintains, "presupposes a centered world; detective fiction, a decentered world. By 'centered' we mean a world which has a center, an anchor, a ground.... In mystery fiction, there is usually one significant scene of the crime (estate, village, railway car); the investigator examines this scene, trying to link its signs (clues) to their root causes. In detective fiction, the investigator invariably traverses a decentered world comprising a variety of physical spaces; he interviews clients, tails suspects, stakes out residences, and so on" (Malmgren, p. 13). Malmgren is evidently deploying the notion of mystery fiction as the equivalent of what Ascari terms detective fiction in order to designate a reliable and intelligible reality, using the idea of detective fiction itself to describe the opposing impulse for destabilization. This divergence at the level of terminology succinctly points to a general lack of agreement among critics and authors regarding the precise makeup of mystery, detective and crime fiction as categorizable entities. In one available perspective, crime fiction can be regarded as the broad genre of which detective fiction, the whodunit, the thriller, hardboiled fiction and courtroom drama (among others) constitute the subgeneric progeny. Mystery fiction, in this context, is often viewed as the branch of detective fiction in which a private eye investigates a crime and, ideally at least, solves it. This kind of narrative is supposed to lay emphasis on the puzzle element with partial or total disregard for specific social and historical circumstances, whereas the hardboiled typology evinces a proclivity for action and an unsentimentally realistic take on its cultural milieu. It is, however, also possible to address mystery, detective and crime fiction as relatively independent genres which may marginally overlap but still preserve autonomous definers. This liberal outlook seems not merely apposite but practically inevitable when one is faced with a hybrid construct like *Mouryou no Hako*. It is indeed hard to imagine how one could even begin to do justice to the anime's prismatic orchestration without devoting equal and impartial attention to as many of its generic sources as humanly possible.

As intimated in Chapter 1, an important aspect of *Mouryou no Hako*'s diegesis lies with its persistent allusions to the ubiquity of human depravity. Dennis Porter's assessment of the "hardboiled detective novel" indirectly provides a fitting depiction of the anime's world view, in this respect. Like that form, *Mouryou no Hako* is indeed sustained by "the metaphor of the spreading stain" insofar as the "initial crime often turns out to be a relatively superficial symptom of an evil whose magnitude and ubiquity are only progressively disclosed during the course of the investigation" (Porter, p. 40). As Malmgren points out, "the contagion of crime eventually affects most of the characters, including the detective. Indeed, at times the detective is the catalyst who precipitates the violent chain of events" (Malmgren,

p. 73). *Mouryou no Hako* exposes an analogous state of affairs not solely by throwing into the relief its society's embroilment with a perturbing diffusion of criminal — or, at any rate, rampantly unethical — practices. In fact, it also deploys the structural principle of multiperspectival repetition in order to suggest that any one nefarious act holds self-reproductive powers which enable it to resurface time and again with dexterous variations. The action intimates that even legitimate investigators, in this dystopian world, might eventually turn out to be implicated in the criminal actions which they apparently strive to stem, and to be finally responsible for triggering or precipitating several of the action's more brutal and perplexing convolutions.

In engaging simultaneously with the centered and decentered worlds typical of the mystery story and the detective story respectively, *Mouryou no Hako* ventures into the province of the crime story as described by Malmgren: i.e., an "oppositional discourse" capable of locating itself "in either the centered world of mystery fiction or the decentered world of detective fiction" and hence pitting itself "in opposition to either mystery or detective fiction" (p. 137). Bound neither by the obligation to make its clues adhere to a rationally calculated agenda nor by an undilutedly transgressive urge to delete all traces of meaning from its signs, *Mouryou no Hako* experiments with a rich gallery of prismatic identities, gliding effortlessly from one to the other with the same glee with which many of CLAMP's own characters keep migrating from world to world. In this regard, even though the anime adopts a prevalently deliberate tempo and sedate atmosphere, its underlying spirit often exudes the same mood of buoyant polymorphousness one senses in CLAMP's own works. Concomitantly, the anime harks back to William V. Spanos' portrayal of the "anti-detective story" as a narrative that endeavors to "evoke the impulse to 'detect' ... in order to violently frustrate it by refusing to solve the crime" (Spanos, p. 154). In this context, any belief in foundational principles meant to foster human interaction and to consolidate the sign systems in which this is embedded is bound to be drastically upset if not exploded altogether. A character's aberrant conduct cannot be dismissed in either a sympathetic or a patronizing fashion as a passing anomaly in an otherwise coherent personality. In fact, it functions as a metonymic indicator of the consummately unstable, fragmentary and ultimately indecipherable nature of the story itself and of its intrinsic zeitgeist.

This composite world view, wherein the mythical and the actual relentlessly intermesh, draws the story into collusion with the realm of what Merivale and Sweeney have described as "metaphysical detective fiction"—namely, a construct eager to raise "profound questions" about "narrative, interpretation, subjectivity, the nature of reality, and the limits of knowledge" (Merivale and Sweeney, pp. 9–10). *Mouryou no Hako* embraces an interrogative venture of this stamp by foregrounding the notion that the product of detection is not so much the unraveling of the crime or series of crimes as a confrontation of the unspeakable mysteries enfolding human nature and human comprehension. Therefore, if readers — or viewers — are also investigators, as proposed earlier in the discussion, it is also the case that they, too, must confront the instability of their personal identities and the fallibility of their knowledge as important parts of the fictive weave. We are thus prompted to wonder what, if anything, we could ever presume to know, how we could unproblematically trust the reality of what we think we know, and how we could supply any conclusive evidence that such wisdom consists of anything more solid and universal than a partial, and therefore inherently arbitrary, ideation of the real.

The *Code Geass* franchise comprises two TV series, *Code Geass: Lelouch of the Rebellion* (2006–2007) and *Code Geass: Lelouch of the Rebellion R2* (2008). As anticipated, this is one of the only two main series examined in this study not to have originated in a CLAMP manga, the other title being *Mouryou no Hako*. In this instance, as in the case of *Mouryou no Hako* itself, the CLAMP artists have operated in the capacity of original character designers, and there can be little doubt that it is largely from their nimble pencils and brushes that *Code Geass* derives its unique atmosphere. This is not to belittle even for a second the part played by Sunrise, the studio responsible for the show's animation, which has actually worked wonders in its own area of expertise, *mecha* design, and in the infusion of the numerous action sequences which pepper the drama with often matchless dynamic elegance. Moreover, the talent of animation character designer Takahiro Kimura contributes crucially to the overall effectiveness of *Code Geass*' cast. His distinctive style announces itself most vibrantly in the actors' stylized movements and in the terse lines of their uncommonly expressive facial features. When necessary, Kimura does not hesitate to imprint the actors' faces with overwrought and anguished expressions which many viewers accustomed only with the cute side of anime would consider unequivocally horrid. The sheer sense of fluidity at the core of

Kimura's animation techniques is intrinsically energizing. It would be hard to refute that *Code Geass* owes its visual energy — an attribute which courses its entire fabric to vitalize even the quietest of moments — to the character designs issuing from CLAMP's and Kimura's joint efforts. CLAMP's designs, specifically, exhibit a distinctively angular and whipcord look, abetted by stylish costumes of alternately martial and baroque flavor. These combine and clash by turns with the anime's pervasive color schemes, where intense contrasts are repeatedly utilized as symbolic means of conveying its society's stark polarization. It is from the character designs, accordingly, that the series' alternate universe comes fully to life. The same can be said of the technologies of subjectivity which sustain the iniquitous ideologies at the basis of *Code Geass*' society, as described in Chapter 1. The characters' stylized silhouettes and gestures — equally critical to CLAMP's initial drawings and Kimura's dynamic ruses — induce us to distance ourselves from the action enough to ponder the conceptual significance of those personae's actions in the context of a specific social formation. In so doing, they concurrently facilitate our appreciation of the anime's engagement with political satire. This pivots on its dispassionate exposure of the strategies through which the government manipulates its citizens' identities by invading each minute facet of their daily lives, relying by turns on explicitly harsh disciplinary practices and secretive forms of media-dominated ideological brainwashing which finally prove no less successful.

The visuals' energy secures the maintenance of a cumulatively engaging tempo even though the anime's pace occasionally slackens to levels which some viewers might deem undesirable — especially in the case of single-installment tangents intended almost exclusively as character-building gestures. Yet, these decelerating digressions do not gravely impair the action since, as Carl Kimlinger observes, "the plot ... is propelled at such a speed that neither its derivation nor its jarring shifts in tone have much time to rankle." This distinctive mood is evident right from the start: "the massacre that rages over the first two episodes sets the tone, never allowing the tension to flag, even as it prioritizes careful strategy over godlike piloting" (Kimlinger 2008). Therefore, even when it indulges in marginal incidents geared toward the consolidation of its actors' personalities, *Code Geass* always appears to be eagerly anticipating its protagonist's next move. No sooner has the show's appetite for action been given full rein than the screen erupts in spectacular set pieces punctuated by flamboyantly melodramatic tropes in both the visual and the verbal arenas.

At the same time, character design lends both dramatic weight and formal cogency to the series' revelations about the tale of political strife which surrounds the world's subjection to the Holy Empire of Britannia and Japan's attendant descent into a state of brutal repression. These are the premises of Lelouch Lamperouge's rise to the status of a terrorist leader, assumption of an alternate identity under the pseudonym of "Zero," and deployment of the power of "Geass" to overthrow the oppressors. In assessing the overall impact of character design on *Code Geass*' development, its hero deserves particular attention. It would be absurd to claim that Lelouch (or Zero as the case may be) is an unproblematically amiable character, and is therefore likely to meet with unanimous approval among diverse anime audiences. However, many viewers would concede that his multifacetedness renders him engaging even for those who might not find his attitude and modus operandi especially attractive. As the account of first season offered by *The Nihon Review* points out, Lelouch "exudes a sense of authority while holding a hidden contempt for authority and has a brilliant mind to boot.... What sets Lelouch apart from the dozen other super geniuses is his frank, down to earth nature. He may be willing to toy with human lives like mindless chess pieces, but when it comes to his friends and family, he unwittingly shows a more vulnerable side that is distinctly human. Practically all of Lelouch's tactical mistakes throughout the series come from dealing with his loved ones. Like most people, he is unable to coldly rationalize and sacrifice those that truly matter to him" ("*Code Geass: Lelouch of the Rebellion*"). Relatedly, even though Lelouch sometimes comes across as undilutedly self-absorbed and hubristic, these unpalatable aspects of his makeup are tempered by reminders that he is also vulnerable and torn — and, most importantly, that he is painfully conscious of the disabling effects of his weaknesses and inner conflicts.

Lelouch contributes vitally to *Code Geass*' evocation of its first season's defining rhythm. The momentum thus established is maintained with the transition to the second season, as the protagonist's crusade to wreak revenge on his father and bring about a better world develops amid countless twists and surprises. In fact, *Code Geass: Lelouch of the Rebellion R2* goes even further than its predecessor in exploiting to maximum effect the series' passion for suspenseful and unpredictable action, by ensuring that virtually every installment climaxes with a cliffhanger. At the same time, it enhances the dynamic impact of most sequences, and not only the overtly theatrical confrontation sequences in which the *mecha* component is accorded pride of place. The kinetic component intensifies with each battle, delivering increasingly ample martial scenarios as the hero's histrionics proportionately escalate to Armageddon-ish extremes. The danger, according to Kimlinger, lies with the action's plausible degeneration to the level of "bloodthirsty sensationalism, preposterous grandstanding and pure excess," especially in the latter part of the show. The collateral hazard carried by these theatrical flourishes is the descent into "absurdity and unintentional humor." Nevertheless, the critic is eager to stress that "even at its most hysterical, and no matter how arduously it courts it, you can't honestly call the series camp" (Kimlinger 2009). It is largely through its character designs that *Code Geass* retains its overall stylishness right to the end of the second season, where CLAMP's art once again reveals its uniqueness through memorable graphic presences.

Homage to CLAMP (iv)
From "Talk About Clamp: Interview."
In *CLAMP no Kiseki Vol. 10*:

Every one of their works surpasses the standard line of entertainment. First, I think that's what it is to be a pro. It's not just absurdity, nor is it acting out to get attention: they always take the royal road.... More than anything, they are people who absolutely will not do a job that they won't enjoy. I think that's a good thing. Because if they're not having fun themselves, they can't make it fun for the readers. The one thing I can say without a doubt is that all four of them love manga. Normally, if someone does something for fifteen years, they start to dislike it a little.... They must have had something steadfast, something unchanging since even before they debuted. —Takashi Iida (2008)

Filmography

Primary Titles

Angelic Layer (2001)

Original Title: *Angelic Layer*. **Status:** TV Series (26 episodes). **Episode Length:** 24 minutes. **Director:** Hiroshi Nishikiori. **Series Composition:** Ichiro Okouchi. **Music:** Kouhei Tanaka. **Original Manga:** CLAMP. **Character Design:** Takahiro Komori. **Art Directors:** Nobuto Sakamoto, Takashi Hiruma. **Animation Directos:** Chizuko Kusakabe, Hiroki Kanno, Hiroshi Osaka, Hisashi Kagawa, Kenichi Imaizumi, Koichi Horikawa, Masaki Hyuga, Naoko Nakamoto, Naomi Miyata, Shigeyuki Suga, Takahiro Komori, Yuka Kudo. **Mecha Designer:** Junya Ishigaki. **Director of Photography:** Atsushi Takeyama, Haruhide Ishiguro, Shuichi Heishi. **Executive Producers:** Fukashi Azuma, Takeshi Yasuda, Tetsuya Watanabe. **Producers:** Masahiko Minami, Shinsaku Hatta, Taihei Yamanishi. **Color Coordination:** Sayoko Yokoyama. **Composite:** Seiji Ishikuro (Gonzo). **Design Coordinator:** Shigeru Morita (Studio Nue). **Editing:** Kengo Shigemura (Gonzo Digimation). **Series Supervision:** Shinichiro Inoue. **Sound Effect Director:** Yota Tsuruoka. **Sound Effects:** Eiko Morikawa. **Sound Manager:** Yoshimi Sugiyama. **Animation:** BONES. **Backgrounds:** BIC Studio, Team's Art. **Production:** BONES, Dentsu Inc., TV Tokyo. **Production Cooperation:** A.C.G.T., Artland. **Recording Studio:** Studio Gong. **Sound Production:** Rakuonsha.

Cardcaptor Sakura (1998–2000)

Original Title: *Cardcaptor Sakura*. **Status:** TV Series (70 episodes). **Episode Length:** 30 minutes. **Director:** Morio Asaka. **Series Composition:** Nanase Ohkawa. **Script:** Hiroshi Ishii, Jiro Kaneko, Nanase Ohkawa, Tomoko Ogawa, Tomoyasu Okubo. **Music:** Takayuki Negishi. **Original Story:** CLAMP. **Character Design:** Kumiko Takahashi. **Art Director:** Katsufumi Hariu. **Supervising Director:** Morio Asaka. **Director of Photography:** Hisao Shirai. **Executive Producers:** Akira Watanabe (NEP21), Yasuko Uchizawa (NHK). **Producer:** Eizo Kondo. **Color Key:** Madoka Katsunuma. **Costume and Card Designer:** Apapa Mokona. **Editing:** Harutoshi Ogata. **Sound Effects:** Shizuo Kurahashi. **Animation:** Madhouse Studios.

Cardcaptor Sakura: The Movie (1999)

Original Title: *Gekijouban Cardcaptor Sakura*. **Status:** movie. **Length:** 79 minutes. **Director:** Morio Asaka. **Script:** Nanase Ohkawa. **Music:** Takayuki Negishi. **Original Story:** CLAMP. **Character Designer:** Kumiko Takahashi. **Art Director:** Katsufumi Hariu. **Animation Directors:** Hitoshi Ueda, Kumiko Takahashi, Kunihiko Sakurai. **Sound Director:** Masafumi Mima. **Executive Producers:** Masao Maruyama, Shigeru Watanabe, Tetsusyoku Ohkawa. **Producers:** Kazuhiko Ikeguchi, Tatsuya Ono. **Chief Animators:** Hitoshi Ueda, Kumiko Takahashi, Kunihiko Sakurai, Masaru Kitao. **Color Designer:** Madoka Katsunuma. **Color Timing:** Yuriko Kadomoto. **Costume Designer:** CLAMP. **Animation Production:** Madhouse Studios.

Cardcaptor Sakura Movie 2: The Sealed Card (2000)

Original Title: *Gekijouban Cardcaptor Sakura: The Sealed Card*. **Status:** movie. **Length:** 79 minutes. **Director:** Morio Asaka. **Screenplay:** Nanase Ohkawa. **Music:** Takayuki Negishi. **Original Creator:** CLAMP. **Art Director:** Yuji Ikeda. **Chief Animation Director:** Hisashi Abe. **Animation Directors:** Hiroyuki Horiuchi, Hiroyuki Kasugai, Katsunori Kimizuka, Kunihiko Hamada, Kunihiko Sakurai, Mariko Fujita, Masaru Kitao, Satoshi Tasaki. **Sound Director:** Masafumi Mima. **Executive Producers:** Naoki Gokida, Shigeru Watanabe, Syuji Miyajima, Yasuki Iwase. **Producers:** Kazuhiko Ikeguchi, Kouichi Tsurunari, Shinji Komori, Tatsuya Ono, Tsuyoshi Yoshida. **Color Designer:** Madoka Katsunuma. **Color Key:** Harue Ono. **Conceptual Work Producer:** Akane Inoue. **Costume Designer:** CLAMP. **Editing:** Harutoshi Ogata, Kayoko Kimura, Satoshi Terauchi, Yukiko Itou, Yurika Tsuchiya. **Sound Effects:** Shizuo Kurahashi (Sound Box). **Sound Production:** Tomoko Nakajima. **Special Effects:** Kumiko Taniguchi, Sachi, Takashi Maekawa, Toyohiko Sakakibara. **Animation Production:** Madhouse Studios.

Chobits (2002)

Original Title: *Chobits*. **Status:** TV Series (26 episodes). **Episode Length:** 26 minutes. **Director:** Morio Asaka. **Script:** Akiko Horii, Genjiro Kaneko, Jukki Hanada, Nanase Ohkawa, Sumio Uetake, Tomoyasu Okubo, Tsuyoshi Tamai. **Music:** Dan Miyakawa (Strings Arrangement), Katsutoshi Kitagawa (lyrics), Keitaro Takanami. **Original Creator:** CLAMP. **Character Designer:** Hisashi Abe. **Art Director:** Chikako Shibata. **Chief Animation Director:** Hisashi Abe. **Sound Director:** Masafumi Mima. **Directors of Photography:** Katsuyoshi Kishi, Takeshi Katsurayama. **Producers:** Tatsuya Ono, Tetsuo Gensho, Yuichi Sekido. **Animation:** Madhouse Studios.

Chobits (2003)

Original Title: *Chobits*. **Status:** OVA (1 episode). **Episode Length:** 24 minutes. **Director:** Morio Asaka. **Script:** Genjiro Kaneko, Nanase Ohkawa, Tomoyasu Okubo. **Music:** Keitaro Takanami. **Original Creator:** CLAMP. **Character Designer:** Hisashi Abe. **Art Director:** Chikako Shibata. **Chief Animation Director:** Hisashi Abe. **Sound Director:** Masafumi Mima. **Directors of Photography:** Katsuyoshi Kishi, Tsuyoshi Kuzumoto. **Producers:** Tatsuya Ono, Tetsuo Gensho, Yuichi Sekido. **Animation:** Madhouse Studios.

CLAMP School Detectives (1997)

Original Title: *CLAMP Gakuen Tanteidan*. **Status:** TV Series (26 episodes). **Episode Length:** 30 minutes. **Director:** Osamu Nabeshima. **Series Composition:** Masaharu Amiya, Mayori Sekijima. **Music:** Mikiya Katakura. **Original Creator:** CLAMP. **Character Design:** Hiroto Tanaka. **Art Director:** Yuji Ikeda. **Animation Directors:** Hideyuki Motohashi, Hiroki Kanno, Hirotaka Kinoshita, Katsuyuki Kubo, Keiichi Ishikura, Masao Nakata, Tetsuya Yanagisawa, Yuichi Endo, Yukio Takahashi. **Sound Director:** Fusanobu Fujiyama. **Director of Photography:** Masahide Okino. **Production:** Bandai Visual, Studio Pierrot, TV Tokyo.

Code Geass: Lelouch of the Rebellion (2006-2007)

Original Title: *Code Geass: Hangyaku no Lelouc*. **Status:** TV Series (25 episodes). **Episode Length:** 24 minutes. **Director:** Goro Taniguchi. **Series Composition:** Hiroyuki Yoshino, Ichiro Okouchi. **Screenplay:** Hiroyuki Yoshino, Ichiro Okouchi, Yuuichi Nomura. **Music:** Hitomi Kuroishi, Kotaro Nakagawa. **Original Story:** Goro Taniguchi, Ichiro Okouchi. **Original Character Designer:** CLAMP. **Character Designer:** Takahiro Kimura. **Art Director:** Yoshinori Hishinuma. **Chief Animation Directors:** Eiji Nakata, Seiichi Nakatani, Takahiro Kimura, Yuriko Chiba. **Mecha Designers:** Akira Yasuda, Eiji Nakata, Junichi Akutsu, Kenji Teraoka. **3D Director:** Tetsuya Watanabe. **Sound Director:** Motoi Izawa, Yasuo Uragami. **CGI Director:** Masato Miyoshi. **Director of Photography:** Souta Ooya. **Producer:** Atsushi Yukawa, Hiroshi Morotomi, Takao Minegishi, Yoshitaka Kawaguchi. **2D Effects Chief:** Hiroshi Furuhashi. **2DCG Director:** Masato Miyoshi. **2DCG Effects:** Makoto Takakura, Mitsumasa Shimizu, Natsuki Nishigai. **3D CG:** Fumikazu Sato. **Chief Animators:** Eiji Nakata, Seiichi Nakatani, Takahiro Kimura, Yuriko Chiba. **Color Designers:** Reiko Iwasawa, Taeko Kumagai. **Editing:** Seiji Morita, Shika Ogura. **Sound Effects:** Masahiro Shoji (Fizz Sound Creation). **Special Effects:** Yutaka Hoshiba. **Animation Production:** Sunrise.

Code Geass: Lelouch of the Rebellion R2 (TV, 2008)

Original Title: *Code Geass: Hangyaku no Lelouc 2*. **Status:** TV Series (25 episodes). **Episode Length:** 30 minutes. **Director:** Goro Taniguchi **Series Composition:** Hiroyuki Yoshino, Ichiro Okouchi. **Script:** Ichiro Okouchi. **Original Story:** Goro Taniguchi, Ichiro Okouchi. **Original Character Designer:** CLAMP. **Character Designer:** Takahiro Kimura. **Art Director:** Yoshinori Hishinuma. **Chief Animation Directors:** Atsushi Itagaki, Daisuke Mataga, Eiji Nakata, Seiichi Nakatani, Takahiro Kimura, Takashi Habe, Yukie Sako, Yuriko Chiba. **Mechanical Designers:** Akira Yasuda (Knightmare), Eiji Nakata (Knightmare), Junichi Akutsu (Knightmare), Kenji Teraoka, Takumi Sakura. **Art Designers:** Takashi Miyamoto, Yoshinori Hishinuma. **3D Director:** Tetsuya Watanabe. **Sound Directors:** Motoi Izawa, Yasuo Uragami. **2DCG Director:** Masato Miyoshi. **2DCG Effects:** Makoto Takakura, Masaharu Okazaki, Mitsumasa Shimizu, Natsuki Nishigai. **3D Animation:** Hironao Ekoshi, Kouji Andou, Minoru Masunari. **3DCG Management:** Yuu Kikiji. **Editing:** Seiji Morita. **Mecha Animation Directors:** Eiji Nakata, Morifumi Naka, Seiichi Nakatani, Tomohiro Kawahara. **Sound Effects:** Masahiro Shoji (Fizz Sound Creation). **Special Effects:** Yoshimi Nomura. **Animation Production:** Sunrise.

Kobato (TV, 2009)

Original Title: *Kobato*. **Status**: TV Series (24 episodes). **Episode Length**: 24 minutes. **Director**: Mitsuyuki Masuhara. **Series Composition**: Michiko Yokote, Nanase Ohkawa. **Music**: Takeshi Hama. **Original Creator**: CLAMP. **Character Designer**: Hiromi Kato. **Art Director**: Hideyuki Ueno. **Chief Animation Director**: Hisashi Abe, Satoshi Tasaki. **3D Director**: Shuhei Yabuta. **Sound Directors**: Masafumi Mima, Toshihiko Nakajima. **Producers**: Akiko Nakano, Eriko Aoki, Jun Kobayashi, Tsuneo Takechi, Yuji Shibata, Yuka Harada, Yukiko Ninokata. **Color Designer**: Harue Ono. **Editing**: Kashiko Kimura, Mariko Tsukatsune, Yumi Jinguji. **Special Effects**: Ayumi Arahata, Kaori Kobayashi, Kumiko Taniguchi. **Animation Production**: Madhouse Studios.

Magic Knight Rayearth (1994–1995)

Original Title: *Mahou Kishi Reiaasu*. **Status**: TV Series (20 episodes). **Episode Length**: 25 minutes. **Chief Director**: Toshihiro Hirano. **Director**: Masami Obari (OP). **Series Composition**: Keiko Maruo. **Scenario**: Keiko Maruo, Nanase Ohkawa, Osamu Nakamura. **Script**: Keiko Maruo (supervisor), Nanase Ohkawa (supervisor), Osamu Nakamura. **Music**: Hayato Matsuo. **Original Creator**: CLAMP. **Character Designer**: Atsuko Ishida. **Art Director**: Tsutomu Ishigaki. **Animation Directors**: Akira Takeuchi, Atsuko Ishida, Hideyuki Motohashi, Hiroaki Nakajima, Hiroshi Kubo, Keiji Gotoh, Madoka Hirayama, Takashi Kobayashi, Takehiro Nakayama. **Mecha Designer**: Masahiro Yamane. **Sound Director**: Yasuo Uragami. **Director of Photography**: Takashi Nomura. **Producers**: Masahito Yoshioka, Michihiko Suwa, Shigeki Nakamura. **Monster Designer**: Masahiro Yamane. **Music Production**: Yuuki Horio. **Sound Effects**: Junichi Sasaki. **Special Effects**: Kou Yamamoto, Takashi Maekawa, Yoshimi Hayashi. **Animation**: Anime World Osaka, Hadashi Pro, IMAGIN, M I, Mizo Planning, Nakamura Production, Soul Kids, Studio Boomerang, Studio Egg, Studio Jungle Gym, Studio March, Studio Wanpack, Tokyo Animation Center. **Animation Production**: TMS Entertainment.

Magic Knight Rayearth 2 (1995)

Original Title: *Mahou Kishi Reiaasu 2*. **Status**: TV Series (29 episodes). **Episode Length**: 30 minutes. **Director**: Toshihiro Hirano. **Series Composition**: Nanase Ohkawa. **Scenario**: Nanase Ohkawa. **Music**: Hayato Matsuo. **Original creator**: CLAMP. **Character Designer**: Atsuko Ishida. **Art Director**: Tsutomu Ishigaki. **Animation Directors**: Akio Kawamura, Atsuko Ishida, Fuminori Kizaki, Junko Abe, Keiji Gotoh, Kumi Sakai, Madoka Hirayama, Masahiro Yamane, Megumi Kadonosono, Satoshi Ishino, Shinobu Nishioka, Takehiro Nakayama, Tokiko Watanabe. **Sound Director**: Yasuo Uragami. **Director of Photography**: Takashi Nomura. **Producers**: Masahito Yoshioka, Michihiko Suwa, Shigeki Nakamura. **CG**: Hiroshi Ohno, Junichi Nakagawa. **Color Designer**: Chiyoko Shimizu, Kaeko Matsuo, Reiko Hirayama, Sanae Kimura, Yuko Nishikawa. **Sound Effects**: Junichi Sasaki. **Special Effects**: Kou Yamamoto, Takashi Maekawa, Yoshimi Hayashi. **Animation**: Anime World Osaka, Hadashi Pro, IMAGIN, M I, Mizo Planning, Nakamura Production, Soul Kids, Studio Boomerang, Studio Egg, Studio Jungle Gym, Studio March, Studio Wanpack, Tokyo Animation Center. **Animation Production**: TMS Entertainment

Mouryou no Hako (2008)

Original Title: *Mouryou no Hako*. **Status:** TV Series (13 episodes). **Episode Length:** 23 minutes. **Director:** Ryosuke Nakamura. **Series Composition:** Sadayuki Murai. **Screenplay:** Sadayuki Murai. **Music:** Shusei Murai. **Original Creator:** Natsuhiko Kyogoku. **Original Character Designer:** CLAMP. **Character Designer:** Asako Nishida. **Art Director:** Hidetoshi Kaneko. **Animation Directors:** Chie Nishizawa, Kunihiko Hamada. **Sound Director:** Yasunori Honda. **Director of Photography:** Shinichi Igarashi. **CG Production:** Shunsuke Fukui. **Color Setting:** Harue Ono. **Editing:** Naoki Kawanishi, Satoshi Terauchi. **Animation Production:** Madhouse Studios. **Production:** D.N. Dream Partners, Madhouse Studios, NTV, VAP.

Mouryou no Hako: Hako no Yuurei no Koto (2009)

Original Title: *Mouryou no Hako: Hako no Yuurei no Koto*. **Status:** OVA (1 episode). **Episode Length:** 16 minutes. **Original creator:** Natsuhiko Kyogoku. **Animation Production:** Madhouse Studios.

Rayearth (1997)

Original Title: *Seiden RG Veda*. **Status:** OVA Series (3 episodes). **Episode Length:** 45 minutes. **Directors:** Keitaro Motonaga, Toshiki Hirano. **Script:** Manabu Nakamura. **Music:** Toshihiko Sahashi. **Original Creator:** CLAMP. **Original Character Designer:** Apapa Mokona. **Character Designer:** Megumi Kadonosono. **Mecha Designer:** Naoyuki Konno. **Sound Directors:** Katsuyoshi Kobayashi, Yasuo Uragami. **Executive Producers:** Akio Izumikawa, Shunzo Kato, Yasuo Katsuki. **Producers:** Fumie Yamauchi (Polygram), Ken Tsunoda (Kodansha), Shozo Yoshioka (Tokyo Movie), Tetsu Kojima (Tokyo Movie). **Art Supervision:** Hiroshi Kato. **Beasts Designer:** Keiji Gotoh. **Editing:** Hajime Okayasu. **Sound Effects:** Junichi Sasaki. **Animation Production:** TMS Entertainment. **Production:** Kodansha, Polygram Japan, TMS-Kyokuchi.

RG Veda (1991–1992)

Original Title: *Seiden RG Veda*. **Status:** OVA Series (2 episodes). **Episode Length:** 45 minutes. **Directors:** Hiroyuki Ebata, Takamasa Ikegami. **Script:** Nanase Ohkawa. **Music:** Nick Wood. **Original Manga:** CLAMP. **Animation:** Tetsuro Aoki. **Designers:** Apapa Mokona, Futoshi Fujikawa, Kiichi Takaoka, Tetsuro Aoki. **Production:** ANIMATE.

Tokyo Babylon (1992)

Original Title: *Seiden RG Veda*. **Status:** OVA (1 episode). **Episode Length:** 50 minutes. **Director:** Koichi Chigira. **Script:** Yoshihiko Urahata. **Music:** Toshiyuki Honda. **Original Creator:** CLAMP. **Character Designer:** Kumiko Takahashi. **Art Director:** Masuji Ikeda. **Art:** Mamoru Kurozawa, Nobuhiro Seikino, Yuriko Ikebara. **Director of Photography:** Hitoshi Yamaguchi. **Executive Producers:** Megumi Sugiyama, Yutaka Takahashi. **Producers:** Kasuhiko Ikeguchi, Yumiko Mashushima. **Editing:** Yukiko Itou. **Animation:** Madhouse Studios.

Tokyo Babylon 2 (1994)

Original Title: *Seiden RG Veda*. **Status:** OVA (1 episode). **Episode Length:** 55 minutes. **Director:** Koichi Chigira. **Music:** Machihisa Honda. **Original Creator:**

CLAMP. **Character Design:** Kumiko Takahashi. **Art Director:** Masuji Ikeda. **Sound Director:** Noriyoshi Matsuura. **Director of Photography:** Hitoshi Yamaguchi. **Executive Producers:** Satoshi Sugiyama, Yutaka Takahashi. **Producer:** Kasuhiko Ikeguchi, Yumiko Masushima. **Editing:** Harutoshi Ogata, Satoshi Terauchi. **Animation:** Madhouse Studios.

Tsubasa: RESERVoir CHRoNiCLE (2005–2006)

Original Title: *Tsubasa Kuronikuru*. **Status:** TV Series (52 episodes). **Episode Length:** 25 minutes. **Directors:** Koichi Mashimo (first season: 2005); Koichi Mashimo and Hiroshi Morioka (second season: 2006). **Original Creator:** CLAMP. **Screenplay:** Hiroyuki Kawasaki. **Storyboard:** Hiroshi Morioka, Koichi Mashimo, Koji Sawai, Masaya Kawa, Tomoyuki Kurokawa. **Music:** Yuki Kajiura. **General Producers:** Shinichi Tominaga, Sou Ichita. **Art Director:** Shin Watanabe. **Animation Directors:** Kaori Higuchi, Minako Shiba, Takao Takegami, Tomoaki Kado, Yoshimitsu Yamashita, Yukiko Ban. **Character Designer:** Minako Shiba. **Director of Photography:** Katsuaki Kamata. **Sound Effects:** Sho Urahata. **Color Designer:** Makiko Kojima. **Animation Production:** Bee Train.

Tsubasa: RESERVoir CHRoNiCLE The Movie: Princess of the Birdcage Kingdom (2005)

Original Title: *Tsubasa Kuronikuru—Torikago no Kuni no Himegimi*. **Status:** movie. **Length:** 35 minutes. **Director:** Itsuro Kawasaki. **Scenario:** Jun'ichi Fujisaku, Midori Gotou. **Original Creator:** CLAMP. **Music:** Yuki Kajiura. **Producers:** Fumiaki Furuya, Ichiro Seki, Masaki Yasuda, Mitsuhisa Ishikawa, Nobuyo Ogawa, Yuuji Shimamoto. **Animation Directors:** Kyoji Asano, Yoko Kikuchi. **3D Animation:** Kazuya Sugiyama, Yuta Seo. **Character Designer:** Yoko Kikuchi. **Director of Photography:** Miki Sakuma. **Sound Director:** Kazuhiro Iwabayashi. **Production:** Dentsu Inc., Kodansha, MOVIC, Nippan, Production I.G, Pyrotechnist, Shochiku Co. Ltd. **Animation Production:** Production I.G.

Tsubasa: Spring Thunder (OVA, 2009)

Original Title: *Tsubasa Chronicle: Shunraiki*. **Status:** OVA series (2 episodes). **Episode Length:** 29 minutes. **Director:** Shunsuke Tada. **Screenplay:** Nanase Ohkawa. **Original Creator:** CLAMP. **Character Designer:** Yoko Kikuchi. **Animation Director:** Akiharu Ishii, Toshihisa Kaiya, Yoko Kikuchi. **Art Designer:** Tomoyasu Fujise. **2D Work:** Akiko Hamanaka. **3D CG:** Chiori Satou, Satoru Kobayashi, Tomoki Tsukamoto. **3D Director:** Makoto Endo. **Sound Director:** Masafumi Mima. **Director of Photography:** Hiroshi Tanaka. **Executive Producer:** Aya Hashimoto. **Producers:** Hiroaki Morita, Masayuki Haryu, Takuya Matsushita. **Sound Effects:** Shizuo Kurahashi. **Special Effects:** Masahiro Murakami. **Animation Production:** Production I.G.

Tsubasa: Tokyo Revelations (2007–2008)

Original Title: *Tsubasa Toukyou Bakuro*. **Status:** OVA series (3 episodes). **Episode Length:** 25 minutes. **Director:** Shunsuke Tada. **Original Creator:** CLAMP. **Screenplay:** Ageha Ohkawa. **Music:** Yuki Kajiura. **Executive Producer:** Rui Kuroki. **Art Director:** Masanobu Nomura. **Art Designer:** Tomoyasu Fujise. **Animation Directors: Akiharu Ishii, Toshihisa Kaiya. **Character Designer:** Yoko Kikuchi. **Monster Designer:** Keigo Sasaki. **Prop Designer:** Kazunori Akiyama. **3D Director:** Makoto Endo. **Director of Photography:** Hiroshi Tanaka. **Sound Director:** Masafumi Mima. **Color Designer:** Yuko Tsumori. **Visual Effects:** Kanta Kamei. **Production:** Kodansha. **Animation Production:** Production I.G. **Background Art:** Biho Co., Ltd. **Sound Production:** Techno Sound.

X (1996)

Original Title: *X*. **Status:** movie. **Length:** 100 minutes. **Director:** Rintaro. **Screenplay:** Mami Watanabe, Nanase Ohkawa, Rintaro. **Music:** Yasuaki Shimizu. **Original Creator:** CLAMP. **Character Designer:** Nobuteru Yuki. **Art Director:** Shuichi Hirata. **Chief Animation Director:** Nobuteru Yuki. **Sound Director:** Yasunori Honda. **Executive Producer:** Tsuguhiko Kadokawa. **Producers:** Kazuhiko Ikeguchi, Kazuo Yokoyama, Masao Maruyama. **Sound Effects:** Shizuo Kurahashi (Soundbox). **Production:** Bandai Visual, Kadokawa Shoten, Madhouse Studios, Marubeni, MOVIC, Sega, Shelty, Victor Entertainment.

X (2001–2002)

Original Title: *X*. **Status:** TV series (24 episodes). **Episode Length:** 24 minutes. **Director:** Yoshiaki Kawajiri. **Script:** Hiroko Tokita, Kazuyuki Fudeyasu, Kenji Sugihara, Yoshiaki Kawajiri, Yuki Enatsu. **Music:** Naoki Sato. **Original Creator:** CLAMP. **Character Designer:** Yoshinori Kanemori. **Art Director:** Yuji Ikeda. **Chief Animation Director:** Yoshinori Kanemori. **Sound Director:** Yasunori Honda. **CGI Director:** Takahiro Miyata. **Producers:** Jouichi Mizuno, Masao Maruyama, Michiko Suzuki, Shinji Komori. **Sound Effects:** Shizuo Kurahashi (Soundbox). **CG:** Takashi Kudou, Tetsuya Sasaki. **Color Coordination:** Ken Hashimoto. **Composite:** Chie Nakamura. **Animation Production:** Madhouse Studios.

xxxHOLiC (2006)

Original Title: *xxxHOLiC*. **Status:** TV series (24 episodes). **Episode Length:** 25 minutes. **Director:** Tsutomu Mizushima. **Original Creator:** CLAMP. **Series Composition:** Ageha Ohkawa, Michiko Yokote. **Screenplay:** Ageha Ohkawa, Michiko Yokote, Miharu Hirami, Tsutomu Mizushima, Yoshiki Sakurai. **Music:** S.E.N.S. **Character Designer:** Kazuchika Kise. **Prop Designer:** Minoru Ueda. **Art Director:** Hiromasa Ogura. **Animation Directors:** Fumiko Urawa, Hiroyo Izumi, Junichiro Taniguchi, Kaoru Agatsuma, Kenichi Ishimaru, Masayuki Nomoto, Minoru Ueda, Ryouko Nakano, Shinsuke Terasawa, Tomoyuki Matsumoto. **Producers:** Ikuko Shikano, Katsuji Morishita, Naohiro Futono, Naomi Sudou, Takuya Matsushita, Toyoaki Iwasaki, Yoshihisa Nakayama. **Editor:** Taeko Hamauzu. **Sound Director:** Kazuhiro Wakabayashi. **Sound Effects:** Michihiro Ito. **Special Effects:** Masahiro Murakami. **Color Setting:** Izumi Hirose, Mina Noguchi. **Animation Production:** Production I.G. **Production:** Ayakashi Research Society.

xxxHOLiC: Kei (2008)

Original Title: *xxxHOLiC: Kei*. **Status:** TV series (13 episodes). **Episode Length:** 24 minutes. **Director:** Tsutomu Mizushima. **Original Creator:** CLAMP. **Series

Composition: Ageha Ohkawa, Michiko Yokote. **Music**: S.E.N.S. **Character Designer**: Kazuchika Kise. **Prop Designer**: Minoru Ueda. **Art Director**: Hiromasa Ogura. **Animation Directors**: Hiroyo Izumi, Junichiro Taniguchi, Kazuya Kise, Minoru Ueda, Ryouko Nakano, Sachiko Kotani, Satoshi Hata, Shinsuke Terasawa, Yumiko Hara. **Producers**: Junichiro Tanaka, Kozue Kaneniwa, Nahomi Sudo, Takuya Matsushita, Tomoyuki Sagawa. **Sound Director**: Kazuhiro Wakabayashi. **Sound Effects**: Michihiro Ito. **Special Effects**: Masahiro Muragami. **Color Setting**: Chie Tanimoto, Daisuke Yamazaki, Hatsumi Okada, Izumi Hirose, Kumiko Akahori. **Animation Production**: Production I.G. **Production**: BMG Japan, KIDS STATION, Kodansha, Production I.G. **Sound Production**: Phoenicia.

xxxHOLiC: Rou (2010)

Original Title: *xxxHOLiC Rou*. **Status**: OVA (1 episode). **Episode Length**: 45 minutes. **Director**: Tsutomu Mizushima. **Script**: Nanase Ohkawa. **Music**: S.E.N.S. **Original Creator**: CLAMP. **Character Designer**: Kazuchika Kise. **Art Director**: Hiromasa Ogura. **Chief Animation Director**: Kazuchika Kise. **Animation Director**: Hiroyo Izumi. **Sound Director**: Kazuhiro Wakabayashi. **Animation Production**: Production I.G.

xxxHOLiC: Rou Adayume (2011)

Original Title: *xxxHOLiC: Rou Adayume*. **Status**: OVA (1 episode). **Episode Length**: 30 minutes. **Director**: Tsutomu Mizushima. **Screenplay**: Nanase Ohkawa. **Music**: S.E.N.S. **Original Creator**: CLAMP. **Character Designer**: Kazuchika Kise. **Art Director**: Hiromasa Ogura. **Chief Animation Director**: Kazuchika Kise. **Sound Director**: Kazuhiro Wakabayashi. **Color Designer**: Kazu Doi. **Editing**: Taeko Hamauzu. **Animation Production**: Production I.G. **Sound Production**: Phoenicia.

xxxHOLiC: Shunmuki (2009)

Original Title: **Status**: OVA series (2 episodes). **Episode Length**: 27 minutes. **Director**: Tsutomu Mizushima. **Original Creator**: CLAMP. **Screenplay**: Nanase Ohkawa. **Character Designer**: Kazuchika Kise. **Prop Designer**: Minoru Ueda. **Art Director**: Hiromasa Ogura. **Editor**: Junichi Uematsu. **Sound Director**: Kazuhiro Wakabayashi. **Color Setting**: Mayumi Satou. **Animation Production**: Production I.G.

xxxHOLiC the Movie: A Midsummer Night's Dream (2005)

Original Title: *Gekijouban xxxHOLiC Manatsu no Yoru no Yume*. **Status**: movie. **Length**: 60 minutes. **Director**: Tsutomu Mizushima. **Original Creator**: CLAMP. **Screenplay**: Jun'ichi Fujisaku, Yoshiki Sakurai. **Music**: Tsuneyoshi Saito. **Character Designer**: Kazuchika Kise. **Prop Designer**: Minoru Ueda. **Art Director**: Shuichi Hirata. **Animation Director**: Kazuchika Kise. **Producers**: Ikuko Shikano, Junji Seki, Natsumi Shirahama, Tetsuya Watanabe, Toru Kawaguchi, Toshiaki Doushita, Yoshihiro Iwasaki. **Editor**: Taeko Hamauzu. **Color Designer**: Sayuri Yoshida. **Animation Production**: Production I.G. **Production**: Dentsu Inc., Kodansha, MOVIC,

Nippan, Production I.G, Pyrotechnist, Shochiku, Co. Ltd. **Sound Production**: Pony Canyon.

Ancillary Titles

Cardcaptor Sakura Video Diary (OVA, 2000)
Chibits (special, 2004)
CLAMP in Wonderland (OVA, 1994)
CLAMP in Wonderland 2 (OVA, 2007)
Clover (special, 1999)
Miyuki-chan in Wonderland (OVA, 2001)
Sweet Valerian (TV, 2004)
Wish (special, 1997)
X: An Omen (OVA, 2001)
X—X2 Double X (OVA, 1993)

Appendix

SELECTED MANGA

Dates:	Title:	Serialized in:
1989–1996	RG Veda	Wings
1990–1991	Man of Many Faces	Newtype
1990–1993	Tokyo Babylon	Wings
1992–1993	Clamp School Detectives	Monthly Asuka
1992–1993	Duklyon: Clamp School Defenders	Newtype 100% Comics
1992	Shirahime-Syo: Snow Goddess Tales	Monthly Asuka
1992–2002	X/1999	Monthly Asuka
1992–1994	Legend of Chun Hyang	Serie Mystery — Special
1993–1995	Magic Knight Rayearth	Nakayoshi
1993–1995	Miyuki-chan in Wonderland	Newtype
1993–1995	The One I Love	Young Rose Comics DX
1996–2000	Cardcaptor Sakura	Nakayoshi
1996–1998	Wish	Monthly Asuka
1997–2001	Clover	Amie
1999–2001	Angelic Layer	Monthly Shounen Ace
1999–2000	Suki	Monthly Asuka
2000–2003	Legal Drug	Monthly Asuka
2001–2002	Chobits	Young Magazine
2003–2009	Tsubasa: RESERVoir CHRoNiCLE	Weekly Shounen Magazine
2003–2011	xxxHOLiC	Young Magazine and Bessatsu Shounen Magazine
2005–2011	Kobato	Monthly Sunday Gene-X and Newtype
2011–	Gate 7	Jump Square

BIBLIOGRAPHY

Because of the intrinsically volatile character of the world wide web, it cannot be guaranteed that all of the website addresses provided in this bibliography are currently available and accessible. All of the sites here cited were, however, active at the time of their consultation in the preparation of this book.

Aarseth, E. J. 1997. *Cybertext: Perspectives on Ergodic Literature*. Baltimore: Johns Hopkins University Press.
Abercrombie, L. 2004. *The Epic, An Essay*. http://www.readcentral.com/chapters/Lascelles-Abercrombie/The-Epic-An-Essay/004.
Ascari, M. 2009. *A Counter-History of Crime Fiction*. Basingstoke and New York: Palgrave Macmillan.
Ashkenazi, M. 2003. *Handbook of Japanese Mythology*. Oxford: Oxford University Press.
Auster, P. 1987. *City of Glass*. New York: Penguin.
Bertschy, Z. 2004. "*Cardcaptor Sakura*—DVD 18: Revelations." *Anime News Network*. http://www.animenewsnetwork.co.uk/review/cardcaptor-sakura/dvd-18.
Bertschy, Z. 2006. "CLAMP Focus Panel and Press Conference." *Anime News Network*. http://www.animenewsnetwork.com/convention/2006/anime-expo/22.
Bryson, N. 1988. "The Gaze in the Expanded Field." In *Vision and Visuality*, edited by H. Foster. Seattle, WA: Bay.
Calza, G. C. 2007. *Japan Style*. London and New York: Phaidon.
Carse, J. 1986. *Finite and Infinite Games*. New York: Macmillan.
Cavallaro, D. 2001. *Critical and Cultural Theory: Thematic Variations*. London: Athlone.
Cavallaro, D. 2010. *Anime and the Art of Adaptation*. Jefferson, NC, and London: McFarland.
Chang, C-C. 2006. "Interview with Ageha Ohkawa and Mitsuhisa Ishikawa." *Anime News Network*. http://www.animenewsnetwork.com/feature.php?id=245.
CLAMP 2004. *xxxHolic*, vol. 1. Trans. W. Flanagan. New York: Del Rey.
CLAMP 2005a. *CLAMP no Kiseki*, vol. 1. Los Angeles, CA: Tokyopop.
CLAMP 2005b. *CLAMP no Kiseki*, vol. 2. Los Angeles, CA: Tokyopop.

CLAMP 2005c. *CLAMP no Kiseki*, vol. 3. Los Angeles, CA: Tokyopop.
CLAMP 2005d. *CLAMP no Kiseki*, vol. 4. Los Angeles, CA: Tokyopop.
CLAMP 2005e. *CLAMP no Kiseki*, vol. 5. Los Angeles, CA: Tokyopop.
CLAMP 2005f. *CLAMP North Side*. Trans. Y. N. Johnson and A. Kirsch. Los Angeles, CA: Tokyopop.
CLAMP 2006. *CLAMP no Kiseki*, vol. 6. Los Angeles, CA: Tokyopop.
CLAMP 2007a. "Different Worlds, Different Pleasures." *Newtype USA*, vol. 6, no. 11.
CLAMP 2007b. *Tsubasa Reservoir Chronicle*, vol. 15. Trans. W. Flanagan. New York: Del Rey.
CLAMP 2007c. *CLAMP no Kiseki*, vol. 6. Los Angeles, CA: Tokyopop.
CLAMP 2007d. *CLAMP no Kiseki*, vol. 7. Los Angeles, CA: Tokyopop.
CLAMP 2007e. *CLAMP no Kiseki*, vol. 9. Los Angeles, CA: Tokyopop.
CLAMP 2008a. *Tsubasa Reservoir Chronicle*, vol. 16. Trans. W. Flanagan. New York: Del Rey.
CLAMP 2008b. *Tsubasa Reservoir Chronicle*, vol. 18. Trans. W. Flanagan. New York: Del Rey.
CLAMP 2008c. *Tsubasa: RESERVoir CHRoNiCLE*, vol. 19. Trans. W. Flanagan. New York: Del Rey.
CLAMP. 2008d. *CLAMP no Kiseki Vol. 10*. Los Angeles, CA: Tokyopop.
CLAMP 2009a. *Tsubasa: RESERVoir CHRoNiCLE*, vol. 21. Trans. W. Flanagan. New York: Del Rey.
CLAMP 2009b. *Tsubasa: RESERVoir CHRoNiCLE*, vol. 23. Trans. W. Flanagan. New York: Del Rey.
CLAMP 2009c. *Tsubasa: RESERVoir CHRoNiCLE*, vol. 24. Trans. W. Flanagan. New York: Del Rey.
CLAMP 2010. *Tsubasa: RESERVoir CHRoNiCLE*, vol. 28. Trans. W. Flanagan. New York: Del Rey.
Clements, J., and McCarthy, H. 2006. *The Anime Encyclopaedia: A Guide to Japanese Animation Since 1917. Revised and Expanded Edition*. Berkeley, CA: Stone Bridge Press.
Cocteau, J. "Pencil Quotes." *Brainy Quote*. http://www.brainyquote.com/quotes/key words/pencil.html.
"Code Geass: Lelouch of the Rebellion." *The Nihon Review*. http://www.nihonreview.com/anime/code-geass-lelouch-of-the-rebellion/.
Cooper, J. C. 1983. *Fairy Tales: Allegories of the Inner Life — Archetypal Patterns and Symbols in Classic Fairy Stories*. Wellingborough, Northamptonshire: Aquarian.
"Crossover Universe." *Tsubasa Reservoir Chronicle Wiki*. http://tsubasa.wikia.com/wiki/Crossover_Universe.
Demko, G. J. "Mysteries in the Land of the Rising Sun." *G. J. Demko's Landscapes of Crime*. http://www.dartmouth.edu/~gjdemko/japan.htm.
Derrida, J. 1978. *Writing and Difference*. Trans. A. Bass. London and Henley-on-Thames: Routledge and Kegan Paul.
Doyle, A. C. 1963. "The Crooked Man." In *The Memoirs of Sherlock Holmes*. New York: Berkley.
Drazen, P. 2003. *Anime Explosion: The What? & Who? & Wow! of Japanese Animation*. Berkeley, CA: Stone Bridge.

Eco, U. 1986. [1973.] "Dreaming the Middle Ages." In *Travels in Hyperreality*. Trans. W. Weaver. New York: Harcourt Brace.
Eisenbraun, C. "Butterflys." *The Symbols One Word at a Time*. http://www.scootermy daisyheads.com/fine_art/symbol_dictionary/butterfly.html.
Fine, G. A. 1983. *Shared Fantasy: Role-Playing Games as Social Worlds*. Chicago: University of Chicago Press.
Fukai, A. 2010. "Future Beauty: 30 Years of Japanese Fashion." In *Future Beauty: 30 Years of Japanese Fashion*, edited by A. Fukai, B. Vinken, S. Frankel, H. Kurino. London and New York: Merrell.
Gifford, K. 2006. "*Naruto: Ultimate Ninja*—Preview." *Newtype USA*, vol. 5, no. 6. June.
Grella, G. 1980. "The Formal Detective Novel." In *Detective Fiction: A Collection of Critical Essays*, edited by R. W. Winks, pp. 84–102. Englewood Cliffs, NJ: Prentice-Hall.
"*Guzen* and *Hitsuzen*." 2008. *On Philosophy*. http://onphilosophy.wordpress.com/2008/10/31/guzen-and-hitsuzen/.
Heard, J. 2003. "E3 Convention: Anime is like the Wired, it's everywhere." *Akadot*. http://www.akadot.com/article.php?a=139.
Heliö, S. 2004. "Role-Playing: A Narrative Experience and a Mindset." http://www.ropecon.fi/brap/ch6.pdf.
Hetherington, J. 2006. "The Art of Gaming." *Animation World Magazine*. http://mag.awn.com/?article_no=2866.
"History of Manga." *Wikipedia, the free encyclopedia*. http://en.wikipedia.org/wiki/History_of_manga.
Hocart, A. M. 1933. *The Progress of Man*. London: Methuen.
Hutcheon, L. 2006. *A Theory of Adaptation*. London and New York: Routledge.
Iida, T. 2008. "Talk About Clamp: Interview." *CLAMP no Kiseki*, vol. 10. Los Angeles, CA: Tokyopop.
Inoue, S. 1996. "Pictocentrism—China as a Source of Japanese Modernity." In *Imaging/Reading Eros*. Bloomington, edited by S. Jones. Bloomington: East Asian Studies Center, Indiana University Press, pp. 148–152.
Inoue, S. 2007. "Talk About Clamp: Interview." In *CLAMP no Kiseki*, vol. 9. Los Angeles, CA: Tokyopop.
jennaria. 2011. "Review: *CLAMP School Defenders Duklyon*." *XamJapan*. http://blog.xamjapan.com/?p=200.
Kamon, N. 2006. "CLAMP As I Know Them." In *CLAMP no Kiseki*, vol. 6. Los Angeles, CA: Tokyopop.
Kanoh, A. 2005. "War of the Worlds." *Newtype USA*, vol. 4, no. 9.
Ker, W. P. [1931.] 1957. *Epic and Romance: Essays on Medieval Literature*. New York: Dover.
Kimlinger, C. 2008. "*Code Geass: Lelouch of the Rebellion* DVD 1–2." *Anime News Network*. http://www.animenewsnetwork.com/review/code-geass-lelouch-of-the-rebellion/dvd-1.
Kimlinger, C. 2009. "*Code Geass: Lelouch of the Rebellion* DVD, Part 3." *Anime News Network*. http://www.animenewsnetwork.com/review/code-geass/lelouch-of-the-rebellion/dvd-part-3.

Kinsella, S. 2000. *Adult Manga: Culture and Power in Contemporary Japanese Society*. Honolulu: University of Hawai'i Press.
Klee, P. "Paul Klee Quotes." *Brainy Quote*. http://www.brainyquote.com/quotes/au thors/p/paul_klee.html.
Kohler, C. 2004. *Power-Up: How Japanese Video Games Gave the World an Extra Life*. Indianapolis, IN: Brady Games.
Koyama-Richard, B. 2010. *Japanese Animation From Painted Scrolls to Pokémon*. Paris: Flammarion.
Landow, G. P. 1997. *Hypertext: The Convergence of Contemporary Critical Theory and Technology*. Baltimore: Johns Hopkins University Press.
Lankoski, P., and Heliö, S. 2002. "Approaches to Computer Game Design — Characters and Conflict." http://www.digra.org:8080/Plone/dl/db/05097.01201.pdf.
Law, J. M. 1997. *Puppets of Nostalgia*. Princeton, NJ: Princeton University Press.
Leach, E. 1972. "Anthropological Aspects of Language: Animal Categories and Verbal Abuse." In *Mythology: Selected Readings*, edited by P. Maranda. Harmondsworth: Penguin.
Lodge, D. 1985. *Small World: An Academic Romance*. London: Penguin.
Mackay, D. 2001. *The Fantasy Role-Playing Game: A New Performing Art*. Jefferson, NC: McFarland.
MacWilliams, M. W. 2008. "Introduction." In *Japanese Visual Culture: Explorations in the World of Manga and Anime*, edited by M. W. Williams. Armonk, NY, and London: M. E. Sharpe.
Malmgren, C. D. 2001. *Anatomy of Murder*. Bowling Green, OH: Bowling Green University Popular Press.
Marc. 2006. "*Tokyo Babylon* Anime Review." *Akemi's Anime World*. http://anime world.com/reviews/tokyobabylon.html.
Marriott, S. 2006. *The Ultimate Fairy Handbook*. London: MQP.
Mashimo, K. 2008. "*Tsubasa: RESERVoir CHRoNiCLE*." *Newtype USA*, vol. 7, no. 2.
Merivale, P., and Sweeney, S. E. 1998. *Detecting Texts: The Metaphysical Detective Story from Poe to Postmodernism*. Philadelphia: University of Pennsylvania Press.
Miyake, I. 2008. "Message Beyond Space and Time." Quoted in *The Mingei Spirit in Japan From Folk Craft to Design*. Exhibition Catalogue. Paris: musée du quai Branly.
Murakami, T. 2005. *Little Boy: the Arts of Japan's Exploding Subculture*. New York: Japan Society.
Niida, J. 2005. "Nippon Ichi's Jack Niida on NIS' Journey to the West: Interview by Brandon Sheffield." *Gamasutra*. http://www.gamasutra.com/features/200508 02/sheffield_01.shtml.
"*Onmyoudou* Introduction." *Onmyoudou Awakening*. http://hushicho.captainn.net/ onmy/onmyintro.htm.
Porter, D. 1981. *The Pursuit of Crime: Art and Ideology in Detective Fiction*. New Haven, CT: Yale University Press.
Reeve, J. 2006. *Japanese Art in Detail*. London: British Museum.
Robinson, T. 2007. "*Tsubasa: RESERVoir CHRoNiCLE*— Vol. 1: Gathering of Fates." *Sci Fi Weekly*. http://www.scifi.com/sfw/anime/sfw15773.html.

Rollins, J. 2006. *Map of Bones*. London: Orion.
Ross, C., and Carpenter, C. "*Card Captor Sakura*." *T.H.E.M. Anime Reviews*. http://www.themanime.org/viewreview.php?id=92.
Schodt, F. L. 1986. *Manga! Manga! The World of Japanese Comics*. Tokyo: Kodansha.
"*Shoujo* Manga: A Unique Genre." 1998. *A History of Manga*. http://www.dnp.co.jp/museum/nmp/nmp_i/articles/manga/manga6-1.html.
Smith, L. 2007. "The CLAMP Invasion." *Newtype USA*, vol. 6, no. 6.
Solomon, C. 2006. "Four Mothers of Manga Gain American Fans With Expertise in a Variety of Visual Styles." *The New York Times*. 28 November. http://www.nytimes.com/2006/11/28/arts/design/28clam.html?ex=1322370000&en=915b5385604af201&ei=5090&partner=rssuserland&emc=rss.
Spanos, W. V. 1972. "The Detective and the Boundary: Some Notes on the Postmodern Literary Imagination." *Boundary 2*, 1, 1, pp. 147–168.
Stern, E. 2002. "A Touch of Medieval: Narrative, Magic and Computer Technology in Massively Multiplayer Computer Role-Playing Games." http://www.digra.org/dl/db/05164.03193.pdf.
Symons, J. 1985. *Bloody Murder: From the Detective Story to the Crime Novel: A History*. New York: Viking.
Tanaka, Y. 2005. "CLAMP The Courier of Dreams." In *CLAMP no Kiseki*, vol. 1. Los Angeles, CA: Tokyopop.
Taniguchi, G. 2007. "A Gleam of Hope." *Newtype USA*, vol. 6, no. 8.
Tatsumi, T. 2006. *Full Metal Apache: Transactions between Cyberpunk Japan and Avant-Pop America*. Durham, NC: Duke University Press.
"The Theory of Parallel Universes." *Dummies.com*. http://www.dummies.com/how-to/content/the-theory-of-parallel-universes.html.
Thomas, F. "Collaboration Quotes." *Brainy Quote*. http://www.brainyquote.com/quotes/keywords/collaboration.html.
Thorn, M. 2005. "A History of Manga." http://www.matt-thorn.com/mangagaku/history.html.
Tiu, D. "*xxxHolic: Kei*." *T.H.E.M. Anime Reviews*. http://www.themanime.org/viewreview.php?id=1108.
Todorov, T. 1988. [1966.] "The Typology of Detective Fiction." In *Modern Criticism and Theory: A Reader*, edited by D. Lodge. London and New York: Longman.
Waskul, D., and Lust, M. 2004. "Role-Playing and Playing Roles: The Person, Player, and Persona in Fantasy Role-Playing." *Symbolic Interaction*, vol. 27, no. 3, pp. 333–356.
Yoshida, M. 1980. "Japanese Aesthetic Ideals." In *Japan Style*. Tokyo: Kodansha International.
Yoshida, M. 1984. *The Hybrid Culture: What Happened When East and West Met*. Hiroshima: Mazda.
Yoshida, M. 1985. *The Culture of Anima: Supernature in Japanese Life*. Hiroshima: Mazda.

INDEX

Aarseth, E.J. 70
Abercrombie, L. 43
Angelic Layer 2, 34, 35, 36, 37, 97, 117, 136–149, 157, 159, 161
Ascari, M. 170, 173
Ashkenazi, M. 6
Auster, P. 170–171

Bertschy, Z. 10, 12, 85
Bryson, N. 149

Calza, G.C. 9, 133–134
Cardcaptor Sakura 2, 8, 25–26, 49, 64, 82–88, 94, 95, 96, 97, 108–109, 117, 150, 155
Cardcaptor Sakura: The Movie 83
Cardcaptor Sakura Movie 2: The Sealed Card 83
Cardcaptor Sakura Video Diary 83
Carpenter, C. 25–26
Carroll, L. 116
Carse, J. 68
Cavallaro, D. 5, 158
Certeau, M. de 148
Chang, C-C. 10, 12
Chibits 2, 159, 164–165
Chobits 2, 158–166
CLAMP in Wonderland 2, 117
CLAMP in Wonderland 2 2, 117
Clamp School Detectives 2, 96, 97, 153–158
Clarke, A.C. 72
Clements, J. 143
Clover 2, 97, 117, 165–166
Cocteau, J. 1
Code Geass: Lelouch of the Rebellion 2, 40–42, 175–178
Conan Doyle, A. 171
Cooper, J.C. 127

Demko, G.J. 169–170
Derrida, J. 63–64

Drazen, P. 43–44
Duchamp, M. 146
Duklyon: Clamp School Defenders 2, 97, 153

Eco, U. 71
Eisenbraun, C. 130

Fine, G.A. 68
Fitzgerald, F.S. 100
Foucault, M. 157–158
Fukai, A. 15
Furukotofumi 6

Gate 7 2, 132
Gifford, K. 144
Grella, G. 168

Heliö, S. 72, 74
Hetherington, J. 146, 147
Hocart, A.M. 127
Hoffmann, E.T.A. 163
Hutcheon, L. 5

Igarashi, S. 3, 4, 10, 11, 12, 78–79, 162
Ihara, S. 169
Iida, T. 54
Inoue, S. 17

Jennaria 152–153

Kamon, N. 42
Kanoh, A. 21
Katoh, H. 61, 69, 70, 141, 157
Kawajiri, Y. 80
Kawasaki, I. 114
Ker, W.P. 51
Kimlinger, C. 176, 178
Kimura, T. 175, 176
Kinsella, S. 17
Kobato 2, 23, 31, 32, 97, 117, 132–134
Kohler, C. 142, 143
Kojiki 6
Koyama-Richard, B. 16, 17

195

Kyogoku, N. 167
Landow, G.P. 60
Lankoski, P. 74
Lanning, L. 146–147
Law, J.M. 35
Leach, E. 7
Legal Drug 2, 117, 132
Legend of Chun Hyang 2, 96, 99
Lodge, D. 52
Lust, M. 68

Mackay, D. 72
MacWilliams, M.W. 148
Magic Knight Rayearth 1, 21–22, 37, 49, 50, 64–77, 78, 79, 82, 84, 94, 96, 97, 99, 100, 117, 128, 136, 137, 157
Malmgren, C.D. 172–173, 174
Man of Many Faces 2, 97, 149, 151, 152, 153, 156
Marc 56–57
Marriott, S. 126
Mashimo, K. 28, 94
McCarthy, H. 143
Merivale, P. 171, 175
Mihara, I. 161
Minami, M. 139–140
Miyake, I. 136
Miyuki-chan in Wonderland 2, 96, 97, 116–117, 119
Mokona 3, 4, 10, 11, 46, 47–48, 53, 76, 104, 140–141, 167
Mori, K. 20
Mouryou no Hako 2, 40, 166–175
Murakami, T. 17

Nekoi, T. 3, 4, 10, 11, 53, 65, 102, 167
Nihonji 6
Niida, J. 145

Ohkawa, A. 3, 4, 8, 10, 11, 12, 44, 45, 47, 53, 54, 60, 61, 65, 84, 85, 86, 102–103, 119, 120, 137, 140, 153, 159, 163, 164, 167
The One I Love 2, 165
Oshii, M. 167

Poe, E.A. 171
Porter, D. 173

Rayearth 22, 64
Reeve, J. 13, 48–49
RG Veda 1, 3, 18, 19, 20, 23, 25, 43–52, 53, 54, 58, 79, 81, 82, 92, 94, 96, 97, 117, 124, 128, 150
Robinson, T. 94
Rollins, J. 129
Ross, C. 25–26

Schodt, F.L. 17

Shirahime-Syo: Snow Goddess Tales 2, 99–100, 117, 137
Smith, L. 3, 4, 8, 10
Solomon, C. 10, 12
Spanos, W.V. 174
Stern, E. 71, 72
Suki 2, 97, 165
Sweeney, S.E. 171, 175
Sweet Valerian 2, 116
Symons, J. 172

Takeuchi, N. 64
Tanaka, Y. 81
Tanbe, S. 163–164, 166
Taniguchi, G. 41
Tatsumi, T. 17
Thomas, F. 3
Thorn, M. 15–16, 17
Tiu, D. 31
Todorov, T. 57–58
Tokyo Babylon 1, 18, 20, 21, 23, 38, 52–64, 79, 82, 97, 120, 124, 132, 151, 156
Tsubasa Chronicle: Spring Thunder 26, 89, 114, 115–116
Tsubasa: RESERVoir CHRoNiCLE 2, 3, 8, 9, 18, 22, 23, 26, 27, 28, 31, 37, 49, 50, 55, 83 88–117, 118, 119, 120, 121, 123, 127, 132, 133, 150, 159, 160, 165
Tsubasa: RESERVoir CHRoNiCLE The Movie: Princess of the Birdcage Kingdom 26, 89, 114–115
Tsubasa: Tokyo Revelations 26, 27, 89, 90, 105–114, 115

Warhol, A. 146
Waskul, D. 68
Wish 2, 102–103, 165

X 1, 23–25, 77–81
X: An Omen 1, 80–81
X/1999 77, 79
X—X2 Double X 1, 77
xxxHOLiC 2, 3, 9, 18, 21, 27, 29–31, 38, 49, 55, 91, 95, 96, 109, 112, 113, 117–132, 133, 167, 168
xxxHOLiC: Kei 118
xxxHOLiC: Rou 118
xxxHOLiC: Rou Adayume 118
xxxHOLiC: Shunmuki 113, 118
xxxHOLiC the Movie: A Midsummer Night's Dream 118, 128–129

Yamaga, H. 20
Yamamoto, F. 50–51, 79, 124
Yoshida, M. 13, 28, 35–36

www.ingramcontent.com/pod-product-compliance
Ingram Content Group UK Ltd.
Pitfield, Milton Keynes, MK11 3LW, UK
UKHW041919140426
5217IPUK00013B/224